PEACE IN THE HEART

PEACE
IN THE HEART

BY ARCHIBALD
RUTLEDGE

DOUBLEDAY & COMPANY, INC.

GARDEN CITY 1949 NEW YORK

TO

JAMES C. DERIEUX

BROTHER OF MY HEART

ACKNOWLEDGMENT

FOR courteous permission to reprint certain parts of this book the author makes grateful acknowledgment to the editors of *The American Magazine, Good Housekeeping, Virginia Quarterly Review,* and *St. Nicholas Magazine*

CONTENTS

❧

ARCHIBALD RUTLEDGE

ARCHIBALD RUTLEDGE lives in a house, but he does not really belong there. His spirit is of the open air. His heart is in the woods. His talk is of the things he has seen out of doors. When he takes a walk, the exercise he gets is the smallest of his compensations, for he is always quietly aert to the pageant of Nature, always seeing things in the daylight and in the dark, always fitting these things into the great principles of life, and deducing from them some meaning for himself and for others.

But he is not a naturalist; he is a Nature lover. His observations of natural events are accurate, but he prefers not to be bound by the restricting rules of science, as his joy is not only in seeing an occurrence, but in interpreting it. His interpretations, more than his science, have made him tremendously popular as a writer. None the less, you will rarely if ever catch him in error! There is no man in America who knows the

deer, the wild turkey, the fox, the rattlesnake, the raccoon, the quail better than Rutledge. He grew up on
intimate terms with these and many other creatures of
Nature.

The South Carolina plantation upon which he spent
his infancy, his boyhood and his young manhood (and
upon which his heart still lives) is two rivers, three
swamps and a pine forest away from the nearest railway
station. The house that was his home, and that he now
owns, is one of America's noblest colonial mansions.
It was built in 1730 by a Rutledge. It has always been
owned and lived in by the Rutledges, long famous in
American history. It was a favorite rendezvous for
General Francis Marion in the Revolution; once he
jumped through a back window to escape capture by
the British. It sheltered President Washington on his
famous visit to the South. It saw the glamorous rise of
the great southern civilization that preceded the War
of Secession, and it saw the decline of the South into
poverty. Weeds crept up to the very steps where once
the flashiest gentlemen and the most copiously dressed
ladies America has known were wont to dismount from
their carriages.

Such is the real home of Archibald Rutledge. Under
the high traditions of this grand house he grew up. His
father, Colonel Henry Middleton Rutledge, taught him
to hunt. His negro companions taught him the ways
of wild things, for negroes are very knowing in such
matters. In the limitless woods and swamps of the South
Carolina lowlands he found the peace and the philos-

ophy which make him decidedly good for the soul. Rutledge knows the mystic quality of night in the forest,
he knows the dull drowsiness of hot days in the pine
lands, he knows the soul-cooling quality of moonlight.

Life wasn't very busy on that plantation. He had plenty
of time to ride and roam about the woods, to explore
the swamps as deep as their impenetrability would permit, to ponder, to see and to reach conclusions. He is
a teacher now, and has been for twenty years. The cata-
logue of his school, the Mercersburg Academy, of
Mercersburg, Pennsylvania, says he is a teacher of
English literature. So he is, and a good one, too. But no
student ever looked forward to holidays more eagerly
than he does, for on these days he takes to the woods,
the fields and the streams. Every Christmas finds him
again at "Hampton," his South Carolina home.

Back of the old house, and high up in a tree, there is a
plank seat fastened to forked limbs. A curious place for
a seat to be built, and visitors often wonder why it is
there. Sometimes Rutledge tells them, though not
always, for fear they might think him a bit off balance
in the head. That seat is his, and he placed it there.
What's more, he has used it hundreds of times on moonlight nights. For years it was his reviewing stand from
which he watched wild things as they roamed at night.
The most wary of animals often will walk immediately
under a tree in which a man is hidden, for the scent
of the man seems not to sink to the earth. Rutledge
knew this, and so he fashioned his perch in a tree on
the edge of a clearing. He watched deer, foxes, rabbits

and other nocturnal creatures as they went about the business of finding food, and as they played. This observing, while unobserved, has always been one of his favorite sports.

Those who have hunted with Rutledge at "Hampton" say that, no matter which way they turned, Rutledge was sure to see a tree, a trail, a pond, a savanna that suggested a story. Here in this patch of white sand he turned a king snake loose and watched him overtake and kill a diamond-back rattler; there on that broken tree is where a wild turkey gobbler with a wounded wing took refuge from the foxes; over on that pond is where a great eagle swooped down and grabbed a wooden decoy duck in his talons; and right by that big pine is where two bucks locked antlers in a desperate fight.

So it goes, stories always. A boy with an active mind, growing up in solitude, used that mind to record the events around him. Later, the same active mind, become mature, interpreted those events.

Such is the source of the philosophy of Archibald Rutledge; such is the background of the peace that is in his heart.

PEACE IN THE HEART

I SUNRISE

IF EVERY human being could be asked what he would rather have in life than anything else, a composite of all the answers would probably show that *peace in the heart* is what we really want. Certainly that is what all intelligent, reflective people long for; and surely, is not the attainment of spiritual peace in a world of many discords the master human achievement?

By striving to read the First Gospel, which is the Book of Nature, I believe that I have come upon peace. Will you let me try to tell you of my discovery? Let us take hands and wander for a day, from sunrise to sunset, together; and for a year, from springtime to autumn. Nature is the art of God; and to enter this stupendous gallery of living masterpieces, all one needs is a willing and sensitive heart. Let us enter it together "without money and without price." Perhaps we shall discover in this universal Taj Mahal of God what all our searchings elsewhere can never secure for us— peace, perfect peace in the heart.

1

A sunrise has always been to me not alone a magnificent spectacle of Nature, having in it the grandeur of the mighty rhythm of the universe, serene and infallible; but invariably it suggests to me the presence of Him who planned it all. And I feel also, every time the morning comes, a sense of the forgiveness of God for all my shortcomings and downright sins. Sunrise is to me a splendid pledge that God pardons me, and gives me another radiant chance at least three hundred and sixty-five times each year. We who speak of Creation as a wondrous work should give closer heed to the greater marvel of the continuance of the lordly achievement of Creation by the still more astonishing immortality conferred upon it. Whatever Man makes seems ephemeral; what God creates stays created. And every morning we are radiantly reminded by sunrise that "the hand that made us is divine." During the accepted span of a human life, the human heart has the privilege of being humbled and being cleansed through seeing more than twenty-five thousand sunrises.

Perhaps if I tell of certain of the sunrises that have meant most to me, I shall be the more able to convey clearly and adequately how much this daily recurring splendor has brought into my life. I ought to say that I am not one of those who believe that the marvelous natural mechanism of our solar system is a mere matter of chance, or of the operation of unguided laws. My reason simply cannot leave God out. Granting that the sun does rise in obedience to law, it is a law established by Him "who pillared the blue firmament with light."

I recall a rather memorable experience with a sunrise

2

that I had in the company of a plantation negro named Sam Singleton. Aboriginal in thought and feeling, plantation negroes are among the most authentic and interesting of human beings. They may be as yet far from what we proudly call civilization; but to me they seem very close to God. Their religious attitude is as unfeigned as that of children. To them the rain, the wind, the thunder, the stars, sunset, and sunrise are matters of great moment. I have many a treasured recollection of what I have heard negroes say of these unfailingly recurrent waves in the vast sea of Nature's mighty symphony.

Sam and I left home at one o'clock one winter morning to paddle down the Santee River in South Carolina to a place appropriately called "Tranquillity," since it is as solitary as being in the heart of a wild delta can make it. Our plan was to drop down ten miles or so with the ebb tide, designing to reach at dawn the lonely hummock in the huge wasteland that stretches mistily between the two sea-reaching arms of the mighty river. We were to spend a few days duck shooting at Tranquillity, and we started at a time which would afford us sport with the morning flight.

A Southern river at night is a haunting thing, with great stars hanging like spangles in the dark pines and the ancient water oaks fringing the river shores. Wider flows the dim stream as it moves through the last reaches of the immense coastal plain. Baffling to navigate by broad daylight, the Santee at night is mysterious. And the peril of it undoubtedly was heightened by the kind of craft in which we were traveling. A dugout cypress canoe, it had as certain a tendency to roll as had its parent log, utterly lacking that virtue of stability that one relishes in a boat, especially when one is voyaging through the darkness of a huge river that seems to be wandering toward eternity.

But the stars that had been shining when we left home were soon obscured by a fog so dense that we could hardly see beyond the bow of our little boat. As we were going with the tide, we felt sure of our general direction, but when once or twice we came near looming shores, neither of us recognized the landscape as familiar. Then for an hour there was no land visible. I knew that we ought to be near our goal. But the waves that began to roll our canoe were suspiciously like sea waves. The roar of the surf that we had heard for a long time now became almost clamorous. Attempts to reach either shore were vain. The fact that the tide had now turned, or was about to turn, confused us still further. The canoe shipped water, gallons of it. The mist blinded us. There was no use blinking the truth, we were in immediate danger. I told Sam mildly that in case the canoe was swamped, we must turn it over and cling to it. How can I ever forget what he said?

"Never mind, Cap'n," that humble boatman told me; "it will be daybreak soon."

What was there in that plight of ours on which we could certainly count? Only one thing there was: the coming of light—daybreak, sunrise! It came in time to save us, though we were really on the brink of the sea when the rosy radiance over the delta disclosed our position to us. Yet it was not alone the coming of sunrise that rescued us; it was Sam's reminding me that it was *sure* to come, restoring thus my courage. And in all these years that have followed, whenever the shadows seem deepest and most impenetrable, I seem to hear, out of the dim celestial past, the quiet voice of Sam Singleton saying to my doubting and besieged heart, "Never mind, Cap'n; it will be daybreak soon."

As a personal experience, none of my own ever surpassed in moving power that beautiful and dramatic scene which, though it lies years back in the moonlit land of the past and of memory, is vividly alive to me now. It happened at sunrise, and it was of a sunrise.

One dearer to me than all else in life had, for days, lain helpless, speechless. Consciousness was gone. We knew that the mortal mists were fast gathering; that the irremediable river must soon be crossed. The last morning of our watching was misty; the day emerged so wanly that we hardly knew that it had come. Suddenly the one we loved so dearly sat up in bed, a strange light on her face of a happiness past all our mortal joy. She stretched abroad her arms, crying in the radiant abandon of spiritual certainty, "The Dawn! The beautiful Dawn!"

Those were her dying words—glad, triumphant. And for me they hold the eternal promise of the sunrise. They glow with immortality. In every sense, our mortal dawn that day was anything but beautiful; but she saw the beginning of an immortal day. Believing in a God of infinite love and of infinite power, I find it natural to believe that death is not a disastrous sundown but rather a spiritual sunrise, ushering in the unconjectured splendors of immortality.

I remember a marvelous dawn in Pennsylvania that filled me with a sense of shame. The night preceding had been filled with the tumult of a wintry storm. Snow and sleet had been driven madly against the streaming panes. The house creaked and swayed. Under the eaves the freezing wind hooted, thrusting its icy snout into every crack. As I looked out, I could barely see the dark trees, tossing their wild arms despairingly. I could not sleep for thinking of the quail, smothered by the snow in some fence corner; the deer, shivering in their search for browsing; the hapless grouse, trying to dive perchance beneath some treacherously shifting drift of snow to keep from freezing to death. A resentment against nature stirred in me. Why should there be tempests and blizzards?

Toward dawn I slept; and when I woke, golden light was streaming over my bed. Not a breath of wind was stirring. Dressing quickly, I went out into the grove of young white pines near my house. When I saw what I did, I was ashamed of my feeling during the storm of the night before. Here were the trees hanging, as Whittier beautifully says, "like crystal chandeliers," the snow and sleet on their brown branches softly taking fire in the calm sunrise. Here was breathless beauty, an innocence and a loveliness that shone with virtue. On no two kinds of trees did the snow cling the same way: the swarthy, heavy-foliaged white pines bent to the ground with their burdens; the silvery branches of the birches were delicately ridged with fairy hills

6

and valleys of snow; the shagbark hickories had caught and were wearing on their windward sides shining garments. The old rail fence that sagged down toward the frozen pasture had arrayed itself in ermine, tinged rosily where the level sunbeams glistened upon it. In the air was a delicious sense of relenting, the thrilling certainty of returning love. Sparkling gladness surrounded me, called into being by the wild storm. However grim the tempest, it passes, and peace ensues, a peace that is impressive because it follows war. After a storm, always a calm; after darkness, light; after the mournful shadows and the berserk wind, sunrise again—not only over the earth but also in the heart.

One night I slept among the sand dunes of a wild southern sea island. I happened to be the only human being in that solitary beautiful wilderness. Deer roamed those tropical woods by hundreds; long lines of wild ducks sped veeringly into its Lethe-like streams; wild turkeys raked the pine straw under the huge yellow pines and fed ravenously upon the acorns of the live oaks.

The place was as perfectly wild as it had been before the days of Columbus. In such a place a man is likely to be keenly aware of all that is about him; yet I had expected to be impressed chiefly by the wild life. It was not so. A sunrise over the lonely ocean stirred me far more than the sight of huge stags, shockingly tame; monstrous pines literally draped with wild turkeys gone to roost; and incredibly placid ponds swarming with wild fowl.

The deep woods of the island marched down to the

rolling dunes; beyond the dunes was a fine stretch of beach, tirelessly trampled by the Atlantic. In a hollow between the dunes I slept, rolled in a blanket. Over me blazed the stars, tremulous with beauty. What woke me was the morning flight of the mallards and the black ducks and the teal; with glad cries they left the lagoons of the island for a sunny day among the sea marshes. I lay looking at them in the pearly morning heavens; like them, what was I but a child of Nature rejoicing in the return of day? Then I turned to face the sea and the sunrise.

The tide was flooding; and as the shoals before me extended for more than a mile, the playing of the white horses was spectral and spectacular. Tossed and snowy beauty, dimly illumined now, made the sea a visionary loveliness. The deep rose of the eastern sky turned scarlet, while long blushes of crimson stole softly to the heavens' high arch; a misty amethyst tinge came over the waters.

Now came the sun, its gorgeous shafts of fire reddening the rolling foam of ten thousand waves. Was there ever so gorgeous an arrival? The whole ocean was burning unconsumed before me, and upon the glossy shore there was not a shell that did not gleam and blossom with radiance. The sea and the sun! I gazed spellbound at these majestic forces, formed I know not by what amazing process of evolution; now harnessed, obedient—the sea keeping his bounds and the sun his destined course. The sea at sunrise! I searched my heart for words to express my feelings at sight of it. The words of the Shepherd King came to me, and they seemed adequate: "The sea is His, and He made it."

Then there was that sunrise that I spent with old Asher, a hunter; a man of sinister reputation; something of a feudist; but in appearance a patriarch of his clan. Tall and full-bearded he was, with a craggy face bronzed by the outdoor life of seventy years. Renowned as a hunter, he was also a leader of the people of the woods; and as such he was frequently in personal encounters. He and I had long been friends; and when I met him at dawn on that fateful morning in Hell Hole Swamp, we naturally fell to talking. I asked him where he was going.

"I got to see a man," he said; and he said it in such a way as to promise no good to the man to be visited. I could see from his expression that the subject was a delicate one. As we stood on the old bank, with the wild greenwood awakening around us, I heard the joyous sweet call of the Carolina wren ringing with silver tones through the morning mist, and I called Asher's attention to it. Apparently, however, he was not interested. Then over us passed in gorgeous splendor a stately flight of snowy wood ibises, bound for the distant salt marshes. Both Asher and I watched them stream away over the lofty pines; and just as they were disappearing the first rays of the risen sun glinted refreshingly on their plumage. The tall beauty of the pines was soon flooded with light. Rapture was in the air, fragrance, serene joy, peace. We could not escape all this, Asher and I. But I did not realize its true effect upon him until, when we were about to part, I found him going my way. He said something about returning home. When we did part a half hour later at his gateway he said:

"I'm glad I run into you this morning. If we hadn't stopped to talk, I might not have noticed the sunrise. But for that, I might have kilt a man. Don't it beat all how hard it is to be mean at sunrise, if you once stop to look at it?"

"Hard to be mean at sunrise." To me they are memorable words; and they came spontaneously yet thoughtfully from the depths of a heart deeply moved. But for a sunrise, Asher might have "kilt a man." It is one of those things that goes with me down the long years, giving reassurance, tinging the commonplace with the mystic bloom of wonder, suggesting to the heart that the pageants of Nature always have in them spiritual power for us if we do not drive through life so fast that we are unwilling to give their silent splendor a chance to redeem our souls.

It is futile to deny that human nature does not crave the sensational; but are we not shortsighted in imagining that in the brief and busy mortal span that is ours we are dependent solely upon ourselves and upon others like us to supply us with thrills? Besides, human performances can be gauged, can be imitated; many of the most spectacular are mere tricks. They utterly lack the superb aura of mystery that invests myriads of the masterful achievements of nature, which are the achievements of God. If we love thrills are we not missing inimitable chances if we fail to perceive many of those spectacular pageants staged by Nature? For poetic beauty what scene presented by man can compare with a sea moon setting beyond white-rolling waves? What form of entertainment can man devise more splendid, more satisfying than a gorgeous sunrise in a mountain land? I especially remember a great pageant that I watched near Mount Mitchell, the loftiest crest in America east of the Rockies.

One of my harmless pastimes is searching for Indian arrowheads; and on this particular morning I had gone down an old mountain trail to investigate a reputed ancient Indian camp site, high on a flat-topped hill over-looking a wild gorge. I found the hill top to be an old pasture, so grown to heavy grass that I knew my search for relics would be vain. But my trip was not, for I met little Ben Lance, a mountain boy who had just driven his cows into that wild mountain pasture. He was shy but friendly; a lad only ten years old, yet he had about him an air of sturdy manliness and independence; a shy friendliness that immediately won my heart. I asked him his name, and he told me not only that but also much about his life in the mountains. He came of ancient English stock, though he did not know it; his manner betrayed a long inheritance; he had an aristoc-racy of manner that only one who is truly democratic of heart can assume. As we sat together on a gray boulder, facing Mount Mitchell, the awful and sublime rose of sunrise began to bloom for us behind the shoulder of that mighty mountain, momentous and huge and black against the eastern sky.

"Ben," I said to my small companion, "you often see the sunrise from this pasture, don't you?"

"I calculate," he said, with his quaint drawl, "that she will be here just the same time I is. I is late sometimes, but the sunrise she ain't never late. I guess that's because God manages that."

I pondered the child's words as we looked together at the flaming waves of heliotrope that were fringing the mountain crest. Every tree on the skyline of those tremendous slopes stood out vividly; dark lay the valleys beneath.

"What do you know about God, Ben?"

He looked at me with clear, intelligent eyes.

"I know He made everything," he said; "and He watches how we behave. I like to be here when the sun comes up," he went on; "it makes me feel how great God is, and then I ain't skeered of nothing."

Childish ramblings, some would call them; yet to me they brought a heartening message. Here was a lonely little lad who felt God in the sunrise; who knew in his own way the meaning of communion. Ben Lance had learned by himself the most interesting thing that all Nature has to teach us: that God is close to us, is all-powerful, is loving. He learned it from the sunrise.

But all the beauty and all the wonder of the dawn would mean little if they did not infallibly suggest to the heart a spiritual dawn beyond our mortal night. In all the vast realm of human concern nothing has any real importance beside the question of personal immortality. If this one immortal hope of man is vain, all other fulfilled hopes are well-nigh futile. Our trust in immortality is our chief bond to God; without immortality, our claim of divinity in our natures is both ludicrous and pathetic. But we feel that we are true children of God. Being primal and native, man's instincts are commonly right; and he has had, in all times and in all lands, the instinct for immortality. He believes that he shall survive the dark passage of the misty river of death. Nor, even to the most practical mind, need this survival seem incredible; for through what varying forms has a man not passed during his few years on earth! Conceived mysteriously, borne about by his mother in palpable darkness; living as an innocent and happy child; then as a youth, then as a man, then as an old man. He has been many persons, yet one person; and always in him, to distinguish him from the brute creation, he has felt the divine fire, the far kinship to the celestial.

Sunrise suggests to me not only the power of God grandly to continue what He has begun but it also conveys the reassurance of the Creator's love returning to us daily, bringing joy and forgiveness; and to any reflective heart it intimates that no night is final; for, since with God all things are possible, His almighty love has, I confidently believe, prepared for us a radiant future beyond the sundown of death. And if we meditate but momentarily upon what He has done and upon what He does do, confidence in immortality is natural, reasonable, and, to my way of believing, to be counted upon as infallibly as the sunrise.

II LIFE'S EXTRAS

TOGETHER we have considered the sunrise. Shall we now look at what we might call life's extras? Perhaps what I mean can best be illustrated by a story.

My casual acquaintance on the train that was speeding across the autumn landscape seemed thoughtful, reflective, a little wistful as we talked about the things we saw from the car window. At last we came to a big meadow wherein were grazing half a hundred beef cattle. I said something inane about the prosperity of the country, the glowing future of the livestock industry, and so forth. "Look at those little daisies," he said, pointing to a bright patch of them in a far corner of the meadow. Then he added, "Cattle somehow can't thrill me. There's more hope for humanity in a wild flower than in tons of beef."

Long after he left me I kept thinking of what he had said, wondering just what he had meant. His idea, of course, was that a wild flower is one of life's extras, one of those things that we do not have to have but which we enjoy all the more for that very reason.

14

The more I thought about this, the more it appeared that Creation supplies us with only two kinds of things: necessities and extras. Sunlight, air, water, food, shelter—these are among the bare necessities. With them we can exist. But moonlight and starlight are distinctly extras; so are music, the perfumes, flowers. The wind is perhaps a necessity; but the song that it croons through the morning pines is a different thing.

The fascinating part about all this is not the tabulating of life's necessities and life's extras; it is rather the question, Who put them here, and for what purpose? Furthermore, shall we not find, through some stories of personal experience, that the curious and significant remark of my casual acquaintance was right? I do not presume that my actual living this mortal life has in any way been unique, especially as regards this matter of life's extras; yet if I can tell what they have meant to me I shall perhaps be voicing the experience and the hope of many.

I remember one October night visiting a friend who was lying very sick. There was a full moon that night; and as I walked down the village street on my sad mission I felt the silvery beauty of it quiet my heart. The world lay lustrous. There was no scrawny bush nor ugly clod that was not transfigured in that glory. A little breeze over the brimming salt tide brought aromatic marshy odors. It seemed to me that some power was trying to make beauty take away my sadness. I found my friend not less aware than I was of the beauty of the night. He could look from his window and see the argent glamour of it all: how it flooded the gleaming

tide with celestial lights; how it ran long white lances
through the swarthy cedars; how it tinged with soft
radiance the locusts and the mimosas. He felt the breeze
too, and delighted in the odors that it brought of the
happy world beyond his window.

As I sat beside him, a mocking bird began to sing
in the moonlight, chanting divinely. I know the song
reached our spirits. On the table by the bed were all
the necessities for a sick man; but he had small comfort
from them. But the moonlight, and the hale fragrances,
and the wild song of the bird—these brought peace to
his heart.

Long afterward he said to me, "Do you remember
that night? I thought it would be my last. But from the
time the birdsong came through that window I felt that
I would get well. I don't talk much about these things,
but I felt that all that beauty and peace were really the
love of God. I guess He does not love us with words:
He loves us by giving us everything we need—in every
way."

It must be as he said.

At any rate, I know that a thoughtful consideration
of life's extras has done more to give my faith in God
actual conviction than all the sermons I ever heard.
My knowledge of theology is hardly more ample than
that of a bushman of Borneo; but I am absolutely un-
shaken in my faith that God created us, loves us, and
wants us not only to be good but to be happy. He ministers to our bodies by the necessities that abound in
the world; and to our spirits by the beauty that adorns
creation. One has no difficulty in discovering, in the vast

scheme of things, an extraordinary, an exciting, provision and prevision. As philosophy, I know not if this will stand; but I do know that a belief in it has brought me close to God.

I cannot regard the "fiery funeral of foliage old" as accidental, nor the gorgeous pageantry of sunset as anything but the manifestation of divine art. I stood recently on the shores of a mountain lake at sundown after a heavy rain, and watched for an hour the magnificence of the west; the huge clouds smoldering, the long lanes of emerald light between them, then isolated clouds like red roses climbing up some oriel window of the sky, the deep refulgence behind it all. Superb as it was, momently it changed, so that I saw in reality a score of sunsets. I looked across the lonely, limpid lake, past the dark forest, far into the heart of the flaming, fading skies. I was sure that God had done that; moreover, that He had done it for a purpose. When did He ever do anything idly? And what was the purpose? Surely to fill the hearts of his children with a sense of beauty and of awe, and to teach them of His loving care.

Neither a day-dawning nor a sunset (with all its attendant beauty) is really a necessity. It is one of life's extras. It is a visit to an incomparable art gallery; and no one has to pay any admission fee. The human mind, being somewhat proud and perverse, may be inclined to reject this kind of proof of God's love. But the human heart can hardly do so. And in things spiritual I do not know but that the heart is by far the better guide.

17

Not long ago, I visited a lonely cabin in the North Carolina mountains, whence the owner had just been taken, charged with murder. He and a neighbor had had a fatal altercation about a line fence, and he had "drawn" more quickly than the other. The accused had borne a good reputation up to this time. Both men had seen service in France. I was rather well acquainted with both families.

As I went up the old gullied mountain road toward the home of the first, I noticed in the wild glen, down which a white stream gurgled and spurted, incessant, vehement and joyous, that the rhododendrons were in blossom. There may be a more beautiful flower, but I have not seen it—taking it all in all, and considering the wildwood setting in which it invariably grows. To look at this wondrous flower and not to feel that God exquisitely designed it, and did it not merely as a vagrant artist but with precision and nobility of purpose is to me incredible. Ere long I reached the cabin, and one of the man's sisters greeted me and talked with me. Over the humble mantel I saw a crude little photograph of him in his uniform; and beside it, in a small bottle that functioned as a vase, I saw a sprig of rhododen·dron blossom. I looked at the picture; then I said some·thing casual about the flower.

"I don't know why," my hostess said, "but to have it there helps me. It 'minds me of God."

I have always loved the eloquence of simple people. What they say, coming from the heart, often goes straight to the heart. "It 'minds me of God!" I never see a rhododendron without remembering that. And are not all of life's extras reminders of the love and the yearning compassion of God?

I mentioned sunsets and sunrises as extras. Almost the whole complex and wonderful matter of color in the world seems an extra. The color of the sky might have been a dingy gray, or a painful yellow, or a plum-colored purple. But it is sapphire; and my philosophy makes me believe that such a color for the sky is by no means the result of mere chance. Granted that it is the result of the operation of certain laws, forces, and conditions; yet behind it all, back of the realized dream, is the mighty intelligence of the Creator, the vast amplitude of the dreamer's comprehension. And let us not forget that the two colors at which we can gaze longest are blue and green. There is about them a coolness, a serenity, a spirit of fragrant peace. And as the blue prevails in the sky, the green does upon earth.

I have often heard people say that they would like to remake the world. Well, I am glad that we don't have to live in a man-made world. If we consider merely the least of the marvelous provisions for our comfort and our happiness, we can realize how impossible would be an earth and a scheme of life that man had made. And wc should feel, also, that David was right: "For as the heaven is high above the earth, so great is His mercy toward them that fear Him." How high is the heaven? Illimitable. And so is God's love.

To a sophisticated person, this sort of belief may seem too childlike. Yet I have the gravest suspicions of sophistication. I have never discovered it in Nature;

and to me it seems that instead of being a proof of enlightenment and culture, it is the evidence rather of ignorance, and perhaps of folly. It is the triumph of shallowness and sterility. The real trouble with a sophisticated person is not that he knows too much, but that he knows too little.

Probably everyone has had some kind of experience with a star, or with the stars. I mean that, at some moment, a star has risen, or has been seen, or has set amid circumstances that made the memory of it a part of one's life. I remember that the morning star I used to see blazing above the plantation pines, when I was up early to feed the stock, or to be about some other work, used to thrill me with the beauty of its startling radiance. It seemed all dewy and throbbing—a thing alive, glorious and immortal. God set it there, I felt, as a reminder of His presence, so that we might begin our day with the thought of Him. So when the evening came, a great beacon of the twilight reminds us of Him again. Our days and nights are sentineled by the splendid warders of God.

I once had a curious experience with a star. I was driving home to the plantation, in the old motorless days, when I was overtaken at dusk by a storm of hurricane violence. Inky darkness shrouded the world. I could not even see the road ahead or behind. The thunder and lightning were appalling. Finally, a bolt struck a pine not twenty feet from my buggy. My horse had stood a good deal from this storm; but now he made a sudden dash. He broke away through the forest, and I could not hold him. In a moment he had run between two pines standing close together, had smashed both shafts, and had torn loose from the buggy and from me. Into the howling darkness he vanished.

The rain came down as if it meant to make a joke of the Flood. The thunder blared. The lightning became most uncomfortably intimate and intrusive. I heard near me great trees go crashing down in the fury of the tempest. Alone I was, defenseless, in profound darkness. I knew in a way where I was, and to locate myself the better I looked toward what I believed to be the west.

Through the heavy arras of the rain, to my amazement, I saw a little rift in the storm rack, hardly bigger than my hand, in the very heart of which the evening star gleamed in dewy-silver solitude. In all the stillness of felicity it shone serenely, saying to my heart, "This storm is an impostor. It is momentary. The sky is here, and the stars; all shall be well."

Amid all the desolation about me, and the seemingly hopeless chaos, here came a celestial message. Shining through the storm rack, its light reminded me of something past our world. Taking heart, I waded out to the road, found my horse waiting for me half a mile down its gleaming length, rode homeward through the breaking storm, and reached the house in full, calm starlight. Stars fill me with a sense of God; and the heart cannot help being grateful when it remembers that the beauty and the wonder of them may be accounted things not to enable us to exist, but gifts of love to make us joyous.

If there is anything in life in which I take a pardon-

able pride, it is in my friendship for certain old woodsmen and hunters; obscure men, as far as the world is
concerned, but faithful friends, loyal comrades. Occasionally one will tell me something intimate about himself; and when he does it is usually remarkable, as I
believe the following story is. I shall give it without
embellishment.

"It happened last June," my friend told me, as we
were sitting together on a pine log in the depths of a
virgin forest. "I tell it to you because I know if you
tell it, you will never use my name. Bill Moore and I,
you see, had had trouble between us for years. The last
time we met in town, if friends hadn't separated us we
would have finished the thing right there. A lot of
things had made us feel as we did; and everything that
happened appeared to make it worse.

"After that night in town, I figured that one of us
would get the other. I knew he always carried a gun,
and I began to do the same. Well, that day in June one
of the field hands told me that Bill said he would get
me. I made up my mind to meet him a little more than
halfway, and late that afternoon I rode up toward
Bill's house, about three miles from mine, intending
to have the thing over. A man can't live in that kind
of suspense.

"A mile from his house, I saw somebody coming
down the road. The man was riding too, and he looked
like Bill. I just turned off the road into one of these
here bay branches, where I would be hid well. There
I sat still on my horse, with the bushes all around me,
and with my hand on my gun and the devil in my heart.

I put up my left hand to pull aside a little limb, when on it I saw a white flower, a sweet bay flower. And I smelt it, too. My mother used to love that flower; and when I was a boy she made me bring a bush from the swamp and plant it in the yard for her. She was buried with one of them same white flowers in her hand. And, you know, I forgot all about why I had come down that road.

"You'll think I was a fool, but that flower set me to thinking about my mother, and about them old days, and about the kind of man she hoped I might be when she was gone. The first thing I knew the man on horseback was right opposite me in the road. And it was Bill, all right.

"But in the few minutes he had taken to come up, something had happened to me. I didn't want to harm him now. I didn't feel that I had to look out for myself. Perhaps I did a risky thing, but I rode out of the bushes, calling to him. Something in the way I came up made him know it was all right. And it was all right, 'cause we made it right there and then; and we are better friends than ever we were before anything happened. Now what do you think of that—and all because of a derned little flower? But it's all the truth, just as I'm telling you."

He "redeemeth thy life from destruction," says the Psalmist, but we do not often think of the deft and beautiful ways in which God works. Beauty is made to touch the heart, a right spirit is renewed, and the life is redeemed. I don't think this is preaching. I hope not, for of all men I am the least capable or worthy to undertake that. It just seems to me like a rehearsal of truth. Surely life's extras not only give us happiness in a positive way but also indirectly: by saving us from the tragic loss of our nobler instincts, they rescue us in times of peril.

There are very few sounds in the natural world that are harsh. Even the massive rolling of thunder has about it something of solemn beauty. In anthems the sea rolls on the beach; and in the sunny shallows there are water harps forever making melodies. The wind is a chorister. Many a wild bird can warble like an aërial rivulet. The world is really a melodious place, full of soft sounds and harmony. Man makes it riotous and blatant.

I remember being especially impressed with this truth when I went one day into the forest to try to escape from a grief that had come to me—the loss of one dearly beloved.

A little way within the borders of that fragrant, dewy forest, where giant yellow pines, tall as the masts of brigantines and full of dim contralto music in their crowns, rejoiced in the sunshine—just here I heard a parula warbler singing. He was in the crest of a bald cypress, high over the dreamy waters of a little woodland lake. The bird's song sounded like a delicate astral flute, sounded softly and sweetly, to lure me out of my trouble. High in the heavenly blue this chorister was, joyous in that halcyon repose that the heart enjoys when it is at peace. Like a voice of a spirit was this music; it came to me calmly yet thrillingly. Like a quiet hand was that beautiful song, to cool the fever of care, to still the pulse's leap.

All about me were the rejoicing looks of the flowers, and the shining hush and loveliness of dew-hung ferns and bushes, and the gentle, pure passion of the sunlight. And music there was from myriads of sources: gossamer lyrics from bees; the laughter of a little stream jesting with the roots of a mighty pine. The wind's soft wand touched the tall grasses and the sweet myrtles into a sibilant elfin choir. Everywhere I looked I saw wild, sequestered grace. The great pines chanted like the sea, their harps of the sky touched like things celestial. And what did the music and the beauty, those extras, bring me? Passing from a state of keenest grief I came to one of quiet reconcilement—to the profound conviction that, living or dying, God will take care of us.

God seemed very near to me in that wood; the beauty of it all trembled with His grace; the music held His voice. I saw there both life and death—in the green leaves and the brown, in the standing trees and the fallen. If one is honest with himself when he asks the question, What is it that perishes? he will be obliged to answer, Everything that the eye sees. In the forest, amid those things that God provided, I came to understand that if we are to hold anything—and in times of sorrow we *must* have something to which we can cling—it must be to the unseen.

For the strength that is permanent, we have to lean on visions; for immortal hope, we have to trust, not the things that we perceive but those invisible things that our spirits affirm.

I remember walking early one July morning down a thickety path. Trees completely overarched it, but far ahead light gleamed. The path was long and straight, and terminated in a wide meadow. As I glanced upward, my eye caught sight of what I supposed to be a knot on the end of a dead limb that hung directly over the pathway; it was clearly silhouetted against the sky line ahead. In a moment something had darted over my head and had alighted on the knot. It was a humming bird on its nest, which hung like a fairy bassinet in the lonely woodland. I looked at the nest and at the bird, with its elfin grace, its delicate sheen of brilliance, its jeweled throat. And I thought: This whole matter of *grace,* of elegance, of delicacy and felicity of beauty is an extra. It is not necessary to have it so. But God has willed it so, because He loves us and knows our hungry hearts need this kind of beauty.

For many years, I had an idea that Nature had for man an active sympathy; but now I have changed my opinion. There seems really a superb indifference about Nature. It is what lies behind Nature that really has sympathy. The rose does not of itself bloom for us; but God has made it to bloom for us. Surely this beauty is not a random affair; it is too authentically a sign and symbol of love. All we know about the highest form of affection we have learned directly from God's affection for us. We not only "love Him because He first loved us," but we love one another because He teaches us how. We originate with Him; and our sublimest art is nothing but attempts to imitate the things in Nature that He has created.

26

Whatever my religion may be worth, I feel deeply that life's extras have given it to me; and time shall not take it from me. Meditating on what we have, not merely to sustain us but to make us joyous and serene in life, I have come to so clear a consciousness of God that of all men the atheist appears to me the most pitiable and foolish. Nor have I come to this faith by roseate paths alone. I know well the Valley of the Shadow; I know the aspect of that Veil which mortal sight cannot pierce. But I know, also, that the spiritual luxuries that we so freely enjoy vindicate the faith that behind the Veil is the God of mercy and of tenderest love.

III LET'S GO DOWN THE ROAD TO MEET THE SPRING!

AT THE beginning I suggested that we visit Nature for a day and for a year. Here is the matter of the seasons. Let's talk about spring awhile, and tell some stories about it. Some people think of this bridal time merely in terms of lawn mowers and garlic and housecleaning. But we who love Nature sense that all seasons are divinely ordered. He who feels aright the meaning of spring will not "lightly turn to thoughts of love." He will begin to discover peace, just as you and I are discovering it. To be joyous and free, one must not only defeat the devil, but love God too; not only conquer fear, but acquire hope. Without a sense of the immediate presence of God, life for anyone is failure. God takes our hands gently in the spring.

Cherokee Sykes, a humble old friend of mine, lives in a wild clearing on a wilder mountain; sometimes I have difficulty in ascertaining where the mountain leaves off and his place begins. His fences, smothered in wild grapevines, are only semi-artificial frontiers of the wilderness. Ruffed grouse, which are supposed to be among the shyest of game birds, ravenously feed on the apple buds right in his back yard. Timid-footed deer take confident liberties with his turnips and his pea vines. He has an almost hand-to-hand fight with foxes for every chicken he gets, and with the wildcats for every turkey he saves.

"They shore did pester me this last winter," Cherokee told me that glimmering April day, when the air had a telltale, relenting warmth, as if but yesterday it had been dallying and romping with the roses and the jasmines in Florida and the Carolinas.

"These here varmints got so bold-faced I pretty nigh concluded that they would be gettin' after *me* next—and me here all alone."

Just at that moment, while we were seated on his porch lamenting the misdeeds of Cherokee's wild neighbors, a gray fox insinuated itself through the sagging bars of the pasture fence. Once through the barrier, the fox paused, head high, one forefoot craftily raised a little. For some reason Reynard did not seem to have a predatory air. Now he moved with silent and innocent grace along the inside of the fence. All wild things have a certain mercurial elegance of movement.

After what the mountaineer had just been saying to me of the rough handling that foxes had been giving his chickens, I naturally expected him to lay hands stealthily on his gun, leaning within his reach. But he did no such thing. Rather, he amazed me by softly exclaiming, almost with that birdlike tone that chil-

dren often use when playing, or when their little hearts
are utterly serene—

"Now, ain't he the beauty? Ain't he pretty to watch?
He can outstep a cat for making no noise! Well, love
his heart!"

And this from Cherokee—a human rock oak with
all the bark still on!

"Love his heart!" What an exclamation, thought I.
And you know why my shaggy mountaineer had used
it: The season was having its way with him. The dewy
balm of spring had entered the man's soul, subduing
ancient—and, at this time, respectable—enmity. "Love
his heart" in this case meant, "God bless that beautiful, thieving rascal. I can't bear to harm him now; the
world's too sweet and fair."

Indeed, spring does seem to have the seductive, virtuous power to dissolve hatreds as well as lingering
snows; into the deepest chill glen of the heart where implacable resentments are supposed to dwell, and sorrows irremediable, the joy of the springtime penetrates:

> And my regret
> Becomes an April violet,
> And buds and blossoms like the rest.

And this is true resurrection from the dead; for
hatred of anything except sin in ourselves limits, in a
final and painful degree, our capacity to love and to
achieve, thus circumscribing our chance to be happy.

The festival of joy's return, spring is the rebirth of
mortal and of immortal hope. And it is a season that
deserves to be celebrated with far more sacred signifi-

cance than mere pagan rites could represent. The pagan failed to comprehend that virtuous Beauty is God's compassion glimmering into visibility. We have a reasonable right to believe that spring is one of the deliberate manifestations, not only of Almighty Power, but of Almighty Love as well. The pagan accepted spring as the animals do—physically. Feeling as he did, he wore garlands, gamboled, shouted, sang, reveled. With a humble and natural grace of heart in the spring, as at a holy shrine, we praise and bless the Maker and Preserver of us all.

Miraculously, after her far journey from the sun, in the deep void of space, keeping noble pace with Neptune plunging through abysmal night, the Earth has brought us all once more safely to the season of spring. For me it is quite simple and natural to believe that God ordained the seasons. In this faith my mind most perfectly acquiesces. Moreover, it seems reasonable to suppose that the spring may serve the purpose of reminding us of our immortality; here, in Nature, is the manifest intimation of our own far survival through the incredible awakening of the world after the freezing death of winter. Thus to impregnate the human heart with a faith and a hope in immortality was the Creator's master stroke.

There is a close relation between the arrival of spring and the laughing renewal of all our earthly hopes. It is not only Nature which reawakens; our own dreams revive, our aspirations. Sun and bird song and wild flower reach us with penetrant peace. Not alone do the flowers blossom, lifting to the sky their fragile faces of delicate beauty; but our own hearts wake from their long winter's sleep, look up, and worship.

Even the humblest heart rejoices and is inclined to utter things poetic. I recall what an old gardener said to me one day when I stopped to talk with him while he was spading a garden. Serene and amiably melting was the sunlight. In the mild air were rainy sweet fragrances. The freshly upturned soil had the deep, rich odor of damp loam—a fruitful odor full of promises of abundance. All about in the yards of the quiet village the pear trees were standing tall and snowing. The peach trees were a song and a silence of pink and white. The coming green was misting the elms and the maples. What innocence, what modest loveliness, was in the solitary narcissus growing by the garden fence! I said something in greeting to Old John. Both of us remarked on the beauty of the day.

"You know," he said, as he leaned on his spade, "the whole world seems sweet sixteen!"

Always have I treasured those words from that modest source. And it is true that spring arrives less like an infant than like a débutante. Almost as soon as she truly appears, she looks like a girl dressed for her first communion.

In the general scheme of things there are compensating forces at work everywhere; and this great fact is nowhere more manifest than in the joy that the coming of spring affords to the inhabitants of various zones of the earth. Excepting the Eskimos, from consideration upon whose emotional processes I am unable to report, it seems true that the farther north one lives, the sharper the demarcation of the season becomes, and, as a result, the more poignant the happiness when the frozen reign of winter is over. In the far South, winter is seldom more than a mellow, pronounced autumn. In middle latitudes, winter is real; in the truth North, it is a serious business, to be prepared for like the meeting of an inveterate and hardy enemy.

Born and reared in the South and familiar with her "golden suns and silver rains," I well remember, after my first winter in college in the North, how eagerly I awaited the spring, how much more the season meant because of the character of what had passed.

Every season is unique; and there is about spring a flower charm that no other season possesses; a sense of virginity, of tremulous ecstasy divinely ordered. Then the floating clouds picture our own soaring hope; then the day is graced by innocent beauty, winsome as the prayers of a child; then the night is jasmine-bosomed, mystical with fragrant rhythms; then every sense and every heart is joy. The world seems suddenly free of envies and malices: they perished in winter's majestic disrepair. Then the strong, cold beauty of the North, that so long has stood stately and immobile against her grand background of steely snow and bleak, gigantic trees, begins to relent. Diana is about to capitulate. A lover from the far South has touched her heart.

"The darkest day," said the old philosopher, "if we but live till to-morrow, will have passed away." It is so with the darkest week, or season. Winter brings the world into shadowy and majestic and cosmic disrepair. The days scowl bleakly by. The nights slump gloomily past. Yet, at the appointed hour, the far, all-animating paternal Voice sounds over the world. The clarion summons is obeyed. Life stirs in the dark soil. In the dim air, high above the mountains' misty throne, there are triumphing wings, as the wild geese go northward. And to us the Voice means eternal recurrence of joy. Singing to us that no human trouble is final, no winter lasting, no darkness permanent, spring is the living and laughing denial of the omega of death.

Once more, amid music and beauteous lights, it runs up the curtain that we had thought fatefully down forever. Indeed, the scheme of things in our world is such that no tragedy is wholly convincing. Human nature is too resilient, and God is Love. The soul feels clairvoyantly her immortality. Spring always returns. And there is something superlatively reassuring to the human spirit in the certainty of the spring's approach. It is almightily so ordered.

And when it comes, it always comes "trailing clouds of glory." About an April twilight there is a special magic that makes us feel that we are privileged to be invited into one of God's glimmering gardens. At such a time the human heart is likely to be ingenuous to an engaging degree. I have long believed the soul to be somewhat nocturnal in its habits; or at least, as daylight wanes, the spirit begins to feel and to manifest certain occult powers. And when a silvern April moon transfigures the world, the soul becomes communicative

34

and childlike. Safe in the arms of God, it talks like a child, its voice one of angel notes.

Well I remember, as an illustration of the truth of this, what an old negro said to me one April twilight. The thought, I believe, had haunted him for years. It took a spring evening to make him utter it. Knowing Gabriel as I do, I had not supposed him capable of a fear so poignant. I will tell you what he asked me.

I had ridden down to the plantation gate, and Gabriel had walked along—just out of comradeship. Calm was the sunset, blooming like a gradual rose of the dim universe. Dusky fragrances came from the twilight pines; the scent of the wild yellow jasmine was in the air. An amethyst light suffused the lonely forest. Both Gabe and I felt the mystery and the beauty of it all. Later, I would return to the Great House, and he would go across the dark ricefield bank to his cabin. As we reached the gate and the deepening shadows cast by the imminent forest, I drew rein; and at that moment, clearly through the spring evening, from far away across the plantation fields, came the voices of negroes singing. Their melody blended with the radiant twilight choral that the pines were softly chanting:

> I will meet you,
> Yes, I'll meet you;
> Oh, I'l' meet you in de Promise' Lan'.

And the music, and wakened memories, and the tender darkness of the holy evening, loosed the tongue of Gabe, so that he asked me a question that must have haunted him many a year. How shall I ever forget the appeal of its utter humility?

"Cap'n," he said softly, "I know for sartain that the time is coming when you will see all those who have gone befo'. You will see little Blue Eyes what died, an' Ole Miss, an' all yo' people. But how 'bout me? How 'bout Gabe? I is jus' a po' nigger. You t'ink de good Lord will let me see them once mo'? Can I get to de Promise' Lan'?"

I could only reach down and take my black man's hand.

"You will see them again," I told him, speaking what I believe to be true; "we'll all be together once more in God's good time."

Gabriel, my dusky friend, with a heart pondering mystery, left me under the stars of that April evening. The air was very still; and from the shadowy road under the pines, as he receded from me, I heard him saying softly—

"Yes, my Lord; in de Promise' Lan'!"

Thus did the humble Gabriel eloquently voice for me the human heart's eternal homesickness for that Other Country, where those who loved us await us.

I remember a spring dawn on a farm. Night had warmly hung over the earth like a dark-blue flower, like a spirit presence, laying velvet fingers on the dreaming world. Long before daylight I was awake, looking in childlike wonder at the superbly blazing morning star, effulgent just above the misty oaks beyond the sleeping meadow. An air odorous as Eden softly moved the curtains by my window. Now the east was brightening with a cool, gray premonition of dawn. Far, peaceful cries were heard from awakening farms.

Now the farm creatures began to stir. The cattle heaved themselves humpily from their couches by the haystack. The turkeys, now off the roost, began their faint fussings. Bespangled with fragrant dew, the pea vines and strawberry plants in the garden began to take shape out of the lifting mantillas of mist. Almost as native to the farm as the cattle and the fowls, as the dawn unfolded flowerlike, a bobwhite, mounted on a fence post in the far pasture, began his ringing wild whistling.

Flaring over the ridge of hills now came the sun. Day on the farm had commenced. And if that, with all its beauty, peace, fragrance, chance for honest toil, palpable proof everywhere of the Creator's love for us—if that does not make life seem worth while, what ever can? In the great words of the Psalmist, a spring dawn on a farm has the power, by divine alchemy, to "renew a right spirit within me."

The worker of the soil, the toiler in the fields, he who feels and sees the springtime fulfilling infallibly the hopes which his heart had cherished throughout the long winter—he has no difficulty in apprehending God. *Not* to believe would be a task too stupendous for his understanding. The gardener is always humble. He walks with wonder, and toils amid poetic miracles.

Well he knows that there's magic in the garden in the spring, and in every field and wood. Out of the rayless darkness of the soil rise sunsets and dawns of bloom. Something there is that whispers to the lonely little seed, "Awake and live." Out of the dust the fairy wild flowers make their artful artless gowns. Out of the dust the oaks and the hickories, the walnuts and the beeches, receive their massive crowns. Here, indeed, is resurrection. Until wakened by God, all the beauty we know slept in dust.

Should not the springtime afford us deep spiritual joy by suggesting to us that only Almighty Love could have designed such a season; and that its purpose and love's purpose in the human heart are one: to lift life to warmth and light out of an ancient cold and darkness?

Spring has always come to me early—perhaps because I have usually gone down the road to meet it. It has come to me early in March on the wings of a warm, wild, rainy wind, full of the smell of sap, the odor of living bark and swelling buds, the fragrant promise of blossoms.

For many years one of my regular spring comrades has been the author of that justly famous poem, beginning—

> When tulips bloom in Union Square,
> And timid breaths of vernal air
> Go wandering down the dusty town
> Like children lost in Vanity Fair.

As surely as the little pools of spring rain glitter in the grassy meadows; as surely as the shy ferns uncurl their trustful, delicate fronds; as surely as the eaves of the apple trees are hung with fringes of delicate blossoms, Henry van Dyke comes to his old haunt in Pennsylvania, Dickey's Run, to fish for brook trout;

and I have learned to associate his coming with the return of spring. Among my happiest memories of this vernal season are recollections of him.

Though, after a fashion, I am a fisherman myself, when this old master comes, I cannot profane art by casting a fly when he is doing the same thing. Alert to notice the things of Nature along the springtime stream, and swift to speak of them with precise felicity, he described, I recall, the wild columbine's flowers as "red chalices"; the field sparrow's singing at dusk as a "song of the spirit"; and the shadowy, gleaming waters of a great hemlock-shaded pool as "a huge amethyst." His keen awareness of the wild life about him, even while he is masterfully casting a fly under a tangle of elders, may be judged from the fact that the only rose-breasted grosbeak that I ever saw along this trout stream he pointed out to me, in an old sycamore.

A poet first and always, this comrade of mine is ever a searcher after ultimate truth. Often, as I walk the bank while he wades the stream, he says little profound things to me that prove that his fertile and comprehensive mind is not preoccupied by fishing. For example, I recall his saying, with that spontaneity which sometimes comes readily to us while we are children once more on Nature's heart: "All the real trouble in the world comes from someone's lack of self-control." And this: "A man should be guided by his admirations, not by his disgusts." And this: "There is always a prophetic certainty which belongs to moral intuition."

Because of my fellowship with this true philosopher, when the slow tide of color brims the earth, when the joy of spring deluges the world with resistless might, I have been constrained to be thoughtful about it all; and to accept it less as an unreflecting pagan. Truly it is God's work, this "bridal of the earth and sky."

I have another cherished comradeship with an old friend who is a cabinet maker. He, too, loves trout fishing; and on afternoons in mid-May I meet him by the trout stream.

One day I found him by the stream fishing in the rain. As he is much older than I am, and as the weather did not seem inviting to me, I was concerned for him, and told him so.

Standing by an old weeping willow, his coat collar turned up, his battered old hat pulled down all around, he let his line drift lazily down the dimpled stream. He smiled at my fear.

"What's a little spring rain?" he asked jovially. Then he added, "Nature never hurt me yet."

The essential, elemental truth of that saying keeps coming back to me. Nature does mother us.

It is generally supposed that spring makes us gregarious, turning our fancies to thoughts of love, and all that. But the soul often delights to wander alone in the spring, through all the new beauty and the new song, seeking out some old haunt of ecstasy, of strolling at will down fragrant lanes fringed by bursting sprays. Spring gently and insistently reminds us that life is to be lived, and not altogether to be toiled away.

Once more it comes to us, this divine miracle of spring. We delight in its outward manifestations, and our hearts feel its profound spiritual import. At Nature's nuptial shrine we renew our faith in the Eternal; and into our hearts these convictions must infallibly and irrevocably take root and sturdily grow: That truth and beauty are the language of God; virtue is the behavior of God; love is the will of God!

THE glorious processional of the seasons comes to us
because of the earth's obedience to the irrevocable laws
of God. All Nature is swayed by the mystic wand in
that Almighty Hand; and the humbler children of
swamp and wood and wild waste field seem more obedient to law than we are. As a result, their lives are
far more sane than ours in those physical features of
identity which make a sensible comparison possible between them and us.

Let us observe with what ready obedience these
children of a supposedly inferior order of things mind
their ancient mother. Will you come with me while we
watch their behavior as they are tempted to disobey?

It was late in the afternoon of a hot July day, and
I should have been anywhere but on the sultry borders
of that broom sedge field, more than a mile from the
plantation house. For some time I had been trying to
make accurate observations on a flock of young wild

turkeys that ranged the pinelands and the sparkleberry thickets adjacent to this beautiful waste field.

I was perched in a small live oak, "spying out the land," when a gray fox passed almost beneath me, paused at an old rail fence, put his forefeet up on a rail just like a hesitating dog or cat, and then insinuated himself between two rails. He entered the sedge field, but his behavior made me think that he meant merely to skulk along its borders. Indeed, several times during the next few minutes I caught a gleam of his tawny coat and a glimpse of his sharply intellectual face as it momentarily peered over the grasstops. His presence and his manner boded ill for the half-grown turkeys that were now not far off.

Indeed, I still had my eye on the master of stealth when I heard the turkeys coming. As they trooped rather drowsily to roost, they shuffled the dead leaves under the big oaks and the hollies; and the old mother kept calling them softly but with an imperious note of wild wariness. She knew the probable fate of a straggler at such a time and in such a place.

Looking into the broom sedge I could see the fox literally peeping through the grass stems and apparently edging himself toward the fence, which he now probably regretted having crossed. The young turkeys were a hard lot to manage. They found grasshoppers so plentiful that obedience to their mother's warning to keep on coming was a difficult task. One young gobbler was especially enterprising. The grasshopper for which he had suddenly formed an attachment flew over the rail fence beyond which the fox was crouching. The turkey essayed to follow his prize. The mother called warningly. The fox slipped forward through the grass, his eyes gleaming. It was his chance to cut one of these birds out of the flock and pounce upon it ere it could take warning or wing.

The situation looked pretty critical to me. But in a moment the aspect of the whole affair changed. The young turkey heard his mother calling; he hesitated for an instant; in another moment he had abandoned his private adventure and was safe within the family fold. The fox, frustrated by the obedience of the young bird, crept through the fence. But the old mother saw him, gave the alarm, and the whole flock scattered in the air, alighting on the limbs of oaks and hollies and pines. There they settled for the night, far out of the reach of any marauder prowling on the ground beneath.

Wild children know how to obey!

I am told that over the entrances to certain encampments the American Marines erected a sign which read something like this: "If you don't listen, you'll get killed." Terse enough and significant surely. But this warning did not originate with the Marines. It is really the life code of wild things. With them to obey is to live, and to disobey is to die.

Almost daily wild creatures are called upon to make life-and-death choices; and they usually choose with celerity and wisdom. Reason and natural laws go hand in hand; and to violate a law of Nature is always to defy reason. It is only because of perverse pride that we humans sometimes imagine obedience to law a proof of the loss of our liberty.

I well remember an experience in a valley in southern Pennsylvania. I was ten long mountain miles from any human habitation, and it was just about sundown. I was driving a car, but it was a rattletrap thing whose mortal race was about run. Its cylinders missed oftener than not. Its gait had a certain abandoned lightness that was neither grace nor health but rather a dizzy agility. At last my debilitated coffee grinder snickered, sneezed, and was silent. "Her heart heaved but once, then forever was still."

As I have not the gift of fiddling with an engine until it starts again, I knew that I should have to wait until the late mail-car came along, at nine o'clock at night. Hours on that desolate road! What was I to do? At first I was troubled, impatient, anxious. But this mood quickly passed. Twilight was closing in; and as I walked down the deserted road, I began to feel that waiting would have its compensations.

The lonely oriel windows of the west were resplendent. About the silent hills there was the mystery of Nature's peace, the charm of her quietness. I had a sense of the beauty of it all; of the perfection of its law and order. Some people speak of Nature and Art as being opposed; rather is Nature the effect of the most divine and exquisite Art. I saw the night mists rise in ghostly delicate bloom. I saw the first star gleam above the mountain crest. Against the rose-and-amethyst of the evening sky I saw a long jetty line of crows going to roost. From a dewy pinewood came the glimmering anthem of a hermit thrush. All was order and repose.

To the eastward of the road was a broad mountain meadow through which ran a spring-fed stream. Into this misty green wilderness I saw two shadows come, melting out of a birch thicket—veritable spirits of the mist. I could recognize them; but I could not follow them with exact observation. Yet so long have I studied wild deer that I knew exactly what they were doing, even though they were but faintly discernible. After resting all day in the coolness of the laurel thickets— a repose broken only by a habitual wariness that is really second nature to a wild thing—a deer will come forth at twilight to browse delicately on tender buds and leaves, on grass, on all kinds of dewy greenery. He will drink deeply from the cold stream. Quietly he will roam for miles the solitary country of the night— never in haste, never gluttonous, never riotous. He does not carouse, then complain next day of a headache. As day dawns, he will retire to the green stillness of his covert, there to abide in quiet contentment until night once more calls him forth upon his wanderings. Not even when sorely tempted will a deer forget fastidious- ness that really is the soul of temperance.

I remember what a cotton planter told me about some deer that had been raiding his fields by night. Perhaps if I give the story in his own words it will be better understood.

"My fields, you know," he said, "run right up to the fence of the Club, on the preserves of which the deer are very plentiful. Finding that they had been getting over a low place in the fence and had begun to eat up my cotton, I tried in several ways to keep them out of the field. I raised the low panel of the fence; I tied an old hound at night near their place of crossing; I hung a big bell in an oak, and every hour or so during the night I would ring it by the long rope that stretched to the house from the tree. But the deer simply wouldn't scare. The original discoverers of my cotton not only returned but they invited all their friends to the picnic.

"At last a neighbor said, 'Try Paris green. Sprinkle a half acre next to the Club fence, and you will have no more trouble.' I hated to do this; but I reasoned that it was my last chance, and that the deer might get only enough of the poison to make them lose their appetite for cotton leaves. With great care I sprayed the half acre, the work being done in midday, when everything was dry, so that the Paris green took well on the plants.

"Early next morning I went down to the field, fearing that I might run into a shambles. Instead, I merely discovered how indifferent a sprayer I had been; for the deer had been over the entire half acre, had taken every leaf that I had failed to spray, and had utterly ignored every leaf that had on it even a drop of the poison! They had given particular attention to the lower parts of the plants, so that the field had a peculiar undressed look. If those deer in my field had had no more restraint about eating than some people have, not one would have recrossed the Club fence."

This story, I think, demonstrates what appears to be, in natural life, the close relation between obedience and wisdom. These deer came to wisdom through obedience. From fawnhood each of them had been taught to abhor certain scents, to forego certain kinds of greenery, to reject as food whatever had upon it the taint of artificiality. Eventually, their obedience saved them a miserable death.

Not long ago, one very windy afternoon, I was on the edge of an oak forest, beyond which lay some rolling fields from which the grass had been mowed, leaving them green and smooth-shaven. Along one of these ridges I saw a farmer walking, literally fighting the wind. It blew off his hat; it shrilled through his coat and shirt; it made him bend low in order to overcome the opposition of its force. Apparently, the wind was a natural enemy that he did not know how to manage.

A few moments later the farmer's collie followed him. But he was not on the man's track. He kept low in one of the hollows between the ridges. He defeated the wind by evading 't. Then, for it was late afternoon, I saw flocks of robins, of starlings, and of boat-tailed grackles coming into the oak wood to roost. This place being an old rookery, I had often watched the birds come in and had noticed that they were usually about fifty feet in the air. But now every individual of every flock was flying close to the ground—hardly more than a foot above the smooth grass. And not only that, but they kept close to the earth, regardless of its undulations. Their flight undulated too so that the wind would not catch them. They skimmed over the little hummocks and dipped with eerie, unerring grace into the hollows, arriving at the wood on time and undisheveled. They came serenely home, whereas the farmer, reaching home with all the good nature blasted out of him, probably kicked the cat and said something disrespectful about his wife's supper biscuits.

This observation may appear a simple one, yet it taught me to know that birds are aware of the folly of fighting against Nature's laws and forces. They fly with the wind whenever they can; and whenever they are obliged to face it, they either take advantage of the help offered by the natural rises and falls of the land or use all manner of resource in the arts of tacking, veering, and otherwise making the hostile force aid them.

I was talking not long ago with a United States forester. When I raised the question with him of the power of Nature's laws, he said, "We have learned that we can never beat Nature. We do not write in a book the laws for a tree's growth and then go out and try to make the tree live up to our specifications. We try to discover what the laws are by watching trees grow; then we report our discovery. Every time in our work we run counter to Nature's way, we get the worst of it. Nature's laws seem always to be the laws of reason; they are irresistible; but they are beneficent and kindly. I can think of nothing more important in life than to discover what they are, unless, of course, it is to obey them when discovered."

One of the genuine beauties of this matter of obedience to law dawns on us when we realize that, among wild things, it is a long inheritance. A little wild thing is trained by its mother; in time, it trains its own young. And this training has all the zeal of live religion. We

49

rather negligently obey certain tenets, believing thereby to save our souls from immortal death; wild creatures obey instantly and vehemently in order to save themselves from immediate death.

On one occasion I caught a family of little raccoons, and from them in their captivity I learned a profound lesson on the subject of obedience. They were large enough to get around; they appeared excessively intelligent; they eyed me with a certain quaint forgiveness. But for several days they would not eat.

In order to keep the pen clean, I had placed the water pan outside, to be reached through a small hole in the wire. The morsels of food in the pen lay untouched. One morning, early, when I was down at the pen, troubled about my elfin philosophers, I saw one of them pick up a lump of sugar, amble sedately with it toward the pan of water, and, taking it in his right paw, push it through the hole in the fence, submerging it in the water. His paw was remarkably like a miniature black human hand. He tried to get the left hand through so that he could give the sugar a thorough washing before he ate it, but the aperture was not large enough.

Then the whole trouble about their appetites dawned on me: these babies were too well schooled to eat food without first washing it. They had been minding their mother. And the poor youngsters had been ravenous for days! Their tiny sides seemed caved in. At once I brought a big pan of clean water and set it in the pen. Yet even then the raccoons went about their repast gently and politely. But I never saw anything much more comical. As soon as the water was available, each one of the five little philosophers picked up a morsel of food, headed for the pan, sat down, washed it thoughtfully and then ate it daintily. These babies had been terribly obedient to a law—far more obedient than human children would have been.

There are those, of course, who will say that a wild creature's behavior is purely a matter of instinct—as if that were nothing of which it might be proud.

Granted that it is instinct, if it leads to obedience, it is a powerful and virtuous force. We too have instincts; and our disregard of them is constantly leading us into difficulty. Indeed, the proud march of civilization does not permit us to leave these instincts behind. Instinct seems to mean our awareness of the laws of Nature. It is a primal virtue.

Having, on one occasion, made up my mind to watch the behavior of a covey of quail for a whole day in order to ascertain the birds' exact routine, I located a covey at twilight in a stubble field. They were just huddling together for the night when I left them. Before sunrise next morning I was again with them. It was a frosty morning, with all the grasses and the wheat stalks rimed with gleaming crystals of ice. The birds had not moved. On cold mornings they often stay on the roost until the sun has begun to warm things up.

I watched them clustered on the ground, saw their bright black eyes blinking as the level sun rays touched them; noticed with what nice discrimination of judgment they stayed comfortably huddled instead of stroll·

ing with naked feet through the icy grasses. But the moment the sunshine began to feel genial, they did move—a wary, joyous band, a highborn family.

A game bird or animal can be excessively cautious, strangely timid. But it is never cringing. When in secretest hiding, it maintains to the last a certain aristocratic distinction. The birds fed in the stubble from eight o'clock in the morning, by actual timing, until half-past eleven. Then, withdrawing from the field, they wandered in their skittish, bickering fashion down to a little stream flowing between ditch banks. Here they drank. Then they straightway retired for a long siesta. Nature seems to demand for most of her children a long rest in the middle of the day. The supposed lords of creation are the only ones that spare themselves but thirty minutes for luncheon. The bobwhite gives himself three hours.

From the stream, the birds went into a sheltered clump of briars on the sunny and leeward side of the ditch bank, where they literally lay down, fluffed themselves out, utterly relaxing. They made little beds in the soft warm sand, dusted themselves thoroughly, drowsed, blinked luxuriously, loafed gloriously. For three solid hours they were in those briars, while I watched them, reading a book to pass the time.

At about half-past two they wandered back into the stubble, trooping with immaculate grace through the tattered cover—alert, trim, ever ready for instant effacement or for instant flight. They fed quietly until the sun was almost down. Then they grouped themselves for the night near the same spot where they had roosted the night before. On the roost they form a compact body; all their tails are together. All their heads are out, so that through the lonely dark hours every bird is a sentry.

When those birds were tiny youngsters—mere balls of fluff—the mother taught them the best routine of life. And those wild children had the grace of heart, the genius, to obey. Surely it takes more sense to obey than to disobey. To disobey is unnatural. *Wild* things are, of all the creatures of Creation, the most infallibly docile to the teachings of their elders, the most persistently obedient.

This routine that I have described is habitual with the quail; it is normal, admirable, enviable. Always there are the two periods for feeding, with the long intervening siesta; and in general it is the common scheme of life of most birds—the nocturnal ones, of course, maintaining a different schedule—but never staying up all night and all day too, as some mortals do. I have often watched, with some amusement, a nighthawk on the branch of a weeping willow in my yard. The whole day long he crouches flat on a limb, deigning once in a while to blink, and sometimes even uttering a queer, drowsy note; but literally lying in bed snugly, with all the covers tucked in, until the coming of twilight summons him forth to hunt his food.

To observe how many of these wild things live does us good, because their way of life suggests to us many improvements in our own. Sane, tolerant, deliberate, happy things they are. Their quiet approval of law appears more like a calm acceptance of a helpful restriction. And this obedience makes them safe and contented.

We surround ourselves by scores of man-made laws, which are good enough, I suppose, for certain purposes. But in trying to obey them (or to evade them), we are often in danger of forgetting those lordlier principles by which the universe itself is tirelessly run. Infallibly recognizing many of those great laws which control life—laws such as temperance in all things, the requirement of rest, calmness of spirit, contentment with quiet and natural joys—wild creatures are law-abiding citizens of the universe. They do not appear dependent on excitement for happiness; they do not jazz their way along from one thrill to another. Their satisfactions are sane and durable, and they have no use for novelty, which, after all, in its highest form, can afford man only the most fleeting pleasure.

And because the children of the wild mind their mothers, because they are not excessive, because they repress with extraordinary self-control whatever riotous instincts they may have, they are never jaded.

In natural life, the strict observance of law is really a matter of life and death. Human laws are infinitely more tolerant and evadable. But natural laws are inexorable. Infringement of any one of them may be a capital crime. For example, the wild thing that is not forever in training, that neglects for a single day the restrictions imposed by the laws of temperate living, is in danger of his life. The gorged lion falls an easy prey to the hunter. I remember seeing one day in the woods a pretty sight that illustrates this point of the absolute necessity for obedience in the realm of wild life.

One morning after a fearful cold wave, brought from the north by a wind of cyclone speed, I went into the mountains near my home in Pennsylvania to see how many wild turkeys of a favorite flock had survived. During the night I had thought of them on their freezing perches, tossed here and there on the creaking frozen branches, icily holding on while the wind tore through their tattered feathers. How many did I find? All of them; and a more contented and preeny flock I never saw. They were no more disheveled nor discomfited than if they had slept in a warm barn. They had been safe because their physical condition had been perfect; and it was perfect because they had lived according to law.

It appears that the Bible not infrequently reminds us that we can correct our conduct by observing the ways of Nature; that we can heal our spirits by returning to the ancient hearthstone, there to rest on the old heart of our common mother, in the old home. One passage from the New Testament has always appealed to me as especially suggestive. "And he was with the wild beasts," we are told of Christ's sojourn in the desert; "and the angels ministered unto him." May this not mean that the Maker was ministered to celestially because he was close to Nature? I do not think it too daring to say that the passage may mean, "Because he went far away from the distractions of life, where only wild creatures were, strength returned to him, and grace, and clear vision, and the courage to face even death." Our chief business in this life is to try to dis-- cover Nature's laws, God's laws, and to obey them.

Our friends of the forest and stream, of the waste- lands and wildernesses, have apparently long since dis- covered that to obey these laws is life and joy, and to disregard them is sorrow and death. They seem to know what we do not: that mortal things on this earth can never make bargains with the Almighty.

It assuredly is not difficult for one to adduce out of the wisdom of the wild a certain philosophy of con- duct. For example, he learns that liberty comes through obedience to certain essential laws, and in no other way, so far as we can see. And it is not only liberty that is thus achieved, but safety, joy, quietness of mind, life itself. Anarchy, a system of no government, might be desirable if our natures were perfect; but constituted as we are, law for us is imperative, and obedience to it vital. Providence has decreed eternal statutes, and to obey them is our best wisdom. Says Dante, with all the weight of thought and none of the weight of expres- sion, "In Thy will is our peace."

To me it is very appealing to discern this same prin- ciple of obedience, by which the planets are sceptered, controlling likewise the babes in the woods. Not long ago I was walking down an old road that was bordered by a rail fence overgrown with vines. A movement on a distant top rail caught my sight. In a moment I had made out a red squirrel. With customary temerity this sprightly elf kept on coming toward me. I paid no par- ticular attention to her until I saw what followed her.

There were five little ones, rather absurdly like their mother. One of these was as white as snow—a pure albino, that I later captured and kept for some weeks. But what interested me now was the extraordinary behavior of these fluffy little infants, apparently out for their first journey.

They were heading toward some good-sized, safe-looking trees; and possibly for other reasons as well, the mother did not wish to turn back. Neither did she want her tiny treasures discovered. Seeing me, she swiftly stopped behind a post, giving at the same time a warning chatter, at which her brood froze fast exactly where they were when the sudden word of warning reached them. The mother peered out at me nervously, fixing me with bright eyes. Every little squirrel crouched breathless on the rail, hardly daring even so much as to look. Indeed, I distinctly remember that one clung valiantly to the rail, his eyes closed tight! A second one had been rather too close to the edge of the rail when his mother had called back to them. Now he literally hung, one back leg down limply—so obedient to be still that he even let that leg hang, incontinently and perilously, in space.

I advanced a few steps. Again came the warning chatter, this time in a different tone. It meant, I suppose, to emphasize the first warning. At any rate, the already obedient and effaced babies further diminished themselves, shrinking against the rail until they appeared growing on it, like patches of lichens. Then, at another call from the nervous mother, every one faced about, performing the maneuver deftly and simultaneously. A moment later, the mother leaped to the ground, where the grass was long. Every little squirrel leaped too. The white one was the last to go. I think he had never taken such a jump before. But he was too obedient not to follow the others.

Nor are wild children ever too young to obey. I recall with what amusement I one day saw a brood of quail that was not quite hatched. As I came upon the nest, the last chick was struggling through the shell. Two other wee ones had half a snowy shell clinging to their backs. Yet when the old mother called from the dewy shelter of the foxtail grass, every chick obeyed. The last one to get into the safety of the grass was one of those carrying a house on his back!

Observing the obedience of wild things, the reflective mind cannot escape the conclusion that these children are aware of the wisdom and the goodness of their great mother, Nature. The reflective mind will sense more: it will become aware that there must be a sky beyond the reach of any mortal wing, a music past the silence of the world.

For the lover of Nature, life is a long inheritance of loveliness; an incredible garden of spiritual springtime, full of perfume and falling waters. He walks with wonder; and if his heart is made to accept agony, his reaction to the pain will be a noble exaltation of spirit, tingeing his character and his work with the divine radiance of consecration. The man who watches with what certainty and grace of heart wild things mind their mother has opened for himself another door in the mystic and beautiful house of life. And what he views there infallibly will strengthen his faith in God. For though his vision, being human, will be dim, he will have palpably manifested to all his physical senses, and ex-plicitly obvious to his spirit, the majesty of Creation.

V BABES IN THE WILDWOODS

In those days I lived on one of the most remote of
plantations; and one of my almost daily duties was the
rounding up of stock in the far greenwood that, like
a gently rolling sea, stretched more than forty miles
southwest toward the nearest town. A romantic forest
it was, where the mighty pines soared steeply; where
all vistas had the allurement of the primeval; where
the wild jasmine rioted joyously over almost every bush
and sometimes climbed halfway up a stalwart tree,
leaning gracefully thence to wave emerald hands at me.
In these woods wild life has always been abundant, from
the splendid shadowy deer to the rollicking Carolina
wren.

At the time, I was young; and while in matters of
judgment youth may be at a disadvantage, the eagerness to observe and the power to do so are then at their
best. My great weakness as a hunter and a finder of
cattle was my tendency to digress: I have always loved
to linger in the woods to watch wild things. For the

some reason I have often failed as a hunter because, at the critical moment, so absorbed was I in the sheer personality of a wild turkey or a wild duck which was approaching that I completely forgot the business of putting my gun to any use. Domestic creatures interest me, of course; but a fawn has always meant more to me than a calf, a baby vireo far more than a hefty chick. Especially have these little wild things engaged my affection and my interest—these babes of the wildwoods. We nestle ours in downy blankets; they have no enemies in the proper sense; the love that brought them into the great world yearns over their mere helplessness, with arms to hold, with prayers to guard, with strength to shield, with faith to guide, with tenderest voice to sing. But how fares it with the elfin infants of the wild? How do they get along in the huge, foe-haunted forest, in the vast and lonely swamps, upon the floods of great waters? Are they, too, guarded by love—that mystic power which alone redeems the world? Must they be taught, even as babes, the secrets of illusive behavior that may mean life or death? What are some of their tiny joys and sorrows? What are their instinctive resources in times of peril?

Perhaps I can best try to answer these questions by relating quite simply some of the observations I have made on little wild things. This matter of observing them has always been a delightful but seldom an easy undertaking; for these infants are precocious, and most of them have the elusiveness, the finesse of spirit, of patrician elves. Nor has the watching of the children of Nature led me to the sad disillusionment that sometimes ensues upon the observation of human existence. In Nature there is no sin, and that fact is a vast and a salutary one. In Nature we do not find that which so often puts us out of sorts with humanity—the sheer inelegance of a love of praise. The mighty triumvirate of birth, love, and death—these are found, changeless and serene, mystically akin to those other illustrious rhythms of existence—to the seasons and the tides, to darkness and light, to the mountains and the sky.

I trust the reader will not condemn me as supersensitive when I declare that this study of the infancy of wild things appeals to me with all that powerful mystic charm that we associate with the miracle of motherhood, which has as much genuine divinity in it as anything else in mortal life. The filmy veils separating human from animal life, if drawn aside with a sensitive, cautious, and sympathetic hand, will often disclose to us scenes of innocent joy, of tender pathos, of tremulous beauty. Such, for example, was my encounter with the flock of young wild turkeys on that brilliant day early in June.

I was driving along in an old buggy through the pine forests, feeling myself a witness of great majesty as I looked about on the incredible green mansions retiring fabulously into the remote and romantic distance. The sunshine was golden everywhere. The air was still save for furtive little hazardous winds, playing a fairy game of hide-and-seek among the lustrous ferns and the gleaming wildflowers. I saw a tall bay tree, appareled in light, standing dewily in the fragrant sunshine. I saw the great pines towering far into the pure heavens.

From fragrant roadside thickets I heard vireos and parula warblers singing. Suddenly the general glamour became specialized, as I saw a wild turkey hen steal furtively into the road. A wild mother, it seems to me, always displays a peculiar quality of wariness which pictures to us defensive love, sleeplessly vigilant. As the turkey paused, gleaming iridescently against the background of white sand in the roadway, ten or twelve tiny little turkeys trooped up behind her, pathetically imitating her in their elfin wariness. They gathered behind her in an expectant group, apparently wondering what was to happen next in this marvelous wide world.

I drew in my horse, stepped from my buggy, and walked forward toward the turkeys. My horse, accustomed to my vagaries, began to browse on the roadside grass. Upon sight of me the old mother turkey darted into the bushes beside the road, whence she immediately began to call with urgent nervous excitement to her winsome little followers. These fairylike children of the wild obeyed their mother's commands so swiftly and with such felicity of understanding, and with so much precision of action, that in a moment they had vanished in the short grass bordering the road. I knew that they had not run any farther, because there was a stretch of open sand in the woods ahead, and they did not cross that. The mother meanwhile kept calling plaintively from the shadows of a watercourse some fifty yards away. In Nature the observer can, after a little experience, distinguish the various calls of wild things, and the meaning of each call. One means, "Look out." One means, "Come here." One means, "Stay

where you are." Only the careless observer will con-
clude that every call is a summons. I could tell from the
quality in the tone of this mother's call that she was
warning her babies to lie close until the danger had
passed.

Near the place where my gleaming pixies had vanished, I sat down beside a pine, knowing that the little
birds were all about me, furtively silent, occultly hidden. Though I did not move, every one of them, concealed by some grass tussock or by some huckleberry-
bush or fern-pine, must have been watching me with
beady bright eyes, for not one stirred from hiding.
Having given the proper warning, the mother had become silent. After at least fifteen minutes of vain waiting, hoping that one of the chicks would venture forth, I
rose and began to walk slowly back toward my buggy.
Almost as soon as I was fairly upon my way, the mother
turkey gave a quick reassuring call. Pausing to look
over my shoulder, I saw the fugitives running artfully
over the clear strip of sand toward their mother. A
few moments later, as I drove by the place, the whole
innocent wild family was happily united; and my heart
thrilled to hear music as sweet and appealing as any
ever heard in the whole realm of Nature: the treble
elfin pipings of little wild turkeys joyously joining their
mother. These delicate little creatures at such a time
are precisely like human children who, coming home
after some adventure, like a first party, "tell mother
all about it" with all the charm of utter naïveté.

Not far from where I saw the wild turkeys I came
one day upon a pretty sight. I was down on the edge

of a tupelo swamp, looking for a black fox-squirrel that
I had seen there some time before—this color phase
being the melanic variation of the standard gray of the
Southern fox-squirrel. Because the best way to watch
squirrels is to sit still, I was sitting on an old pine log
with my back against a cypress. I love a cypress, partly
because of the rich, woodsy aroma that it exhales;
partly because of the almost eternal character of the
wood; and also because I can never see without the
thrill that beauty brings the incredibly green mantilla
that this superb tree wears. The foliage of the cypress
is always delicate, gleaming with enchanting lights. For
tired human eyes such a color is like fragrant pity,
spiritual compassion. I was watching the splendid crown
of the cypress when I sensed that I was being inspected.
Then a long, yellow flake of cypress bark fell into my
lap. Looking up the bole of the tree, I say a gray fox-
squirrel coming down. Nor was it alone, for behind it
came a tiny squirrel. Judging by its size and by the
tremulous manner in which it clung to the stem of the
great tree, I was sure that it had not had many out-
ings before this one.

Apparently the old mother was bringing her baby
to the ground, but I intervened. Meanwhile the baby
quaked perilously, and I actually got ready to catch it
if it should lose its grip. When I moved, the mother
turned and ran up the tree again, chattering in fright.
She passed the little one and apparently called to it to
follow back to the nest in the hollow above. But the
tiny climber had difficulty in making the turn. In attempting it he lost his grip with three of his four hands

—a squirrel's paws always seem to me more like hands than feet. For a moment he dangled head downward, swaying. He seemed just a ball of gray fur, so light that his delicate weight would not sway him back against the tree. But in his peril his mother came to him. She got below him, came up under him, managed to get him safely back against the tree. Then she told him to follow her.

About a yard down the tree was a heavy limb that ran straight out for perhaps thirty feet, its end merging with the limbs of many other trees on the swamp edge. A glance sufficed to show that it was the kind of branch that is a regular highway for squirrels. Along it the fluffy infant followed the wise old mother. I am sure that it was his first lesson in acrobatics and aeronautics. But, though both an infant and an amateur, he handled himself on that limb as no human child ever could.

At last the mother came to where the cypress leaves almost touched the balmy leaves of a sweet-gum. Crouching, she took a lithe leap into the green shelter of the gum. Then she turned on the end of the limb and waited for her baby to follow. The gray woodland elf came to the jumping-off place. He hesitated. That gulf looked so profound, that leap so prodigious! But on the farther side was his mother waiting. I was near enough to see her eyes, maternal love making them wide and beautiful. The little squirrel gathered himself up, leaped, and landed all in a smother of green leaves. Distinctly I saw the mother reach out her hands for him, and clearly I saw one of her arms literally about him as he struggled manfully for a footing after his homeric flight! The two disappeared in the green fragrance of the tall sweet-gum.

Another memory that I treasure is the recollection of the nest of wild rabbits that I came upon. There were six of these babies. I discovered the home through seeing some of the soft fur that the mother had pulled from her own breast sticking up in a patch of dead grass. Upon investigating, I discovered a small, shallow excavation lined with fur. In this pigmy pocket were six palpitant little bunnies. I marveled that they could be comfortable in a place so small that the typical modern apartment would be spacious beside it. I wondered also over the absence of the mother; for though I ranged the near-by woods carefully I could discover no sign of her. As I was obliged to pass by the same place late in the afternoon, I decided to watch for a little while to see if the mother would return home. My vigil was happily rewarded.

The first evidence of the approach of the mother was a violent upheaval in the hole itself—like a miniature earthquake; for all the little rabbits either heard her approach or somehow became occultly aware of her coming. I saw the grass and the tufts of fur jumping gladly, convulsively. Then the mother stole up to the nest with a wondrous light in her beautiful, gleaming eyes. With one front paw she gently drew aside the tiny mat of grass and fur that covered her precious babies. I knew, of course, that it must be suppertime, and I wondered just how the wild infants would be fed. To my surprise the mother gently stretched herself over the aperture, lying there passively while her little

ones nursed avidly. Life, I thought, was giving itself
for other life: so it ever must be in this world of ours.
Here was a mother, surrounded by a thousand perils,
coming faithfully to her waiting babies, sustaining them,
comforting them. I do not know that I ever saw in Nature a more appealing sight than that. And as I watched,
the twilight deepened; a throbbing star began to gleam
in dewy silver solitude; a dusky, fragrant wind breathed
softly out of night lands. Wonder was upon the world:
wonder of beauty, of silence, of coming starry darkness, of mother-love; but the greatest of these was
mother-love. Among those mystic bypaths down which
faith approaches the human heart is the glimmering
bypath of wonder.

I am aware that writers on Nature subjects are sometimes accused of being sentimental (as if having sentiment were a crime!), and I am among those who have
thus been stigmatized. Yet all life is interrelated, and
surely to attempt to interpret these subtle and mystic
relations and to express honest convictions concerning
them is not moonstruck business. It is exceedingly difficult to determine to what degree we can attribute our
own feelings and emotions to our wild cousins. But
it has always appeared to me that those who know Nature best are most willing to concede a close kinship
among all her creatures, a man included; and most children, wild and human, being ingenuous in their behavior,
have an astonishing number of traits in common. For
this reason I cannot look at the nest of a warbling
vireo as if it were merely a cleverly constructed basket
of lichens, mosses, and skeletonized leaves, smartly

tied to a limb; rather it is a fairy bassinet for some tiny woodland princes and princesses. In the great fact of having *life*, they have practically all that I have. They, too, are children of God. They, too, love the winds and the skies and the sunshine. I cannot fathom the mind of the atheist. A single humming bird is enough to rout all his arid philosophy, a violet can confound him; if he could only be honest with himself, he would be completely condemned by the mystery and wonder of the beauty of the world.

A friend of mine, who is an enthusiastic sportsman, tells me a pretty story of a covey of young quail that wandered into his yard one day. It would be supposed that, of all birds, young or old, the quail would be the wildest. But these babies proved to be exceedingly confiding. By some chance they had lost their mother; and my friend, seeing the little elfin visitors running about his yard, left the porch, and, stooping down at the foot of the steps, made a cup of his hands on the ground, all the while giving softly the sweet, alluring note of the mother bobwhite. Than the delicate contralto of this bird, what sound in Nature is more charming? The whole covey, fourteen babies, with carefree yet timid unsuspicion, came running eagerly and climbed into the sportsman's hands, where they crowdingly nestled delightedly, piping in a faint treble to their foster-mother their pledge of understanding and obedience. When he would open his hands, they would troop gently out; but always they would return at his soft whistle. At last the real mother began to call from a near-by pea patch, and the tiny, graceful guests ran across the yard and disappeared under the fence.

Most beautiful and most gentle of all American wildfowl is the wood-duck, which seems invariably to nest in a tree. Sometimes the nest is placed in the strong forks formed by larger limbs leaving the trunk; sometimes it is in a hollow; and in this case the wood-duck has often been known to use the deserted nesting and sleeping hole of the lordly pileated woodpecker—and even of the great horned owl, that chimera among marauders. Almost always the nest is near the water; often it is over the water itself; but occasionally a nest will be found a mile or more from the nearest pond or river. This bird, however, uses nice discrimination in choosing the kind of water near which it likes to build: a pond, a lagoon, a backwater, or a still estuary is what it likes, for it knows well enough that those little black balls of down that are going to be born must be sent to swimming kindergarten in quiet bays and not in swift currents. I know of one wood-duck nest on the North Carolina coast which is built in a hole in a holly tree in a man's front yard. This confidence manifests that the wood-duck is not afraid of man when it can sense that man will not molest it. This heartening fact is true of practically every wild thing.

One April I found a wood-duck nesting in a shallow hole just above a crotch in a cypress, the tree standing in the temporary water of what, even in the rainy season, was nothing more than a shallow pond. The depression was just the basin of a savanna that had filled with the spring rains. I watched the nest carefully, somewhat concerned over the fledgling ducks far out here in the pinelands. By the time they were ready to leave the nest (and that was when they were but a few days old), the pond had completely dried up. These water babies were at least a mile from the Reserve, a fine inland lake that, in the old days, was artificially formed for the purpose of flooding the rice fields. How were these tiny, bright-eyed ducks to make the journey to that placid paradise? They could not go overland, through the dense broomsedge and the wild growths of gallberry and huckleberry, past all the enemies that they were sure to meet on the ground. They could not fly. But where strength fails and the mind falters, love begins. It is a supernal power. I have seen its miracles too often to doubt its character or its might.

One day I was going toward this wood-duck's nest when I saw the mother flying low through the pine-woods. I had never seen one take the same kind of flight; usually one will rise until clear of the tree tops and then make off gracefully on faintly whistling wings. But this duck was flying horizontally, not more than twenty feet above the ground. Moreover, there was an unmistakably purposeful quality in the manner in which she headed straight for the Reserve. Taking my place not far from the nest, I soon saw her returning. She flew straight to her nest, alighted on the big limb by it, thrust her head into the hole, and withdrew it with a little, fluffy, black ball gently but firmly gripped in her bill. She took a few moments to get her burden nicely adjusted, to look about her with a mother's care, meanwhile murmuring, no doubt, reassurance to her palpitant chick. Then off she flew, the tiny, precious baby in her bill. Because I have long studied the habits of the wood-duck, I am certain that the father was at the receiving end of the line, taking care of the infants as fast as the devoted mother brought them.

I remember some other little wood-ducks that I saw early one morning when I was roaming down the edges of a lagoon, all lustrous and gleaming in the new beauty of the summer's dawn. I had come to an old wire fence that sagged its way into the lagoon when I heard a slight noise before me in a small group of cypresses. I thought at first that some gray squirrels were playing in the trees, for they are fond of eating the tender leaves of the cypress and of romping in these sheltered retreats. A second sound, however, told me that I had come upon a family of wood-ducks. One of the cypresses was much larger than its fellows; and in a low fork of this, I now observed, the mother duck had her nest. The nest itself was a slight affair, set tightly in the crotch and deeply lined with down from the female's breast. I saw the proud but anxious mother on one of the adjacent limbs. She was talking in a curious way to her babies, which could barely be distinguished as a dark group in the nest itself. The male duck I did not see. Suddenly the mother—how graceful and gentle were her movements!—stooped over the nest, picked up one of the young in her bill, lifted it carefully, held it clear of the limb and over the limpid water beneath, just a few feet below; selecting with bright eyes a place where her baby could safely fall. Then she dropped her precious burden. The little black ball shot downward, landed with an infantile splash in the water, tipped up, rocked violently, immediately righted itself, and at once began to paddle about gaily and happily. In this precise manner the mother warily dropped from the nest the entire brood. The little ones were about the size of baby bantam chicks and were black.

When the brood of nine was on the water, with a delicious motherly note of relief and contentment the wood-duck herself settled there. Then I became aware of the gorgeous male, which must have been near all the time; but like most males, in critical domestic matters he was more of an observer than a participator. He came swimming in all his unreal beauty out of a patch of sunny marsh and wampee, joined his family gracefully, and all of them moved quietly off into the glimmering lagoon.

I can never forget those winsome water babies. It was a scene that my mind must have photographed, for it is as vivid to-day as when my eyes first saw it. Babes in the woods were those little ones—tiny children of the wastelands and the lonely waters, beautiful and appealing. I wish I could tell more distinctly how that scene impressed me; but our hearts are greater than our vocabularies. Much that all of us feel is too deep and inclusive for human speech. Moreover, there remains for us a mystery about loveliness that is incommunicable.

Another incident that I should like to record has to do with a family of woodcock, one of the shyest and most intelligent of American game birds. Every year a few pairs of these nest in my woods, though it is customary for most of them to migrate before they breed. This pair that had a nest one spring in the dense shrubbery near the plantation house was a source of the rarest and most romantic interest to me. I watched it until the four young hatched, and was amused to see how solemn the tiny fledglings looked, with their large heads, their big round eyes, and their long bills pointing almost straight downward. One day, when the birds were about a week old, upon going as usual to investigate their progress, I was troubled at finding only two in the nest.

Suddenly I heard a delicate music of whistling wings, and the mother, after an unerring hazardous flight through the thicket, settled on the ground near her babies. Her eyes shone with that intelligence and determination that I have nowhere seen in Nature save in a mother intent upon caring for her young—which is, wherever it may be found, only a miniature of the colossal and cosmic business of continuing the race.

The woodcock now approached the nest, nuzzled the young gently with her beak, looked off through the thicket to make sure of her line of flight, opened wide her bill, built for probing, gently took hold of one of her downy little ones, and flew away through the sun-dappled woods. She held her baby just as a cat holds a kitten. Within a few moments the fourth baby was removed in the same manner. My visits had become too frequent; she was carrying the children to a safer place. I knew myself the cause of this hegira, from the wary, bright-eyed, determined look she gave me.

Her flight carried her across a marsh. Following the

line of it, I saw her coming back from the farther side of Warsaw Creek, which has the depth and breadth of a river. She knew its dark-flowing tide would stop my inquisitiveness. But to think of her flying across those dangerous waters with her infants! Yet even the casual observer of Nature easily discovers that in the wild natural heart is the same love, the same protecting care, the same intelligent guarding of children that we find in human families.

Perhaps the most appealing of all babes in the woods is the fawn of the Virginia deer. There is an old English superstition that if a fawn ever hears a human voice and feels the touch of a human hand, it will desert its own kind to follow man. This belief has some truth in it. At least, in the wildwoods, I have found that these delicate and beautiful little creatures seemed to have no inherent fear of man. I have had one rise on swaying legs and come forward to meet me, eagerly licking my hand as soon as I held it out, and tugging at my finger voraciously. I once raised a fawn that I called "Flight," but the name was a misfit. The little thing never tried to get away from me. At night, after I had given it its bottle, it used to sleep on top of my bed. In the morning it used to steal out to a patch of oats in front of the house, curl up contentedly there, and could be counted on to be found there.

This matter of staying in one place has a romantic and pathetic interest; for the doe, when she leaves her fawn while she goes away to feed, must tell him not to stir. So, even in captivity, with the mother far away, the fawn by instinct is obedient.

75

The observations I have recorded will be interpreted by the scientist in a manner different from the way in which I read them. I can only tell how these things affect my own heart, and what they mean to me in terms of human life. Face to face with Nature, we are face to face with God; and I for one believe Him to be the God of love as well as of law. That I cannot see Him troubles me not. I find Him in His works, in His constant abundant blessings, in the nature of the human soul. Putting aside all else and considering nothing but the babes of the wildwood, we have enough through our understanding of them to convince us of the power, the affection, the mysterious and matchless compassion of the Creator of all.

VI STORMS

As FAR as mere animal life is concerned, physical comfort is the great goal to be attained; but our own real
triumphs are in the realms of the spirit. Because of
that fact, we need difficulty for development. And do
not storms in the natural world typify those dark chal-
lengers of our souls, to meet which calmly will bring us
into the country called peace? Just as virtue is always
tested innocence, so genuine strength of heart comes
from our withstanding, with all the dauntlessness we
can summon, the storms of life.

Far back into the lonely mountains I had driven to
see an old friend of mine, an aged German cabinet-
maker who has a tiny shop in the depths of the wilderness. The shop is equipped with modern machinery, the
power being supplied by water from a trout stream
that has been dammed.

After I had secured the black walnut plank for which
I had searched the valley towns in vain, and was saying
good-by, he looked southwestward with the just ap-

praisal of a man who knows weather, his kindly blue eyes glinting with sudden brightness.

"You will be in a storm," he said; "it will be on you before you are halfway home."

"Do you think I ought to start?" I asked.

"I would like to have you stay with me; but a storm will not hurt you."

A far light came into his eyes, speculative, philosophical: "A storm does good. Something in here," he tapped his broad chest, "something in here rises up to meet it. A storm makes a better man of me."

A half hour later, when the tempest overtook me, I experienced what my old friend had said. With the rain rushing like a river, and with the wind wildly bowing the tree crests; with the stark spearheads of lightning riving the lost landscape, and the deep thunder detonating grandly, a wild joy was in me—wakened from I know not what obscure depths of being—a feeling that I was at war with one of the ancient devastating forces of Nature. . . . Something in the heart does rise up to meet a storm, and no other kind of occasion appears to call it forth. Blessed are storms. They rend and mar; but they strengthen and they mightily build.

At the far turn of a golf course, recently formed out of valley land totally wild, there stands, on a little hill, a massive white oak. Its age cannot be under two centuries. A tolerant old giant it is, rugged, hale, and conquering. Two features about it impressed me most: one is the fact that it grows literally out of the rocks; the other is that, because of its extremely exposed situation, on a hilltop with no windbreaks near, it is powerfully writhed. The living limbs are gnarled; the trunk is quite visibly turned and twisted. Tenoned in the rock, implanted in the very foundations of the world, plunging its life-bringing roots far into forbidding places, it is a proud and ancient patriarch, illustrious and invincible.

Here is an outpost that has escaped no storm. Its strength has been shaped by hardship. A champion, strong, it is the product of those very forces that we usually consider to be the most destructive and discouraging. Here is a powerful warder of the vale. Here is a grand old bugle horn, summoning the mortal spirit straightway to arise and to meet, as it has done through the centuries, whatever storms may come—learning grace from the sunny days, and power from the tempest. Rugged triumph!

Old oak, you speak to me of what you have faced, endured, overcome. And that furious rage that was the storm's has now passed, by your resistance, into your own being, to abide there as gracious and seasoned power. Perhaps, after all, the Indians were right in believing that the valor of the enemy that they overthrew became a part of their own strength.

The more natural people are—in the sense that they live close to Nature—the more closely they watch the approach of storms, the better they understand them, and the more elemental is the ingenuous joy with which they prepare to meet them. I try never to lose an opportunity of associating with such people: they teach me much of the ancient wisdom of simple and humble humanity. I love the forest because of the people who live in it; I admire their objective way of living, their obvious motives, their honest struggle for existence; the hard hands, the clear eyes, the manly thought, the hale, direct speech. One of my woodsman friends never says, "The wind is rising." Looking with falcon eyes that are wont, in not unfriendly fashion, to estimate all Nature's doings, he marks the untidy clouds in the west, where the stormy glory of a wild sunset is burning. He sniffs the rainy, cool air. "She's going to put the blower on," he says in his hearty way, as if he doesn't care, even though Boreas jerks the lid off of his whole box of tricks.

I like to see the big racks of wood that are to hold in check the shock troops of winter's advance; and in dim cellars to see piles of apples glowing, and gleaming rows of jarred fruits.

Because of the nature of my life through a long period of years, storms called me forth. Instead of seeking shelter, I had to see that the stock had it; and to this day, because of the strange primal exhilaration in it, I'd much rather be in a storm than out of it.

I've seen interesting behavior of wild life when storms were at their height. During a very heavy snowfall, while walking noiselessly up a mountain pathway, I once saw a big red fox, on the lee side of a tangle of wild grapes, raking away the snow sedulously, making a bed. I saw him crawl in and snuggle down serenely. On another day I followed the track of a buck through a storm, and found him standing on bare ground under the dense and dark canopy of a huge hemlock.

In the midst of a three-day West Indian cyclone, I saw my old horse walk out of his comfortable stable, take a stance in the open with his back to the storm and with his head and tail down, and there remain for hours. He had, I'm sure, heard the stable give some alarming crackings, and perhaps had felt it give some sick heavings, and he made up his mind that he would be safer in the storm than under perilous shelter.

When I was a boy between eight and fourteen years of age, I had to ride seven miles to school every day on horseback; and, as was natural, I encountered all kinds of weather. I used to love the balmy spring days, almost breathless with opening beauty, when the bees were buried in the jasmine bloom and the little wild glades were carpeted with violets. I loved also the misty days, when all the woods were strange and ominous; when wild creatures, thinking dusk had come, were unwary; when from the glistening needles of the pines the moisture slipped in gleaming drops; when the faint rainy wind moving in the tall pines made music like that of soft violins far away.

But, after all, what thrilled me most was a storm. How many a time, a mile or more from home, a tempest would roll up behind me. My horse understood our problem as well as I did; indeed, the degree of his eagerness to get home often made me aware of a storm's coming. At such a time, I used to hold in Redbird deliberately, until I felt that the business was going to be a real race. Then I would give him his head, and away we'd gallop madly, flash through little streams, sweep along pine-scented stretches of road, the world darkening over us; and instead of opening the gate I used to let Redbird run for a low place in the

fence, over which he would sail in delighted excitement.

Then up the avenue he would thunder fleetly, his
mane and tail flying. Straight to the front door he
would rush, stop suddenly, turn his head to look at the
storm, his neck arched proudly and defiantly, snort with
the disdain of a victor, his eyes wide, his thin nostrils
dilated and quivering. Who has not had the same
tingling thrill over beating a storm home?

As a color to rest the eye, green is delightful; but
when it tinges a cloud, beware. One afternoon I was fly-
fishing in a lonely mountain meadow and had been so
engrossed in the sport that I had not noticed, until the
wild old fields suddenly darkened, that a storm was
upon me. The hills surrounding the meadow are not
high, but they lend a sense of protection; yet the moment I saw the emerald lights in the cloud, and the red
fringes, I knew that the hills would not help me. Because of the danger from lightning, I have always dis-
liked taking shelter under a tree during a storm.

Looking quickly about for some kind of cover, I
saw, a hundred yards downstream, a massive sycamore
that some previous storm had laid prostrate. Some of
its roots still had a good hold in the damp soil, and
about half the top of the tree, flat on the ground, was
in new leaf. In a few moments I was on a tiny pebbly
strand that edged the stream under the fallen tree. I
jumped a rabbit from a heap of dead leaves there and
startled two phœbe birds that had begun to build. Indeed, I felt as if I had entered a new and private world,
under that fallen lord of the meadow. Crouched there,

close to the earth, I could almost feel the green, luxurious silence of the grass. Storms often drive us into places which otherwise we should never visit, affording us an opportunity to see much that we should else completely miss.

Meanwhile, the storm rushed on apace. From the fateful color of the cloud, the whole landscape took on an eerie tinge, a strange lurid glow of green and saffron suffusing the gentle stream, the wild flowers in the peaceful meadow, the dark rock pines on the slopes of the hills. Here indeed were beauty and mystery, terror and the unknown fast approaching.

Great, scattered, thumping drops of rain pounded the earth. The wind began to snort like a frightened horse, and again would moan gustily close to the ground, and then would whistle fiercely, then grieve softly through the limbs of the sycamore and through the little bending alders. From my homely but serene shelter I had a full view of that green-bosomed storm, the full force of which struck the hill crests to the north of me, about a half mile away.

The tempest cloud, like some vast galleon of the sky crowding her gorgeous canvas mightily, bore down on the doomed hill. Thunder shook the earth. Lightning, enigmatically swift as the tongue of a serpent, darted earthward its fiery flashes. The whole sky seemed winged with red lightning and tempestuous rage. Sublimely the storm smote the wooded crest.

With the rising of this storm, I felt my feelings rise; the human spirit rushes with the wind, wildly fathoms the blank unknown, as does the lightning, drives with the slanting rain. And all this is for the reason that a storm, in terms of the human spirit, is a challenge, and God made us ready to meet challenges, giving us power to oppose whatever seems to menace us.

I remember going one October day into an immense lonely field of broom sedge across which a faint wind out of the pine forest was drifting. The wreck of an old stake-and-rider fence shambled through the waste field; and on this I sat, supposedly watching for wild life, but in reality "inviting my soul." It was early; the dew still gleamed in the fairy forests of the sedge. Over the world there rested that virginal beauty that apparels all things when the morning is still in her maidenhood. I do not recall that I ever saw Nature more serene.

But this is a world in which change is a certainty. Within a brief half hour, out of the far southwest the dusky funnel of a cyclone began to drive toward me with tattered and ominous funereal splendor. The bloodshot clouds converged fearsomely toward the tip of a huge green and purple vase. For all the peace that environed me, a shattering storm was coming.

It looked safer to stay in the field than to go into the forest, and there by the fence I stayed while this giant cloud came powerfully rolling on. The dark pines rocked, and wild music awoke in their crests. The gold of the broom sedge was tarnished by sick shadows. In a few moments the stormful vanguard was upon me— wrathful wind, hail, torrents of rain, darkness. Certain great pines went down with sloshing crashes. I could hear a fearsome snarl of wind off to the northward, where the funnel of the storm was passing. Hemmed in by the gale, I thought of Emerson's clairvoyant phrase: "the tumultuous privacy of storm."

In less than a half hour, peace and sunshine had been restored. The broom grass was humbly bowed in misty gold. Birds, coming out of hiding, seemed to hasten to express in song the joy of deliverance. The sun flared splendidly on the wet forest, setting millions of dripping pine needles glinting. Beauty, order and peace were restored. And in my heart was rejoicing over the wonder and majesty of it all.

I remember going up a mountain path one day when I met a mountaineer with an ax in his hand. We were so high that there were few large trees above us; only rocks, a sparse growth of craggy and gnarled bushes and stunted trees, and the immensity of the blue sky above. As we were going the same way I walked with him, and eventually asked him what he was going to cut.

"I need a piece of timber to fix my timber wagon," he said. "You know that does the heaviest and most rackingest kind of work, and the tree that grows on the top, where the storms hit it hardest, is the tree that has the toughest wood. If ever you want to get a piece of timber to stand all the jolts and strains, cut it from a place where all its life it has been obleeged to stand the same kind of roughness. A tree that ain't shielded," he said, "is the last one to fall. It has stood so much in the way of storms, little by little, that when the big gale comes, it can weather it."

The mountaineer had hold of the same truth that Tennyson expressed when he said that the knights used to choose their lance shafts from trees "storm-strengthened on a windy site."

A storm compels a man to seek shelter, to try out his anchors, and it appears to me that storms develop the fine spiritual fiber of faith.

But storms also afford us the opportunity to shelter others. In a stormless existence, how should we develop our sympathies? It is not strength alone that we gain by struggling against the adversities of life but a certain enlargement of heart that is worth all the physical strength in the world.

The mighty Linville Gorge, in the mountains of North Carolina, is a majestic and mystical place. The deepest wooded gorge in America, through it roars the Linville River, at normal times little more than a mountain trout stream, warbling along among the rocks lining the bottom of the cavernous gulch. It would seem an easy thing for a man to traverse this gorge, but it is said that only two persons have ever been daring enough to do so. One was a woman.

The length of the defile proper is about twelve miles; its sides are almost sheer. What constitutes the peril is the fearful rapidity with which the gorge fills. At one moment there may be a purling rivulet, searching out a channel among the west rocks; within a half hour, a wild-crested flood will be ramping grandly down the narrow defile, storming thunderously through the drowned gulch, roaring resistlessly seaward. There are jewels to be found in the Linville Gorge, and beautiful Indian relics. But its nature is such that a storm, even of moderate violence, will render it a most perilous place.

Once I saw happen the thing which explorers of this splendid defile dread. I was on a pinnacle of rock over-looking the gorge when, far to the west, I saw the magnificent gloomy pageant of a thunder-storm. I watched the sublimity of it—like some dark, disastrous blossom of the sky, growing, bursting into lurid bloom, fading away.

That storm never came near me. Yet within two hours I saw its effect. It had been in the Linville watershed. The first intimation I had of what was coming was a deepening of the roar of the waters far below me. Watching, fascinated, I saw the gleaming friendly stream turn suddenly turgid, white-maned. Thunder was now in its stride. Little waterfalls became tall cataracts. Rocks and bushes in the gorge vanished. Under my very eyes the stream was transformed. Now it was a lordly river, gulping the sheer canyon walls, storming in wild splendor down the magnificent gorge. . . .

I thought: Here was a storm that never came near me. Yet the flood it started would drown me. It made me think of the deeds of others, reaching far, affecting the lives of many. It looks to me as if someone, some-where, has to sustain the shock of every human deed. A virtue practiced may make some utter stranger strong; a vice in me may be disastrous, not only to those I love, but to people I shall never see or know.

Granted that storms leave scars, they are what old seams and sword cuts are to soldiers. Symbolic are they of encounter and resistance. And always, because of

the analogy from Nature, we have a right to believe—
and to be comforted by that belief—that Eternal Light
can, by mortal storms, be obscured only for a little
while. Cardinal Newman must have had such a thought
in mind when he so beautifully wrote:

> So long Thy power has blest me, sure it still
> Will lead me on
> O'er moor and fen, o'er crag and torrent, till
> The night is gone;
> And with the morn those angel faces smile,
> Which I have loved long since, and lost a while.

There's always something masterful and mighty
about a storm; even the quiet snowstorm has about it
an aboriginal, resistless power. If its strength is not
tumultuous, it is at least insistent. And whatever
strength there is manifested calls forth in us the same
kind of virtue to meet it. We are closer kin to the elemental forces than we know. We are blood-sisters and
blood-brothers to the winds and the tides, the snow
and the rain. Does the gale rise? So do our spirits. Does
the snow whisper driftingly down through the needles
of the pines and the hemlocks? So do our spirits float
whitely with the snowflakes, as innocent and as peaceful
as they.

The storms that sway the huge pendent world; the
great primal forces of Nature—these are not for our
destruction. These are but lordly magnets drawing from
the depths of our being similar virtue of spiritual vigor.
As the persuading sun irresistibly compels the vitality
of the buried seed to awake, so the storm rouses in us
obscured and latent virtues.

With children, who are always, it seems, blessedly close to wholesome and natural and authentic racial instincts, the coming of a storm always means excitement. Even a little child will sense the approach of a tempest, and in its own way will rise to meet the occasion. Here is a three-year-old girl in a city apartment over which, for days, a bronze-misty sky has hung torridly. It is now after sundown. A storm is coming.

She sees it, and though she only half comprehends it, it fills her with the need for urgent preparation. She begins to run here and there, chattering excitedly, laughing, starting to do a number of things and finishing nothing. With an eager tenseness she tingles. Suddenly the wind comes. Doors bang. Windows rattle. The little child slings chairs against the doors, runs to the windows, shouts with glee, and in every way manifests the human excited reaction to these magnificent shows of Nature that are staged for our uplift, enjoyment and awakening of heart and mind.

Watching this naïve behavior of a child, one can see portrayed the whole cycle of human emotions about a storm. She had first sensed the thing coming then she became excited, then charmed; then she began to wonder what it all was for. All of us wonder. . . . Perhaps, after a while, we shall learn that apparent triumph and disaster are only impostors. What makes an event important is its effect on the human soul. Death, presumably the supreme disaster, the final storm, cannot, I think, affect the virtuous soul adversely.

Without storms there would be a certain lassitude of existence that would be monotonous in the extreme.

I love storms for the changes that they bring. As Henry Van Dyke beautifully says, "the wind of sorrow will often fan the flames of love into warmth and brightness once again." I love storms for the beauty that follows them; the sense of danger passed; the sense of God prevailing after all. Sometimes at sunset, after a rain, an angelic evening arrives to the earth; and throbbing stars blaze softly on the dewy, silent fields, and night folds tenderly the misty river, the jeweled wood, the purple herd's grass. The peace after a storm makes the heart rejoice that the danger has been survived; we feel a closer comradeship with those who have shared the peril with us; we feel as if a refuge and a rest had been earned.

VII   HIGH WATER

BUT storms are not the only perils of existence. There
are deluges, for example. It is a most curious and interesting thing to observe the behavior of wild creatures
in flood time; to see with what courage and calm in-
trepidity they meet this elemental peril. Nor is the
advantage of such observation to us a mere acquiring
of knowledge; rather should it teach us a more serene
contentment with our lot. For what dangers do we
meet greater than those encountered by Nature's children when their homes and their hiding places are inundated?

One day I set out for a big hunt, my only companion
being a negro woodsman with whom I've enjoyed a
sporting comradeship since boyhood days. Our hunting
ground was to be on the great delta of the Santee. A
high flood had inundated the country. A day of rare
sport was promised us. But to cross the Santee in flood
is to take a chance.

When we were halfway across the stormy and treacherous river, I reached back for my gun, though I did not turn to look back. When one feels in a dangerous position, the eyes in the back of his head begin to function; at least, I felt sure that my good negro boatman needed help. And a man can do something with the stock of a gun, properly wielded as a paddle. But my weapon was not in its familiar place along the gunwale. As the business of shifting my weight in the tippy craft was perilous, I sat still until the canoe finally slithered through the yellow marsh that fringed the farther side of the river. Here, beside a broad raft of dead sedge drifted tight against a canebrake, we came to a halt. I then looked back at my boatman.

"The gun, Prince—where is it?" I asked. "I told you to put it in. You surely haven't forgotten it, have you?"

When a negro is guilty, his expression, instead of being one of contrition, is usually one of amused bashfulness.

"I is fergit," he confessed.

Here, indeed, was a pretty situation! The wide Santee was in flood. Ten or fifteen square miles of delta country were submerged. The vast swamp to northward was deeply invaded by the stealing tide. Thousands of wild creatures, I knew, were marooned on the tiny islets, on the stumps, on the trash piles, in the swaying tops of drowning bushes. The ancient and inscrutable swamp had at last been forced to yield all its mysteries. A man with a gun paddling about in a boat could take choice toll of the hordes of fugitives. But the weapon had been left at home.

I had leaned my gun against a tree by the back door, and had told Prince to put it in the boat. He had promised; but his mind was somewhat distracted by the sickness of two of his younger children; as a result, we found ourselves weaponless on the wrong side of the river. The gun was at home, miles away, across a fairly desperate stretch of water. . . . Before us was the strange drowned delta country, always a fascinating region because of its almost prehistoric wildness—and now superbly so because of this primeval disaster to its inhabitants. The deluge had recurred. Such a catastrophe divulges blankly the creepers and the crawlers, the insidious crafty ones, the skulkers and the dodgers —not to mention myriads of less serpentine behavior.

The river that we had just crossed looked entirely too threatening to recross for the sake of a gun. Not only was it menacing because of the affluent rupture of its powerful tides, ramping in barbarous abandon to the sea, but also because it was wildly freighted with huge snaggly trees, ponderous cypress—timbers, monster yellow-pine logs—runaways from lumber camps in the swamp to northward. A good ram from any one of these would make a canoe look as if somebody had spilled a box of matches.

But why, I wondered, shouldn't I take advantage of the situation to observe the distracted wild life without harming it? Why shouldn't Prince and I make a day of it, after all? How did these creatures really manage in such an urgent case? Were there among them genuine heroes and heroines, daring hearts, philosophers, cravens? Well, I shall try to tell you exactly what we saw on that wonderful day; and by recounting as simply and as clearly as I can what Prince and I observed of the conduct of these refugees from the flood, I hope to be able to share with you some of the vivid enjoyment of what was really my most exciting and unusual outing.

My boatman agreed to my suggestion: the sentiment of it had an appeal for him. The negro's understanding of animals is profound, almost occult; and my aid on this occasion was a man who, from the time when both of us were boys, had taught me many a lesson in wood lore.

The very first refugee we saw repaid us for our crossing of the dangerous river. The marvel of her really got me. That sounds romantic, I know. But of all wild mothers that have ever come under my observation, she was the finest and the ugliest. This fugitive from the flood was a full-blooded wild razorback—all bone and bristles and lean bacon. Her snout was so long and sharp that it gave her the appearance of smoking a pipe. Her sides were plainly slatted. Her *ensemble* was, for all her uncouthness, indescribably fierce. Her startling fringe of bristles was a sort of menacing triumph. Formidable indeed she looked—morose and vindictive —standing gingerly there on a sodden log, wedged precariously by the freshet tide into the low crotch of a water oak.

Brush and sedge and the tree's limbs had made a tremulous islet that swayed in the rushing waters. Behind her, under her, quaking in the shelter of her mighty flanks, were her little ones—nine of them. She could easily save herself. But she would not leave them to

94

perish. I wondered much what would now happen. These hogs, you understand, were perfectly wild; therefore we approached behind a fringe of cypresses, in order to watch their natural behavior.

Knowing that the old mother could swim miles to safety, I made up my mind to save at least some of the pigs. They were only about two or three weeks old; and in their present situation they looked to me doomed. . . . But perhaps no living thing is doomed as long as it has a mother.

You really ought to have seen this one. The waters were fast rising. The old savage creature knew well that she and her trembling brood must soon be dislodged from their quaking, frail support. About a half mile away, across a clear stretch of water, there was some high ground known as the Pine Ridge. I saw her looking at it. She was appraising the risk incurred to reach it. She had, I knew, determined to swim to the Ridge. But she wasn't going alone. Lowering her hideous, formidable head, she tenderly nuzzled the pigs, one by one. To them she grunted deep and placid reassurance. She kept nudging them until all of them were in a huddle.

Then suddenly I saw her plunge off the log into the stormy tide. About thirty feet she swam—fiercely and with head high, as a hog always swims; then she headed around, and in a few moments had returned to the log. She climbed it, streaming. As surely as I was watching her, I believe that she was instructing her babies as to how the thing was to be done; and she was showing them how easy it was. Again she took gentle counsel with her nursery.

Slowly now, and with infinite caution and patience, she herded them down toward the water. She was actually in it, among the stranded sedges, for a moment or two, before she was satisfied that all her brood were with her. Then, grunting easily, very slowly she began to swim. She didn't swim like a hog; for she was now the solicitous mother. All her tiny pigs were in the lee of her great flank. Seeing to it that they started on that side, she broke the current for them, and they swam as if they were in a backwater. She did not appear to be trying to save her own life, but theirs. It was a beautiful sight to watch—that grim old monster mothering her babies across that stormy tide! Self-preservation is said to be the first law of Nature. But from the operation of that law shall we not have to make an exception of mothers?

An hour later Prince and I found our gallant old sea-going heroine on the Pine Ridge. She had every little pig safely with her. I looked with genuine admiration at the gaunt, grim creature; but Prince, remembering his empty smokehouse, regarded her with an economic, languishing glance.

A somewhat similar evidence of a wild mother's crafty solicitude I saw one day in the pinelands near home. I was on a deer stand, and heard a great outcry in a small thicket near me. One member of the oncoming pack of deer hounds had encountered an old razorback sow, and within a few moments the traveling circus, heading my way, came into full view. The old mother had with her five tiny pigs. Close behind this semi-wild family the hound bawled—eager to close with his apparent game, yet seemingly wishing for his comrades to join him, so that the contest would not be too unequal. Deciding to interfere, I stepped forward and drove the hound back into the deer thicket. Then followed a very pretty and amusing sight.

The razorback eyed me with hardly any less scornful apprehension than she had manifested toward the hound. She faced me truculently, champing her lantern jaws. But I knew that all her savagery was but the sword and shield of her heart's affection.

Quietly I withdrew, watching her. Feeling that she was fairly safe from her two enemies, she began to give a series of peculiar grunts. At the first of these, the tiny pigs behaved as if they had been acted upon by magic. They suddenly ranged themselves in single file in front of the mother; then, at another grunt, they broke into a full run. The five were in perfect line, about two feet apart; each had his tail screwed up tightly on his back; each behaved as if he had suddenly been wired for.

The strange part about it was the fact that these babies led, with amazing certainty and celerity, this elfin escape. The grim old mother, merely by trotting along, could keep up with her infants' flight. She kept up her admonitory grunts, and they got the full meaning of her message. She sent them ahead, of course, so that she could cover their flight. She was the rear guard.

A flood makes strange bedfellows. However high a freshet may rise, there is always dry footing on the Pine Ridge of the delta. And the great community of the

wild knows this. This long sandy elevation is almost
bare, and it has a giant pine sentineling its northern end.
Certain bushes give a sparse undergrowth; but this is
kept severely down by the myriads of refugees that over-
run it in time of high waters.

In order to get an idea of their heterogeneous character, and also to estimate the number, I had my negro
put me off at the southern point, directing him to paddle
to the Lone Pine, and then push the canoe along the
edge, driving the fugitives before him. At this particular time the edge was exposed for three hundred yards,
and for some fifty yards across. I could see a confusion
of creatures from my stand; and as Prince moved down
alongside the ridge, these took shape and identity.

Of course the first thing to appear was a wild turkey. This great bird is supersensitive to inspection; and
while raccoons snooze unconcernedly in the face of
danger, and while deer pause curiously to look back,
a wild turkey, exercising the occult art of shadowy
avoidance, slips away. I once heard an old woodsman
declare: "When a wild turkey says, 'Put! Put!' he's
serving you notice that he's going to quit the world!"
Surely, when it comes to a sleight-of-foot vanishing act,
this splendid bird has no equal.

My turkey, coming down the ridge, was alarmed;
therefore, he had drawn himself up very erect, and his
form was slim and trim. His matchless eyes searched
avidly for the slightest movement that would betray
the presence of the enemy. I was standing against a
black stump—which afforded me less effacement than
it would have afforded a man of my paddler's complex-

ion—and delicately toward me the wild bird came. His neck shed iridescent colors; and from his wings and back rippled and waved away a bronze sheen. He was far ahead of anything else on the ridge. Silently, gorgeously, he came stealing along.

He was within thirty yards of me when I must have made a slight movement; a wild thing nearly always identifies a man by sound or scent or movement—seldom by recognition. Without the least hesitancy, the mighty bird, after a little run, took wing, rising until he was seventy or eighty feet above the yellow freshet tide. He was heading for the far-off mainland, more than a mile away. His flight was so superb and swift that I knew he would be there in less than two minutes.

I have timed turkeys flying down a mountainside, and have found them doing a little better than a mile a minute. In straight flight, as nearly as I have been able to estimate, after a turkey gets fairly started, he does not go at a rate less than forty miles an hour. . . . But in making such a hazard, I always recall, by way of reservation, a wise saying of one of my old woodsmen friends:

"How fast does a wild turkey fly?" he repeated before answering my question. "That depends on what's after him, and how close to him it is."

By the time the wild turkey had disappeared, down the ridge came the razorback family already mentioned, and with them a mincing doe! Quaint troops of swamp rabbits moved down the ridge—most of them employing the rabbit's peculiar method of sly advance. He will be crouched, let us say hunched up. Sedulously he will extend his forefeet to the limit of his reach, resting them gently on the ground; then, for all the world like a measuring worm, he will draw his body up to his forefeet. I had often seen a rabbit perform this sort of maneuver, especially when stealing silently in or out of a thicket. But I had never seen the thing done in concert before; it seemed that a procession of accordions was approaching. The impression that it gave was very odd—as if some dim rite were being performed.

After the animals came birds—woodcock and Wilson snipe, flying and lighting down—king-rails walking. The woodcock behaved like proud little turkey gobblers. I saw several of them strut, with wings lowered and fan tails spread.

When Prince came within sight, I motioned him away from the ridge, as I didn't want the fugitives driven into the water. He fetched a semicircle and picked me up. But even while I was waiting for him to come, I saw approaching a visitor whose presence every refugee except two would dread—these two being the deer and the hog. This new voyager was a rattlesnake, an old inhabitant of the moldering swamp that was now flooded. Superbly he swam; indeed, there's hardly a more expert swimmer. I noticed that his sheaf of rattles was held high above the water—to keep the sinister chime dry, of course. I have never yet seen a rattlesnake swimming that he did not have his rattles out. His head, too, will be somewhat elevated.

An aquatic creature often behaves like a submarine,

showing now the periscope, now the turret, now the back—now nothing. A land creature that is forced to swim always seems to elevate as much of himself as possible.

Leaving the ridge, we paddled up to a small bushy-headed cypress, among the limbs of which my paddler had located an acquaintance. Snoozing serenely among the branches, utterly oblivious to the world and the "thousand natural shocks that flesh is heir to" was an old raccoon. Early in life the coon becomes a philosopher; and he has a calm acceptance of things that reminds one of Kipling's requirement for a man:

> If you can meet with Triumph and Disaster,
> And treat those two impostors just the same . . .

Here, indeed, was ample cause for excitement, for haste, for frantic effort. But a raccoon prefers to amble, to snooze, to insinuate his indolent, genial way through the world.

As we approached them, most of the fugitives from the flood fixed upon us their beady black eyes, or their liquid, imploring ones. But this fellow was profoundly, absurdly asleep. I told Prince to lift him into the boat.

Holding a cypress limb with one hand, Prince took the sleeper by the scruff of the neck with the other. There was no wild struggle, no hectic awakening. The coon complained drowsily, and seemed intent upon maintaining that snuggly position into which he had been curled. The only thing which really appeared to perturb him was the fact that we were arresting his slumbers.

In the bottom of the canoe the raccoon curled himself, there to resume his dreamful ecstasy. What did he care about men and floods? When I touched him, he drawled amiably and luxuriously, for all the world like a boy who is an adept at pulling the covers up over his head. While I admire an animal that is constantly alert, and that is radically so in time of general peril, I also admire a creature that possesses a certain stubborn geniality.

Not long ago I heard a rather pompous, absurd individual say that he had never encountered a situation that he could not dominate. The raccoon is not of this dominant strain; but he gets vast enjoyment out of life. This one, for example, snoozing calmly in my boat: though captured by his archenemies, he must have his nap out.

Ancient civilizations depend much upon little customs: the Englishman must have his tea in the afternoon. . . . The raccoon belongs to a more ancient civilization than man, in a sense; and his siesta to him is a sacred thing. Man is developing all the time (so we understand); but from time immemorial the raccoon has been using his full mental and physical capacity. I am not one of those who believe that ere the advent of the automobile and the rifle wild creatures had an easy time of it. Civilization is the foe not only of the raccoon but of the raccoon's old enemies as well. Nature's balance has always been kept; and where man is not, other grim enemies are found.

I recall another raccoon that equaled this one in his *savoir faire*. I was walking one winter down a cause-

way in Blake's Marsh, a vast reedy waste, now a part
of a great game refuge. In a gnarled red cedar I came
upon a raccoon basking in the genial sunshine. As he
was in a low fork of the tree, I reached for him and
lifted him down by the back of the neck.

Snuggling him against my hunting coat, I walked on
unconcernedly. At first I heard one or two low snarls
of sleepy complaint. Then all was still. After a while
I heard what seemed to be further growls. But my
captive was fast asleep, and was snoring confidingly,
contentedly in my arms! Somehow, that sort of experience with a wild thing gets me more than all the
hunting and trapping in the world. I may have become
too sentimental over that raccoon, but he made me
think of Beaumont's beautiful lines:

> They have most power to hurt us whom we love;
> We lay our sleeping lives within their arms.

This whole country, that was now submerged by the
flooded Santee, used to be planted in rice; and where
the ancient banks once were are now lines of trees and
bushes, marking the limits of the fields with perfect
accuracy. Some of the bushes were deluged, or lay level
on the flood like a mermaid's streaming hair. Wherever
there was a tree top or a bush top showing, there was
some wanderer lodged. We came to a sweet-gum tree
over which smilax vines had rioted. The top of this
was some seven feet above the tide. Crouched in it were
three handsome king-rails and five swamp rabbits!

These little brown bunnies, quite distinct from the
jaunty cottontails, are famous swimmers, and they are

good climbers as well. I have known one to go as high as twenty feet in a hollow tree. What interested me about these refugees was the fact that they had not only climbed out of the water but had not rested until they were high above it. Three of them were in the vines near the very top of the bush. It seemed to me that they had taken into account the possibility of a further rise in the water. Thus ensconced, a rabbit will sit for days, nibbling the twigs and vines within reach, with pathetic yet genuine patience awaiting the subsiding of the waters.

I was interested in seeing how many of the refugees were real swimmers; and I dislodged a good many of them just to test their ability. There is honestly no such thing as a wild creature that cannot swim. The king-rails would step off into the tide, and go gliding away in a swift serpentine fashion; the bunnies would take a frantic, timid plunge; but once in, they swam with remarkable speed and grace; we passed a drove of razor-backs heading for the mainland shore. They always swim as if they are racing, their snouts high, crowding each other—occasionally one overriding the back of another. They are powerful swimmers—and apparently tireless. Though I have known thousands to swim, I never knew one to drown, except by being caught in some kind of natural trap. I once found the body of one of these creatures fixed in the tight fork of a tree—wedged in such a way that it was clear, that, attempting to swim through the crotch at a time when the flood was flush with it, he had been caught. The subsequent rise of the waters had drowned him.

Cattle are good swimmers—and sheep also; goats, too, though they dislike water as much as cats, and are as canny about getting wet. I have also seen a wild turkey swim—not a wounded one, either. But Prince and I were now to come to a real master of the art.

A little inundated swamp was ahead of us; and as we entered this the trees made paddling difficult. I tried to pull the canoe along by catching the saplings and drawing on them. The waters here had a glassy glide, broken purlingly by the trunks of the trees—broken also by the swimming of fugitives. I had seen so many rabbits that I paid little attention to them; and when I saw what I took at a glance to be another bunny, I gave him no attention. But suddenly I heard Prince behind me say, "Otter!" The lithe swimmer was then within fifteen feet of the boat—a long, glistening creature, with head held high, with white whiskers gleaming. He's a swimmer *de luxe*.

For a moment I saw him thus, marking his sinuous grace, marking also his gorgeous rich fur; then he humped himself like a diver in a jackknife dive, and was gone into the dim heart of the flood. His long furred tail made identification of him certain. We waited for him to rise, but he did not come up again. For underwater swimming, I don't think a fish has much on an otter; and of all wild creatures inhabiting the delta, this obscure, elusive, elegant aristocrat is to me one of the most appealing.

More than once I have found their slides—the long smooth slopes of mud on some remote bank, down which they glide gleefully. There is not a more playful animal. Once, near the old abandoned place on the delta called Tranquillity, I saw a family of otters sliding. The slide was perhaps fifteen feet high, glistening smooth, and overhung by marsh. Not far from its foot were the mud-covered timbers of an old, abandoned wharf.

The otters would slither down the bank, strike the water with a joyous kind of splash, and then swim over to the timbers, which were almost flush with the tide. On these they would crawl and preen themselves luxuriously in the sun. I say "preen," for that is the impression their toilet making gave. An otter is very fond of licking his exquisite fur; and in the sunlight after such a burnishing it glows radiantly.

Few animals, barring the wildcat, are so secretive in their habits; and otters may live for years close to human habitations without having their presence suspected. I love an otter. He is the most graceful and joyous of creatures; and I never see one in a lonely creek or on some solitary bank without feeling that suddenly the soul of the place has uttered itself in beauty, that the palpitant heart of the wastelands has suddenly divulged its most intimate secret.

Considering once more the flood, it is interesting to know to what degree the more hapless of the mariners may be borne far away, literally into other lands. Having taken a curious interest in this matter, I can say that I knew of a buck to be caught by a drifting tree and drowned, and that his body was found a week later on a sea beach some twelve miles distant. Sea islands which formerly had no snakes have gradually become infested by them, because of the freshet tides that carry them, like so much flotsam, out into the ocean and then back upon the beaches.

Some thirty-five miles from the mouth of the Santee there is a popular bathing beach; and not long ago the seashore beauties were horrified to see a grim bull alligator riding the breakers as serenely as any summertime Adonis of a bathing resort. He, of course, had been floated out to sea by a fresh-water flood; and, as he is quite as much at home in salt water as in fresh, he had journeyed on a sea voyage down the coast for his health.

Of those creatures that seem to love a freshet, none is more loud in its praise than the tiny marsh-wren—a little brown wisp of a songster. This frolic youngster lives, I imagine, in terror most of the time in the shadowy country of the marsh. But when it is flooded, and delightful rafts of sedge are drifting about, he is as engaging and as independent as our village Central. He is the Ariel, as the alligator is the Caliban, of the delta. He bobs up and down on the sedge, carols a truelove ballad, inspects with refreshing pertness the sedges for the tiny insects that are his fare, and cares not a whit how the waters rage. Of course he has his wings. A thing with wings can afford, I think, to take life somewhat more jauntily, more angelically, than we can.

In the presence of an ancient menace like a flood, our brothers of the wild have a certain native felicity of resource, a certain deft precision of judgment. When one of these mighty waters moves down the river, immersing the swamps and the low-lying lands, the life in those regions is very far from being terrorized. Indeed, the only things that I ever saw utterly demoralized by such a crisis were domesticated stock. In the face of a freshet's stormful, proud advancing, most wild creatures are resolute, resourceful, calm; they swim; they climb; they wait with infinite patience; yet I believe at such a time wild ducks are likely to be somewhat demoralized.

They are dependent upon sunny sandbars, reed-hung glassy creeks, well-defined regions. They do not seem to know what to do in a vast sea of rushing waters. I have observed at such a time myriads of wildfowl hurrying in long distracted lines, they knew not whither. In most cases, after much vague and circuitous flight, they betake themselves to the quieter backwaters of the flooded swamp, where they gorge themselves upon the luxurious foods that such a place offers. But when a deluge first takes the delta I have seen countless thousands of mallards, black ducks, and widgeons thronging wildly and tumultuously, embarrased by a satiety of their native element. . . . Yet in the presence of its deadly peril a raccoon will enjoy his sleep serenely.

It was Mithridates, I think, who used to take small doses of poison, so that when some traitor should serve him with a spoonful of arsenic, he would not notice the delicate attention. He who knows of the troubles that one has to expect in life will be neither surprised nor stunned by them. They will be like things that he has long since experienced and sustained.

After we had left the ridge with its inhabitants, Prince and I paddled northward over the drowned country, passing scores of groups of just such fugitives as I have described. We came at last to the gray, gloomy, but alluring margins of the great swamp, steeped now in this stifling tide. Here, we knew, were wildcats, foxes, and bears; for the last, Prince had no especial relish. One thing we saw before we had skirted the swamp a hundred yards. A tall alder bush had a crown of smilax, and this was swaying in the current some six feet above the water.

As we drew up, we discerned a creature curled up in the vines. Of course we thought it to be a raccoon. But it was a fox! Doubtless, in swimming out of the submerged swamp, he had come to this refuge, and had climbed up into the cradling vines. He saw us coming; but he did not move. I could tell by his peaked ears that he was watching us intently; and soon I discerned his brilliant feline eyes. But he had no intention of moving if we passed him by. He seemed to me a very good sport—to hold himself in check while his fellest enemies drew near. He had been in the vines some time, I knew, for his fur was dry and fluffy. There he lay luxuriously—secure in a certain felicitous and admirable guile.

The fox, I think, moves in a mental orbit outside that of most creatures and of most men. His mental attitude is distinctly Oriental. Some people make a ponderous passage through the world by butting the bull off the bridge; others insinuate themselves around and over and under difficulties—secret and serpentine and delicately crafty, capriciously certain. To the latter class belongs the fox. Our cradled friend we left on the lonely swamp edge, swaying in a hammock above the tide.

On our homeward paddle we picked up several rabbits that seemed worn-out with swimming, two tame pigs, and another raccoon. All of these, upon reaching the plantation landing, we set free. Each in his own way left us; the pigs grunting unconcernedly, the raccoons pacing thoughtfully down the edges of the freshet, the bunnies hopping off among the leaves, pausing to lick their wet fur and to wash their faces with their paws.

Our hunt was at an end. It had been the most interesting one I had ever enjoyed. And we hadn't killed a thing! Like the liberated wild things, Prince and I made our way from the river to our hearths and homes —I to the big house near the river—he to his cabin amid the wistful autumn fields, fast fading now in the twilight, dewy and still and fragrant.

As I walked up to the plantation house, thinking of what my strange cruise had meant to me, I came upon my gun, leaning against a tree. Somehow I was glad that it had been left. For if a man takes a gun into the wilds with him, he may leave his heart at home.

WHEN we were looking at those wild refugees from the flood, you will recall that my good boatman was Prince. Will you let me tell you a little more of him? He is so close to Nature that he deserves to be numbered among the elemental verities. Dear comrade is he, whose faithful affection has often brought to my heart a peace the world could not give. To be stilled in spirit, and joyous, do we not sometimes have to depend on the love of friends? God meant them for no better purpose.

My association with Prince Alston has been lifelong. He is the son of Martha, for forty years our plantation cook, and of Will, for a longer period our wood-bringer and fire-builder. Prince and I are of the same age. But his infancy, though he was supposed to be relatively unimportant, was far more dramatic than mine. Nature often seems to overlook with the most exasperating candor many of those very distinctions upon which we most fervently insist. One day, while I was sleeping in my carriage in the front yard, Prince was being plunged, in the back yard, into a huge caldron of hot pea soup. He thus early attained over me an ascendancy in point of authentic interest; and, although I am supposed to be the master and he the man, perhaps he has maintained it to this very day. I owe him much. For forty-four years now our comradeship has lasted, and it is one of deep affection. For my part, I see no reason for the termination of it, either on this or on the other side of the grave.

Prince's affair in the caldron happened quite naturally. His mother reported to mine that the baby had a spasm. Recognizing at once the child's desperate need, and knowing that an immediate plunge into warm water was the best first-aid remedy, my mother called for hot water. None was forthcoming; but Martha suggested that in the back yard peas were boiling. My mother, with little Prince in her arms, hurried down the back steps. Before her under a huge live oak was the momentous-looking caldron, just beginning to steam gently. Dipping in her finger to determine the temperature of the water, and finding it tepid, she laid the black baby among the steaming pea pods, holding him gently but firmly in place. Almost at once his crying stopped. Prince was saved; moreover, a certain glamour was shed over his infancy, and for years he went under the strange and distinctive appellation of the "Pea-Soup Baby."

Prince's inheritance is a good one; I mean his spiritual inheritance. His mother is possessed of a primeval faithfulness and affection, and his father of an almost heartbreaking humble loyalty. How can I ever forget what Will did in the matter of the trunk that held the precious trousseau?

We were to have with us on the plantation a bride and groom; and all arrangements were complete save that of transporting the bride's trunk. It had to come by boat from the city to the Carolina seacoast village, and thence brought by ox wagon to us, ten miles farther on. On this delicate errand of bringing the trunk from the village to the plantation I dispatched Will, with many injunctions. He was told that, whatever happened, the trunk was not to get wet. When many hours passed without his return, and when certain clouds began to spring leaks, I got on a horse and rode down the solitary forest highway to meet Will. By the time I had gone five miles the drizzle had become a downpour. I could hardly see thirty feet ahead of me. At length, quite suddenly, I came upon the wagon in the road. The oxen, with placid bowed heads, were taking the drenching. Neither Will nor the trunk was in sight. I felt sure that there must have been an accident.

But as I rode to the wagon, I saw a figure sprawled on its floor, the rain beating down mercilessly on it, and winter rain at that! It was Will. Under the wagon, resting on the dry sand, was the trunk, all decorated with white ribbons. It was dry. The negro had dragged it from the cart, rolled the vehicle back over it, and then had lain down over it to keep the rain off.

"You done say dis trunk ain't for wet," Will told me, almost in self-defense. There he was, miles from home, performing an obscure fealty. And his son Prince has always had that kind of spirit in him.

Through childhood and boyhood my Black Prince and I were inseparable companions in a thousand plantation escapades: we were thrown from the same woods' pony at the same time; we were together pursued by the same infuriated bull; nearly drowned in the same pond when our canoe upset; and in the matter of gleeful butting, the half-wild goat that we had captured made no distinction between us as victims for his sinister jesting. Whenever our frolics came to the attention of the elder generation, we were mutually reprimanded. My father repeatedly scolded us as one, especially on the occasion when we knotted together the tails of two semi-wild boars that were feeding at a trough, with their backs close to a convenient hole in the fence. And Henry Snyder, the negro foreman, a very superior person, for whom I early acquired a dreadful respect, used to be very severe with us—chiefly because we delighted in ruffling his oppressive dignity.

Our worst offense occurred on the day when, borrowing a set of deer horns from the frieze in the hall, and draping two deerskins over us after the manner in which the Seminoles camouflaged themselves while deerstalking, we burst into the barnyard, where scores of negroes were threshing rice, superintended by Henry. We charged the crowd with wild, weird shouts, scattering madly the gravest and most sedate of them, especially Henry, in whom, as the leader of his clan, a peculiarly high and sensitive kind of superstition had been developed. Henry's ability as a runner, jumper, and general escaper had never been publicly demonstrated before; but he showed on that day the power to lead, in rather magnificent style, a precipitous retreat. We paid dearly for our fun, for to make a man lose an assumed and cherished dignity is of all insults the most deadly.

But mischief did not occupy us wholly. We planted a little garden together; we had scores of curious pets, such as alligators, raccoons, fawns, foxes and minks; we rode together after the cattle; visited the solitary spacious pine woods to get lightwood for the fires. We also, from earliest times, hunted and fished a good deal together, though I cannot report that we supplied the plantation table with commendable regularity. Our failure to do so was not due to any lack of fish and game, but rather to our discursive natures; for no sooner were we well started on a hunt, or well settled by some cypress-brown, bass-haunted lagoon to fish, than some new interest of the wildwood or of the wild water would divert us. Thus I remember that we spent a whole half day trying to see how many deadly cotton-mouth moccasins we could catch with our fishing tackle. We did well, but when we presented our catch to Martha, in a somewhat darkened kitchen, her reaction was decidedly volatile and picturesque.

Young as I was, even in those first years of my association with Prince I recognized in him a decided superiority in certain matters. A plantation negro is as close to Nature, I suppose, as any man in the world; and close in an intimate, authentic sense. He is still a child, folded on that ample bosom; he hears and obeys the voice of the ancient mother; he has with marvelous accuracy what we slangily but felicitously call the low-down on all the creatures of Nature. The knowledge of them that came to me in some small degree after many years of patient observation and study, Prince appeared to have instinctively. His understanding of wild things was, and is, not scientific, but natural; I have always noticed that he speaks of an animal as if it were a human being; he fixes no gulf between the two neighboring kingdoms. His eyes in the woods used to surprise me; now they amaze me. My own eyesight has always been normally good, but it does not clairvoyantly apprehend as does his. As boys together, he was almost invariably the one to warn me when I was about to step on a snake; he could take me to the spot in the sunny wild field of broomsedge where a little fawn lay; he could see, on the topmost tiny spire of a towering yellow pine, that wisp of gray that betrayed the presence of a scared fox squirrel; it was he who took me to the den of a huge bull alligator on a lonely island. He had heard that Minotaur roar, had discounted all the ventrilo-quistic quality of that weird bellow, had located the singer accurately, and to the formidable monster he guided me, when he was not more than eleven years old. We caught the huge reptile, Prince and I, with a hook and line. We drew out Leviathan with a hook.

Because of our close and genuine comradeship, I used to go to Prince's cabin about as often as he came to my home; and as we were together every day and usually until nightfall, each one would go halfway home with the other. The way led through the woods, and along

the edges of the melancholy plantation burying ground
where, for more than two centuries, the negroes of the
place had been interred. There the mighty pines towered tallest; there the live oaks stood druid-like; there
the jasmines rioted freely over hollies and sweet myrtles, tossing their saffron showers high in air. As children, Prince and I dreaded this place and I can remember going along this dusky road many a time, my
love for him taking me farther from home than my
reason warranted; and his love for me overmastering
his fear of the graveyard, so that often he used to come
with me all the way to the plantation gate. We used to
walk that road holding hands; and even now I can remember how the hands of those children, one black and
one white, used to tighten as a dewy, strange wind
gushed by us, or as an owl would begin his haunting
twilight note. (We are still holding hands, Prince and
I, as we go down the mysterious road of life; and the
grip tightens, as it did of old, whenever we feel that
danger and the unknown are near.)

All things human change; and the time came when
a temporary parting was inflicted upon Prince and me.
I was sent away to school and to college; he remained
in his old wild, free life. His prospect looked to me
as halcyon as mine was forboding. It was years before
we were able to renew our companionship. When opportunity was once more afforded us to be together,
we were both grown. Whatever, in a deeper sense, my
growth had been, I do not think that essentially it was
very far in advance of his; and certainly in physical development he had immeasurably surpassed me.

Whence got he those mighty shoulders? Whence came that iron grasp? Whence got he that huge and rugged forearm, that splendid depth of chest? Though not of great height, his stature, leonine and massive, would set all the athletic coaches of America agog if they could see it. While I had been delicately pursuing French verbs to their dim lairs, and trying with many a headache to determine whether pragmatism was a true philosophy and relativity a true scientific theory, Prince had been felling forests, digging canals, driving mule teams, and, with the sun at about 115°, he had been plowing down knee-high crab grass, shouting and singing as he worked. Standing to the thighs in fetid, snake-haunted swamp water, all day long he had sawed huge cypress logs, he and his fellows laughing and joking as they toiled. Or out in the lonely forest of yellow pine, from daylight to dark he had brought thundering to earth the giant trees, tall as the masts of brigantines, and full of nameless aërial melodies in their crowns.

Black, rugged, independent, Prince was a man long ere I became one. Years and other matters had parted us; but when we met, we clasped hands with the old affection, and perhaps understood each other as perfectly as two human beings ever do. Death's is not the only veil through which we cannot see; impalpable arras separate most of us. The human soul seems a shrouded thing, and most solitary. Love alone is capable of destroying isolation and of breaking down every barrier.

That Prince is a real psychological study I have, of

late years, come deeply to appreciate. There is, for example, his mastery of animals, which has in it a spiritual legerdemain fascinating to behold. No man who watches this negro with dogs or mules can be persuaded that magic is dead. On occasions that are literally countless I have shamelessly referred to him dogs that were of the most incorrigible sort, dogs that would not even make up with me. Immediately he would establish a definite relationship with them, partly by firmness, partly by kindness, but chiefly by an occult and complete fathoming of the dog's mentality. I recall how he made Blossom mind him when she would pay me not the slightest attention.

This hound was new and strange, and Prince and I took her into the woods for a ramble. Young, diffident, headstrong, she was prone to race pell-mell after any alluring scent that assailed her delicate nostrils from the damp sandy road. We were in wild country; and to have her escape on a trail would have been serious. I was about to suggest that we put her in a leash when she suddenly left the road on a dead run. A fresh buck track explained her joyous haste.

At thirty yards a shout from Prince brought her to a bickering halt. She was too far away for him to catch her, or even to threaten her effectively with the long lash that he carried. The hound did not want to come back. Yet, while ignoring me, she deigned to give Prince a bright, undetermined look, as if inquiring politely the reason for his impertinent interruption of her urgent business. Knowing that it would be a vain thing for me to try to lure the dog, I left it all to him—I usually leave anything to him that's difficult—watching closely to discover by what mental artful sleight he would accomplish the miracle. Clearly, it was to be a spiritual, not a physical, struggle.

"Blossom," he called, "come here, chile. Here, Blossom, come here to me. You is the prettiest, fines', most 'bedient houn' I ever did see. That's a good girl; come on now. Come on, honey Blossom. I know you wouldn't leave me here in the road all by myself. That's a sweet Blossom."

Flattering wiles, couched in tones that reached the hound's very soul, accomplished what force and anger and less delicate deception could never have done. But there was more than that to the performance. Into the immense solitude environing the individual Prince had suavely obtruded himself. All creatures will, I suppose, respond to blandishments; but they must be of the intimate and understanding variety. The hound Blossom was completely taken by Prince's tones. She turned toward us; then she approached step by step, a little contritely. At last she made a little run, frisked about Prince, leaped up on him affectionately, licked his hand I had had, in college, a course in practical psychology, and one in animal psychology. But my knowledge had left me helpless, whereas Prince knew what to do without ever having been taught.

Watching Prince handle the biggest, stubbornest mules in a timber camp, I have come to believe that the secret of his mastery over them arises from his ability subtly to establish in them a definite conception of their inferiority. He then takes it for granted that they will work, his attitude being objective, hale and natural. He talks to them also, as it were, in their own tongue, and to his raillery they respond with astonishing willingness. To manage mules should be accounted something of an artistic *tour de force.*

I remember the first time I ever saw Prince operate on a stubbornly planted mule. It happened down in a little seacoast village near home. A farmer's mule, hitched to an infirm and staggering wagon, loaded heavily with a Saturday's purchases, had made up his mind that the prospect of seven long sandy miles ahead did not appeal to him. The animal balked in the middle of the village street, right between the post office and the general store, so that the performance created a considerable stir. At such a time, all local and loafal celebrities are exceedingly fertile in advice. To this scene of hopeless *status quo* Prince and I arrived after some very heroic measures had been used without the slightest response on the part of the immobile mule. He had been cruelly beaten; his harness had been taken off. The wagon had been rolled back. But there he stood violently rooted, with a certain exasperatingly virtuous expression on his countenance. Curses and shouts left him unmoved. Even a small fire built under him had had no effect at all as a persuader to progress. The city fathers had become less assured of tone as one after another of their solvents for balkiness failed. The affair had come to an impasse when Prince stepped quietly forward, while I watched fascinated. Approaching the mule with gentle assurance, he insinuated one arm around the stubborn neck. His touch was affectionate. Putting his mouth to the mule's left ear, he said something to the miserable statue. Instantly the creature's rigidity relaxed, and almost blithely the mule stepped forward from the position which for more than an hour he had sullenly maintained. When Prince came back to me, I asked him what he had said to his friend. The negro only laughed, for he never seems to take seriously any of his feats with animals. But his must have been the magic words having the exact wave length of the dull creature's obscure and baffled soul.

For many years I had searched in vain for a specimen of the black fox squirrel, a variant in color of the gray. It is in reality a color due to a condition known as melanism. Mentioning to Prince one day my wish, I was surprised to have him say, "I show you one to-day." Together forthwith we went to the woods. It was mid-March, and the leaves gave the forest an emerald-misty look.

Prince took me up a long watercourse through the woods where grow many tupelos, gums, and redbud maples. Ere we had gone a half mile we had seen gray fox squirrels, big handsome fellows. Each one was in a maple tree. At last my companion pointed to what I should have taken for a spray of dead Spanish moss. It hung almost drifting from among the ruby buds of a maple. It was a fox squirrel, black as ebony.

"How did you know it was here?" I asked.

"He been here las' summer," Prince answered, "and the year befo', when he was a baby. A fox squirrel," he added, "this time of the year will come a mile or mo' to get the redbud."

Woodcraft of this kind Prince gathered during those years when he was a worker of turpentine; and no kind of toil is more exacting in the matter of compelling the worker to traverse almost every foot of the forest. He must literally go from tree to tree. Being a keen and accurate observer, and not only seeing but actually entering into the lives of the children of the wild, he has gathered an astonishing amount of first-hand information about Nature, and this knowledge, like all information acquired through experience, has become a part of his character. Many men use their knowledge of Nature merely as an intellectual decoration; this negro guides his life by that knowledge and by those ancient laws. Because he does live by those laws, ordinary physical obstacles have for him no substantial existence. Long since he has learned, without any mechanical device, how to annihilate distance.

One afternoon I said to Prince that he and I ought to go deer hunting the next day at daylight. I could see that my request embarrassed him a little. But he said he would join me, adding, "I will be back by then."

"Back?" I asked. "Where are you going?"

"I have to step up to Jamestown," he answered.

This place is twenty-three miles from home, and swamp miles, too, over corduroy roads which are usually inundated. Prince walked the forty-six miles, most of them in the dark; and at daylight the following morning was in the plantation back yard before I was up. In fact, what woke me was the joyous yowling of the hounds which announced the arrival of their beloved lord and master. Prince thinks nothing of walking twenty miles to buy a plug of tobacco, a pound of bacon, a sack of flour. And usually in making his journeys he does not follow roads; as short cuts he knows all the animal paths through the forest. When he needs wood, taking his ax he will go to the pine lands, perhaps a mile or more from his cabin, and will return with a massive section of a lightwood log on his shoulder. He does things directly, quietly, in Nature's way. When I read stories of negroes who are little more than minstrels, I do not recognize in them blood-brothers to my Black Prince. Though superstitious in a piquant way, as all elemental human beings are, he is not afraid of the dark. Moreover, without being able to name a single star, he can guide himself by them; and, lacking starlight, he retains an uncanny sense of direction even in the deepest woods at night. Well I remember the time that he and I, taking an acetylene lamp, went to the forest to try to discover and to count the deer that we could shine with the light.

It was late October; the dying year was beautiful only as lovely things departing can be beautiful. It had rained that afternoon; and as we set out on our expedition, a sodden yellow evening with sallow lights was faintly gilding the ruined trees. Pale lilac gleams suffused the fading woods. By the time we had left the inner plantation bounds, night had come down, starless, occult, mysterious. Before we had gone a mile farther, our blazing light had disclosed for us five deer, airy shapes of the fabulous darkness, delicately roaming the forest. I was wearing the lamp as a headlight; and it disclosed to us not only the deer but our own surroundings as well. Prince said he knew where we were, though we were in virgin timber, a long way from any road. On we went, deeper and deeper into the double night of the forest and of the darkness. I heard the muffled joyous gurgling of a stream; the earth deliciously exhaled dewy odors. Other odors there were too, strange and pungent. Suddenly on my arm the hand of my woodsman closed like a vise.

"Cap'n," his soft voice said, "step back this way."

I obeyed, knowing that he had detected something that I had not.

"I smell a rattlesnake," he said; "I think he is in them huckleberry bushes ahead. We must go around him."

It may be that I owed my life to Prince that night; but I doubt if he even remembers what I so vividly recall. I can still feel his hand, hear his voice. It is a voice I infallibly trust. It is a human voice that has never deceived me. Its tones are akin to the tones of Nature.

Not far from that patch of bushes that we wisely avoided, my light began to sputter. Then something behind the glass flared, blinked, and was gone. In vain I tried to rekindle the flame. We were in abysmal darkness, there in the far-off silent woods, inhabited by creatures less appealing than deer. I was as lost as if an airplane had dropped me in the Brazilian wilderness. But I did not have the sense of being lost, for I had with me an infallible guide.

"Do you know where we are, Prince?" I asked.

"Yes, sah, I know."

"Can you find the road?"

"Yes, sah."

"How do you know which way to go?"

"My mind done tell me."

By the expression "my mind" a negro does not mean his thinking capacity, nor yet his knowledge. He seems to mean his prescience. At any rate, in a half hour we were back in the familiar plantation road. It was not that we had been actually delivered from any special peril, for with daylight we could have found our way; it was rather that Prince demonstrated to me that he had a sense of direction that would function even in the profoundest darkness; and there's always something miraculous in one person's doing what a supposed superior cannot. Here, indeed, is a child of Nature. And there is no more pretense in Prince than there is in a good black furrow or in a boulder or in a sunrise.

Of him as a spiritual human being, I have no misgivings. I know his heart too well. But most wives are exceedingly dubious concerning the state of their husbands' souls. It is so with Prince's wife. She unburdened herself to me one day.

"Prince is good," she said, in her gentle, compassionate voice, "but he cannot acclaim himself a Christian."

"Why not?" I asked, surprised.

"Because," she said thoughtfully, "he is a deer hunter. With Prince, deer hunting is religion."

But her subdued indictment of her husband was delivered with a faint smile, with a patient delicate tinge of humor, as if the future state of her sinful deer hunter did not seriously alarm her. As a matter of fact, Prince's faith would put to shame the religion of many a supposed pillar of the church. The faith of this humble negro is aboriginal, complete. How often have I heard him say simply, without a trace of professional unction, things like these: "God is good enough to do anything"; "The weather is so dry that I have a doubt mind, but if we trust in God, He will help us"; "God don't take no care of a man if he don't take no account of God"; "Cap'n, we gwine understand everything when we done reach the Promised Land."

About such a human being there is an atmosphere of permanence. He is one of the true inheritors of Nature's bounty. When I go home now after all these years and find him there, he impresses me with his changeless unspoiled quality, like that of a sentinel pine, or of the primal pagan night. Much of life is a matter of waiting, and partly for that reason we yearn toward the things in Nature which, like mountains and forests, wait with a lordly patience. Surely for the wild mortal heart to await quietly is an illustrious achievement. Prince has the ancient patience of the pioneer.

Some of the language that Prince uses would not be easily apprehended by the ordinary listener. I have made little attempt in this article to give his tones. They are musical and soft; and in addition to the "gullah" of the Carolina coastal negro, he uses a few words as strange as any ever heard in America. These are of genuine African origin, as their sound will connote. For example, when he says, "Cap'n, I yeddy one madindie in dem jubrocroo," he means that he hears a cottontail rabbit in the gallberry bushes. "De wedder giffie" means that the weather is uncertain. "Machinchie"

means small; "bungiewala" means a dragon fly; "bofemba" means a swamp rabbit. It would hardly seem
credible, and yet it is true, that Prince used often to
say to me, when we were boys, "Let we go hunt dem
machinchie bofemba an' dem blue bungiewala."

I owe to Prince what I hope is a fair understanding
of life's deeper values. I hear him say, "When I take
a man into my heart, I can't hate him no mo'." I find
him in a freezing drizzle, far from home and at dusk,
making easy in the lonely wood the bed of an old cow
that is sure to die that night, and I know that such a
man's religion is a living thing, prompting him to act.
I hear him going through the ghostly woods at night,
whooping in a voice so melodious that it would set
jaded opera-goers tingling, and I know that his spirit
is wild and free and joyous. To get on into middle life
retaining a free spirit is a thrilling accomplishment. To
range the wildwoods singing, and with the heart singing, is no light thing; for to do this is to be a child of
God.

That I enjoy the companionship of Prince must be
apparent from all that I have said; but there are those
of my acquaintances who cannot understand what I
see in this humble man that so deeply endears him to
me. To begin with, he has all the reticences that make
comradeship possible. His life refutes the common
but abysmal error that to be obscure and lowly is to be
gross in word, thought and act. We are, of course,
united by memories of old; we have always loved and
understood each other. What better bases for true affection can exist than sympathy and understanding? We

belong to alien races. But we are brotherly. As I take it, the truest affection may exist between those who, naturally, or adventitiously, are far removed in life's stations. In matters of the heart, all distinctions are impostures; but other distinctions are necessary.

And if a man shall openly doubt the depth of affection that I feel for this modest comrade of mine, I am going to refer him to John Randolph of Roanoke, who, after a long and distinguished career, declared that he knew no deeper and purer human affection than that existing between himself and the negroes on his old Virginia plantation. That I, of a later and a far different day in the South, am sharing his experience is not (as I wish it might be!) a testimony of my spiritual kinship with Randolph, but to the essential humility, downright goodness, unfaltering faithfulness of the heart of the plantation negro, as I have known and loved that type of humanity in Prince.

IX STRANGE COMRADES

My COMRADESHIP with Prince represents human fellowship, though there are those who think us strange
comrades. But all life seems to crave companionship;
and in Nature we find the same necessity for association. Quaint indeed are some of the friendships made
by loneliness.

Shall we not find in these displays of affection a justi-
fication for our own preferences, quaint though they
may sometimes be?

It is said that nothing used to divert the populace of
Eighteenth Century London more than to see those
amazing comrades, old Dr. Samuel Johnson and Top-
ham Beauclerk, walking together. Nature had made
them different, and circumstances had strongly developed the characteristics of each. Johnson was a monstrous scholar—uncouth, ragged, shambling in his gait,
given to mutterings and to wild gesticulations; a sort
of gigantic tramp of a man, the very sight of whom
would send all the dogs of the neighborhood into a

frenzy. Beauclerk—with the blood of the Stuart kings in his veins, with charming manners, delicate tastes, wealth, and social distinction his—was the veritable "glass of fashion and the mold of form." A leader of the gay and fashionable world of London, he had divorced the greatest beauty in England to marry her only rival. But despite all his fashionable distinction, and despite Johnson's abysmal social shortcomings, these men were the most devoted friends. Johnson tolerated Beauclerk's punctilious ways and his sarcastic quips, his urbanity and his love of gossip; nor was Beauclerk much disconcerted, when he was bowing to fashionable acquaintances, to have his companion desert him in order to rummage in the piles of garbage on the street in search of orange peel, for which he had a strange, engrossing passion.

"Sir," said Johnson to an acquaintance who had apprised him of Beauclerk's sickness, "I will walk to the extent of the diameter of the earth if it will help him." And down his rugged cheeks coursed the honest tears of manly affection.

Human comrades often seem strangely matched; and it is a real question whether likenesses or differences in character produce affinity. Strange, too, are the comrades that we often find among the children of Nature. I have observed some exceedingly quaint friends among the wild hearts of the wastelands.

Hearts both wild and human, it seems, have a natural deep yearning for sympathy and understanding; but often individuals, families, clans and species will be separated by artificial barriers. When once these fences are removed, association becomes easy and delightful. Even those enmities which are supposed to be of ancient and implacable origin vanish as soon as the artificial conditions producing those enmities are removed.

I recall with what amusement and astonishment I used to watch the behavior of Nymph and Music. Before I became married and partly civilized, I used to delight in keeping all kinds of pets, especially those of wild and strange varieties; and these friends of mine used to cause consternation among certain members of the household. For a negro cook, soulfully singing as she sweeps a room, it is an appalling thing to see suddenly, seated sedately on the top of a door and rolling his eyes at her, a great horned owl. And for a colored maid, dozing before a fire, to stroke caressingly in her lap something that she thinks is the cat only to discover later that it is a raccoon or a fox, is a memorable spiritual experience.

My gray fox Nymph often brought me into disrepute by her ghostly exits and entrances, her uncanny slyness, and her tendency to be light-fingered. But even the negroes, who, always associating a fox with a graveyard, take no delight in this beautiful phantom's artful ways, agreed that Nymph's behavior with Music was a strange and appealing thing to watch.

Music was the best foxhound I had. Whenever I took her into the woods, as I did almost every week during the winter months, she knew as well as I that we were fox hunting. A deer she disdained. Though sometimes she would gulp avidly over the hot scent of a wild turkey, she would not follow the great bird. But in following a fox she was indefatigable; she went about it with that stern joy which the true artist alone can feel. With every fox, Music seemed to be at natural and implacable hostility—with every fox but Nymph. They were almost ludicrously fond of each other.

On our front porch we had some big hickory rockers with cushions in them. The hounds and my pets were supposed to resist the temptation to sleep in them. But many a time I found Music and Nymph curled up in the same ample chair, fast asleep, practically with their arms about each other. Music, like most dogs, very patently felt her superiority over the whole feline tribe, a superiority that I have often gravely doubted.

Nymph seemed perfectly aware of her comrade's tendency to be high-hat sometimes; and she retaliated in the best manner possible; she used to laugh at the hound! I am sure that you will agree with me that she did, when I tell you of the favorite trick she used to play on Music.

The hound knew that she was committing a breach of etiquette when she climbed into the chair; she was therefore always more or less guiltily alert when she was in that forbidden place. A sound or a glimpse, or some movement, would make her leap to the floor of the porch and make off hastily, even though the alarm was a false one. Nymph seemed to take in the full significance of all this; and she decided in that wild little heart of hers to make some amusing use of it. One day I came up to the porch and saw Music asleep in a chair in the sun. Under the chair was Nymph; and she did not see me. There was on her face a mischievous, whimsical look. I could see that she was up to some trick.

Suddenly she set her front paws sharply on one of the chair's rockers, tilting it back violently. With something like a frightened yelp, Music jumped over the back of the chair and came scurrying down the steps. Seeing me, she naturally concluded that I had in some way upset her. She sidled past me in a most crestfallen way. Nymph meanwhile lay under the chair, flattened to the floor, an expression of demurest mischief on her quaintly sharp, intelligent face. She had shown that superior friend of hers which one really had mental capacity!

It is astonishing and reassuring to see how much fellow-feeling there is among the children of Nature. Barriers between all hearts, wild or human, seem for the most part purely artificial; and though often they are formidable, they are seldom insurmountable. Who, for example, would expect that a strong affinity could be developed between a duck and a goat? This odd companionship sometimes made me feel as if my eyes were deceiving me. Yet I believe that I fathomed the real cause of the friendship of these two interesting creatures.

A friend of mine had an ample yard in which wandered many domestic things, and among them these two. Each one appeared to be lonely; the goat because everything else, including the dogs, feared his satanic mien; and the duck because it was so greedy and quack·ful.

The goat was sinister, and the duck was incessant; a wide berth, therefore, all the other denizens of the yard gave them.

As a result, each one became lonely; consequently, they sought each other's society. Perhaps the alliance was slightly militant; at least I noticed that the duck's eyes were a good deal sharper than the goat's, so that the bird with vacuum-cleaner table manners nearly always spied first a chance for feasting. He would, quacking loudly, lead the goat across the yard; then as the two approached the feeding place, the duck would fall discreetly back. The goat, lowering his head with the sharp menacing horns, would continue the advance, the duck waddling beside him. Reaching the food, they would feast greedily, especially the duck. The goat had a sparing, selfish way of eating.

Sometimes my friend who owned this menagerie would see these odd comrades getting more than their share, and would cross the yard to drive them away. At such times, the duck would give stentorian quacks of warning, at which the two culprits would retreat in good order.

When this goat would lie down in the shade of a huge live oak to chew the cud, blinking his cold, glassy eyes, the duck would often snuggle against him; and several times I saw the duck squatting on his back, preening his feathers. On one occasion I heard a distressed outcry from the duck, and upon investigation discovered that the goat was walking the top rail of a fence, eating poison ivy. His comrade was apparently protesting against his aërial maneuvers. As soon as the goat jumped down from the fence, the duck quacked softly and contentedly, and with a fond delight.

When we study odd companionships, we have to be on our guard against what may appear friendships but really are not. Not long ago a friend of mine called me into a back room of his store to show me what he called "a wonderful sight." He said that he had a cat and a rat that seemed to be intimates. In a big barrel was a full-grown rat, and across the barrel from it was a big gray cat.

My friend explained that he had dumped the rat from a trap into the barrel, and had then dropped the cat in, thinking that thereby the last chapter in the rat's life would be speedily written. But, he went on to tell me, the two had been in the barrel an hour, and nothing had happened. When I looked in the barrel, I saw the rat crouched against one side, the cat crouched against the other. A wire screen had been placed over the top to prevent the possible escape of the rat.

Looking through this screen, I studied the situation. Of the two, the rat seemed the more self-possessed. The cat looked bored, and I thought I detected in her attitude something curiously craven. When the screen was lifted, she shot a quick glance upward, and then sprang for the top of the barrel, clambered over the lip of it, and disappeared behind some boxes.

"The cat seems scared," I said to my friend.

He looked puzzled.

"I looked at them a half dozen times," he told me, "and I thought surely that they were making up to each other."

What appeared to be a curious liking was probably nothing more than a contretemps; the cat did not like the idea of tackling the rat in such a place. Indeed, it is commonly true that sly killers like cats insist upon choosing their own fighting ground; and when denied this advantage, they will slink away from absurdly inferior foes. It seems to be true that nothing likes to fight, cornered. They will when driven to desperation; but a voluntary encounter is almost always an open encounter.

I once had a cat that showed remarkable ability to form quaint comradeships. This creature was a fine gray male of extraordinary sagacity. When I was at my summer home, ten miles from the plantation, this cat literally took to the woods, and for six months lived the life of a wild, predatory creature. But if I returned to the plantation for a day, he always appeared; and as soon as I moved back, he took up his abode in the house once again. Seeming capable of a distant but profound affection, a genuine attachment to me, though never an intimacy, this cat always made me think of ancient wisdom, and explained to me why the Egyptians found it easy to worship cats.

Among my pets was a great horned owl, a momentous bird of druid-like aspect and deportment. I had captured it one day when it had become hung in a wire fence, and for months I kept it. In a way, a horned owl is a disconcerting thing for a man to look at, for if he is at all sensitive he is made painfully aware of his abject inferiority. I never looked at my owl without pitying myself.

It would be natural to suppose that this great bird would be at royal enmity with my lordly cat. But such was by no means the case. Though I sometimes let the owl fly about in a room, I kept it usually in a huge box with a wire front. On several occasions I found the cat lying suspiciously in front of the box; usually she would be eyeing the owl with basilisk fascination. Of course I interpreted her design as a sinister one. However, one day the owl was on the floor of his cage and close to the wire. Against the wire the cat was closely pressed. Here was no crouching incident to a coming spring; here was a loneliness, a yearning for sympathy.

Opening the door of the cage, I pushed the cat in, keeping a close watch on developments. The cat lay gently down, looking at the old oracle of the woods with an affectionate deference that amazed me. For his part, the owl seemed not the least disconcerted by the cat's proximity. It is, indeed, hard for an owl to lose his immense dignity. For a half hour the two ancient enemies—in the sense that one was of the feline tribe, and one of the feathered—remained close to each other, apparently quite friendly. And almost every day that cat would take his sun bath in front of the owl's cage.

Certainly it is not in an owl's nature to be effusive or demonstrative; but he had an unmistakable liking for the comradeship of the cat. Watching their odd friendship, I wondered whether they were not somehow spiritually akin; the wisdom of each was of old: occult, mysterious; both lived by their silence and their stealth; both were at home in the deep of night. Both had hunted the same woods. They had shared with Night her pale celestial reign. They seemed to me to meet on terms existent only between those whose natures are subtly allied.

This cat of mine had another acquaintance of most engaging personality. This was a toad that lived at the foot of the back steps. I used to see them often at twilight, for then I loved to sit on the steps, especially on a spring evening. It was then that I used to hear, far across the river, the subterranean, Minotaur roar of the bull alligators; terrible, weird, but fascinating. Then through the sweet-shrub bushes the last bees would be blundering homeward through the dusk, after a long day of flowery toil; then the ponderous ruby pillars of sunset would be glowing; then the whippoorwill's shadowy song would come from the dewy heart of the darkening woods. Then, too, the cat would come down the steps, to sit for a long while beside the doorway of the toad's retreat; and usually, while the cat was waiting there, the toad would come dimly forth.

Here assuredly were two genuine people of the mists and the twilight, two spirits of the dim and ancient night. I never noticed any intimacy between these two; but I often saw them side by side; they certainly appeared friendly; and they had a way of joining each other at a mystic hour, as if they had a secret tryst of some kind. Most small reptiles are the natural prey of cats; but here was an odd friendship, of which I would have known nothing had not I loved the twilight as these two did. Of course they had come forth to seek their meat from God; but I believe that they too enjoyed the dewiness of the evening, the sense of beautiful fading, the strange power of the night.

I am conscious that most of these anecdotes have been about domesticated or semi-domesticated creatures; the reason therefor being that in a purely wild state creatures are more rigorously separated by inexorable barriers. Man is essentially an iconoclast; and when he begins tearing down barriers, many new and apparently strange relationships are quickly established.

Not long ago, while at the really fine zoo in Rock Creek Park, Washington, D. C., I observed two birds making up to each other; and I suppose a similar approach has never been noticed. Several very large, handsome cockatoos, pink and white in color, had some time before escaped from one of the bird houses; but the keepers told me they kept hanging around. Indeed I saw three of them, and heard them crying raucously. They would fly from tree to tree, staying rather high up; I could not be sure whether they were altogether satisfied with their lonely freedom. While I was near the huge cage where the eagles and vultures are kept, one of these cockatoos came over and alighted on a high, bare tree, where she called harshly but apparently with good cheer.

Suddenly out of the misty December sky a wild crow dropped, alighting on the tree near the angelic vision with the fearful voice. The two birds were just of the same size; but there their similarity ended. The crow was just a crow; but the cockatoo was a dreamlike thing, almost unreal in beauty. As for their voices, neither had the advantage as far as music was concerned.

I saw the two perfectly strange birds eyeing each other with interest, the head of each cocked to one side. After a few minutes, the crow hopped nearer; his approach was as awkward as he was democratic. But the proud beauty was pleased. She must have missed the companionship of the many birds in the bird house, and must have longed for fellowship, even with a sable-coated gentleman. It was clear to me that each bird had a genuine attraction for the other. Yet how oddly they were paired, and how bizarre they looked—as if a plowboy and a princess should fall in love with each other.

On a second visit to the zoo, a month later, one of the keepers told me that the cockatoos were still at large. Then I asked him if he had seen a crow with one.

"That old crow?" he said, smiling; "why, he's just crazy about the parrot, and the parrot about him. Some of these days there's going to be an elopement. I never knew that two birds so different would be so friendly as that."

Whenever we study Nature, trying to fathom its ways, we realize that the way of it is the art of God; and we realize also that the Bible has satisfying answers for almost every problem that we raise. For example, here is this matter of the unaccountable affinity of representatives of different families or species. What lies behind it? Is it not a faint but tangible evidence of the certainty of a coming millennium? The Bible declares that the lion and the lamb shall lie down together; that a child will some day be able to play safely by the deadly den of the asp. I never see an odd companionship but

I think, "Here is a faint but thrilling glimpse of what shall be the way of the world when the millennium comes. There shall be no more *fear,* which is always a severing force between hearts."

One day, while I was casting a net for perch and bream in an old canal, I heard a curious rustling and elfin trampling coming toward me out of a dense strip of marsh. I thought an otter might be coming through the reeds toward the canal. To my surprise, however, out there crawled, in very excited childish wriggles, about twenty tiny alligators. Doubtless they had just been hatched, back on the mainland edge of the marsh, and were now making a break for their favorite element. Almost before I could collect my wits they were in the water, paddling delightedly, and floating luxuriously. I threw the net over the entire crowd. When I drew it ashore, I found that I had caught twenty 'gators at a cast—no mean record. But as the little things were a size smaller than the meshes of the net, all but three of them crawled away safely. They were back in the canal in a twinkling.

My three captives I took home. They were made comfortable in a huge half-hogshead in the yard, nearly full of water, a receptacle in which we were wont to keep terrapin. At that time there was a large terrapin in the tub. I had two boards across the width of the tub, and flush with the water, so that the captives could sun themselves. I marked the tiny alligators in order to discern whether any difference in behavior could be detected. One of them was decidedly smaller than the others; it must have been a runt. It was this baby that established a comradeship with the fresh-water turtle.

Among creatures so cold-blooded, and apparently so cold-hearted, friendliness would seem unusual; and it does strike one as odd, especially when it is displayed by a member of one species for one of another. But over a period of months, during which I kept and ob-served these pets, I became assured that what we call sympathy and affection can be felt even by the most taciturn and phlegmatic creatures. If it were not so, why was it that, while the two stronger alligators always basked on the boards, the forlorn little one would never be content unless he lay high and dry on the back of the drowsy terrapin? If they were not friends, why was it that, while the two strong brothers fed voraciously and without any regard to table man-ners or the rights and feelings of others, the baby, when meal-time came, would climb down from his perch on the terrapin's shell, and would eat with the terrapin?

Among wild creatures there are cases of strange comradeships for special purposes at certain times of the year. Leaving out wholly the perfectly normal mat-ter of the mating of the sexes, we shall find that, from the close of one season to the mating time that follows, perhaps nearly a year later, the old males have a way of consorting. I have long noticed that with the white-tailed deer two old stags are very likely to be found to-gether between February and September.

Two bucks that may be the bitterest rivals and ene-mies during the mating season become old cronies dur-ing the summer months, and are often to be seen evi-dently on terms of the most intimate friendship. As deer have an exceedingly limited range, and as they are very fond of their home woods, individuals can be observed frequently. I ramember two grand old stags that I roused on a half dozen occasions. I saw them feeding together, running together, standing side by side, and lying down together. This last observation I made in the depths of a pine thicket when the deer suspected no intruder in their sanctuary. Far under a glimmering canopy I saw them lying on the brown pine straw.

Each one was lying on his right side; and they were lying back-to-back. Thus each old strategist could watch through a certain arc for the coming of enemies. I believe this posture in which they were crouched was by design; they were double-teaming it on the sentry business.

There is something of deep and poignant appeal about an unexpected comradeship; for there is manifested a freedom of trust, an absence of fear that are the testimony of the presence of affection. We are off our guard with those we love; and I find that strange comrades enjoy a spiritual relaxation that only mutual sympathy and faith can give. For one heart to have faith in another is a beautiful thing. Even among human beings whose love for each other is natural, it is a beautiful and a great thing, for love means utter confidence, the utter risking of all.

One April morning when a shower was falling, and when the songs of robins were mingling with the rain; when the pine trees were hanging in a mist; and when all Nature seemed to be sweetly submissive to the fragrant ministration from the clouds, I wandered out into a pasture in search of two odd comrades of which a farmer friend had told me. He said that he believed that either the pig or the turkey was demented; perhaps both. At any rate, during the winter, when both had spent much time in the sunny stable yard, an intimacy had sprung up between them; and as soon as they had been turned out into the meadow, instead of separating they had apparently sealed a compact of fellowship. I wanted to see these two friends together.

Under a hawthorn bush in a sheltered part of the meadow I found them, partly sheltered from the misty drizzle. The hog was half buried in a loamy bed; the turkey stood near, very slim and glistening in the rain. The pig eyed me with a pig's drowsy but bright-eyed insolence; the turkey beadily watched me. I decided to make them perform for me. I stooped, pretending to pick up a stick. Both started from beneath the shelter, the pig with an awkward rushing gallop, the turkey with a stately waltzing gait. When they had gone about thirty yards, both stopped and looked back at me with undetermined bright eyes. Then they moved off together, contented in their strange fellowship, two creatures utterly dissimilar yet bound by some mystic attachment, some unaccountable tie of kindness and good will.

How mysterious, indeed, is all attachment, all sympathy, all devotion! When I ponder the strange comradeships I have seen, life seems richer, more exciting in its promise; I feel that there are myriads of veils which we should lift so that we may catch fleeting glimpses of divine meanings and purposes in all our relationships. I find life full of arras marginal to mystery. And I find that we have in us strange, perhaps divine, reservoirs of strength; but these are never tapped until we ourselves throw the joyous levers of trust, of comradeship, of unselfishness. Then only can we feel the very strength of God moving in us gladly. Only when we love another can we feel vital and immortal.

X WILD THINGS AT PLAY

THERE are some writers who tell us that animals are simply animals, and that it is absurd imagination to credit them with human motives and behavior; there are other writers who invest animals with almost every human endowment. Somewhere between these two positions probably lies the truth. Lower than we are in some respects, these wild creatures are nevertheless marvelously akin to us. If God awakens in man, He stirs in the brute. Perhaps the most delightful manifestation of our general kinship is the manner in which wild things play, though they never, like some of us, make a business of playing—their chief business is living. But in times of relaxation they have the innocent and charming diversion of frolic. Lest the reader hastily convict me of fervid fancy, I must tell of some of the quaint games I have seen, every whit as whimsical and as amusing as Rip saw the Little Men playing in the heart of the Catskills.

When, of course, we speak of play, perhaps we

should consider it in its broader sense—activity which expresses a delight in life so deep and joyous that some manifestation of it must be made. Such was the behavior of three ruffed grouse that I saw at daybreak one balmy November morning. I had left my car at the last farmhouse at the entrance to Bear Valley, that splendid wild nave in the mountains where not a human being lives. But deer love the place, and wild turkeys, grouse, and squirrels. For fourteen miles a mountain stream cascades crystally under the oaks and pines—a voice of the forest, singing joyously even in the wilderness.

As I walked up an old logging road through the woods, the fragrant mist of morning was still veiling all the underbrush. The tips of aromatic pine boughs brushed me with dewy fingers spicy and cold. There was that delicious hush over the wildwoods that enters the very soul of a lover of Nature. Here and there in the forest the sun of the Indian Summer, persuasive as only gentle and wistful things can be, gleamed softly through the mist, turning the hearts of silent thickets into little golden rooms. Long rays came gleaming in, like fingers pointing. I cannot travel fast when magic affairs of this kind are going on. I stopped by a hemlock to look and to listen. Within a few moments I heard a damp rustling below me, toward the stream; and as I looked downward through the lifting mist, in the tender radiance of the mellow sun, in a tiny parlor of the forest, I saw three ruffed grouse—a cock and two hens. They were not feeding; they were not tensely crouching, making themselves one with the tawny leaves on the ground about them; they were not drowsing and blinking luxuriously, as birds love to do in the genial warmth of the autumnal sun. I should say they were playing. Their joy in life was such that they simply had to show it; and they did this by spreading their beautiful tails, by fluffing out their feathers and partly lifting their wings, by making little graceful struts. The females playfully chased the male, and he retaliated. I saw one hover flutteringly over a tiny bush, as if he were playing leapfrog over it. Here these innocent, beautiful, and most charming children of Nature were simply having a little frolic, all by themselves, in the heart of the solitary mountain, in the early morning. As I watched, the sun blazed forth strongly, his flaring beams gaudily firing the twinkling dewdrops that spangled the dripping trees. The beauty and wonder and delight of life were too much for the cock grouse. He took a short run, a short fly, and came to rest on an old chestnut log. Here he lowered his wings, lifted his ruff, and began to drum softly—not with his customary whirring challenge, but almost as if he were singing for happiness. I like to recall that little scene; nor does it appear to me an exaggeration to say that these beautiful birds were playing.

These grouse were full of natural joy, even at a time when love and mating were far distant, and when winter was fast approaching. When the virtuous passion of the virgin springtime arrives to these children of Nature, there is a special reason why their wild hearts are filled with happiness. The mystery of love, the strange, almighty injunction to continue the race, is upon them. It is then that every dawn is a caroling one, every twilight a natural vesper service.

In April, no bird takes my fancy more than the gorgeous Baltimore oriole, just arrived from the far South. His play—for well it may be called such—is really fascinating to watch; for he plays hide-and-seek with the mate with whom he is as yet unacquainted. An April never comes but I eavesdrop upon the wild minstrelsy of this flaming chanter.

Some morning at sunrise he awakens me, his song like a bright banner streaming down the fragrant air. I see him burning in a swamp-oak, hear him calling wildly, but not with the faintest hint of lament. I know that he has come north before the sober-clad females. He flames in an elm; he flares in a dusky pine, bringing music and glamour to its brilliant darkness of mystery. He is never still. His restlessness has all the activity of the searcher and the lover. What is more blithe than his triumphant call, thrilling through the flowering woodland? The Seminole Indians called him "Sanguillah." The name has the romance that properly belongs to this resplendent chorister. He climbs up; he climbs down; he peers into every tree; he flaunts his beauty with charming naïveté. He is looking for Her, calling Her, announcing his splendid presence to Her. I, for one, can never hear this oriole delightfully, blissfully caroling without saying, "Here is a true playboy of Nature." How could he say more distinctly, more irresistibly, "Come, my Corinna, let's go a-maying!"

This behavior of the oriole is a sort of natural coquetry of a kind that we discover constantly in Nature.

When children, especially little girls, display a certain winsome and purposeful charm, amusing because its motive is so apparent, we are prone to think that the artificial touch of sophistication is beginning to reach even our babies. Nothing could be further from the truth. Coquetry of this kind is far more natural and ingenuous than cold common sense. Nature herself is a most incurable flirt, and we come by this trait of radiant demureness by inheritance. More than that, all this innocent allurement is but the reflection of eternal beauty's shadowy fascination.

There are places, even to-day, where wild life seems to throw off every care, to relax in confident repose, and to play the hours away. Such is the remarkable paradise known as Bird Bank, a snowy sand bar about a mile off the mouth of the Santee River. I have often haunted that part of this mighty tidal river, and have seen afar, gleaming beyond the white cavalry of the surf, the glimmering sands of this wonderful wild-duck refuge; I have always wanted to visit it, but have never done so. Yet I have seen the mallards and black ducks throng out to it in happy clouds; and at sundown I have watched the hosts of these splendid wildfowl thronging back joyously into the vast marsh fields of the delta, there to spend the night feeding on wampee roots, lotus seeds, duck oats and acorns, drifted down from the oak swamps up the river.

A friend of mine who spent several weeks near the river mouth catching some half-wild cattle gave me the following account of his visit to Bird Bank. I shall not quote him exactly, but this is about what he said:

"I waited until I got a still night; then, taking in my canoe a shovel and a load of dry sedge, I started for the bank by moonlight, just before daybreak. By the time I got there, the east was red. Pulling my canoe up on the middle of the bar, I hollowed out a shallow trough, into which I set the boat so that its gunwales were not more than a few inches above the sand. I then carefully spread the sedge over the boat, crawled inside, and lay down to wait.

"I didn't have long to watch. It was hardly daylight when long lines of ducks began to stream over Murphy's Island and over Cedar Island, heading my way. Behind me the rim of the sun was just beginning to rise beyond the waves. There was no sound but the soft washing of the water. The day was to be a calm, bright, and warm one. Here I was, all by my lonesome, a mile offshore, watching the whitecaps redden as if their manes were catching fire; snuggled down in my boat, covered by the salty sedge, waiting for the arrival of the ducks. From the river mouth to Bird Bank a duck travels in about a minute.

"This sandy bar has probably been a wild-fowl refuge for countless years; and the fact that it is covered by every high tide does not affect the visitors' love of it. In fact, before they leave the delta they apparently know, by the condition of the tide, whether the bank will be showing. It was an amazing sight to behold those clouds of splendid birds streaming my way. The first to light were some green-winged teal. They came like bullets, veered downward dizzily, swept along the edge of the bar just above the miniature waves in the shallows, and came to rest on the beach itself. What took my eye was the way they behaved when they landed. They had lost, somehow, the vivid alertness which I had always noticed them display on the delta, and now appeared in a mood of complete relaxation, care-free as children on a friendly seashore.

"When wild ducks alight on the water, under ordinary circumstances they begin at once to eye their surroundings warily, and usually they swim away from the place where they have come to rest, as if they could not free themselves from the dread of enemies. But on Bird Bank all was different. It struck me that these ducks had come here to play; and here, for a fact, was an ideal playground. A flock of sixty mallards came down on the beach, quacking loudly, jovially; and immediately, on the leeward shore, they began to parade along the wet sand. All the while they kept up their garrulous gaiety, for all the world like a party of boys and girls from the inland, visiting the ocean for the first time.

"What was true of the teal and the mallards was true likewise even of the shy canvasbacks and redheads. About ten redheads came down the bank within twenty feet of the canoe, and there in the warm sand chased each other playfully. I would not say that they were playing tag, but it looked that way; and they were having a mighty good time at it."

Even to the casual observer there is apparent much playing among flying birds; their wing maneuvers are often too obviously for the sake of enjoyment than for aught else. The tumbling of pigeons, the strange wild soaring in the mating season of the male mourning-dove, the proud sleeping on motionless wings of the poised hawk in the central blue; the roaring descent of a cock grouse from some coign of vantage on a wild mountain to the far sanctuary of a kalmia-lighted gorge a mile distant—all these are not merely manifestations of flight but are examples of the enjoyment of flight. I recall watching, one day, a flock of wild turkeys coming over a mountain ridge, and I felt that they weren't merely flying—they were disporting themselves like masterly aviators.

There must be in flight a peculiar joy which is subtly related to the solitary nature of the soul. Flight is always a lonely and venturesome thing. In it the spirit asserts its strange, inviolate individuality. Wings are symbolic of immortality; they also suggest the sacred-ness of personality.

These great birds that I saw on that gray December day had evidently been startled by some woodsman in the valley beyond the great ridge which towered five hundred feet above me. I saw them first just as they were crossing the lonely pines fringing the crest. Eleven wild turkeys, a thousand feet above the topmost tree on the lofty ridge! They rose superbly over the great barrier of the mountain, showing a certain triumphant mastery that I had never seen these majestic birds display before in flight. At the utmost pitch of their victorious rise they appeared to delight in their splendid achievement. But their next maneuver was even more thrilling than the superb soaring over the ridge. With some difference in the angle, each noble bird set his wings for a tremendous volplane down the vast slope to the far valley. Their great wings were deeply arched, their necks extended, their feet straight out behind them. But in the roaring speed of their grand descent, their bodies were motionless. Now and then, indeed, I could detect a slight veering, a momentary faint lifting or slight lowering of a wing; but chiefly there was a serene aërial coasting, confident, proud, almost flaunting, as if these splendid birds, so seldom on the wing, delighted in showing their skill and their power as voyageurs of "the long savannas of the blue."

I do not know that I ever saw a more impressive sight in Nature; and what made it especially appealing was my consciousness that these gallant sailors of the sky were getting a great thrill out of their daring performance. I was on a bench of the mountain, about one third of the way up, and the wild turkeys passed directly over my head. They were going at dizzy speed; and because of their weight and the fact that they were coasting, their momentum was startling. Yet, two hundred yards below me, they swerved gracefully, almost airily, and came to earth without a sound in a little shadowy glen. A moment later, after their wild gay ride in the heavens, I heard them giving a few customary guarded calls as they gathered once more as a flock on the forest floor.

In Nature's great household there are those who, like some people, think it is playful to scare others, or to bewilder them. Of these players of pranks none is more sardonic in his wit than the blue jay. I remember a pair that had a nest in a hemlock tree just beyond a little porch on which I used to spend a great deal of my time. I used to call the male Uncle Sam because he had two of the vital colors in his coat, and because he was always bold and enterprising. On a still June day, when the woods were hushed, when the gentle phœbes were calling timorously, when the vireos were warbling like little rivulets in the trees, and when flocks of goldfinches were caroling in an elfin chorus, Uncle Sam, returning from some brash foraging expedition, would come dashing into the halcyon sanctuary of the hemlock, yelling bloody murder, stridently imitating the fearsome shrill and defiant cry of the red-tailed hawk. I used to watch this flaunting mountebank during this performance, and it was easy to see that he was just pretending, and enjoying thoroughly the consternation which his coming brought to the neighborhood. When he was thoroughly satisfied that his rude joke had succeeded—a success marked by the fearful silence of the erstwhile innocent singers—he would chuckle to himself, rap loudly on a limb with his strong bill, and then give a few notes in a subdued minor, as if he were saying, "Come on out of your holes. I was just in fun. There's no hawk here!" Poets declare that there is no laughter in the natural world; but the blue jay certainly chuckles. And if the yellow-breasted chat isn't a jester, no one ever wore cap and bells.

I used to go down to a water course in a meadow where hazel bushes grew, my journey being undertaken solely for the purpose of listening to the ludicrous and delicious fun that this bird was having with himself. He just used to chortle. Coming near, I would hardly be able to credit my hearing because of the weird yet jovial concert going on in the dusky heart of the green thicket. Presently the mountebank caroling would cease, and out of the hazel shade a bright-eyed bird would peer at me demurely, his head on one side, as if he were asking me what made me think he had had anything to do with the wild jargon which had just ceased. As a musician, the chat is a great joker; and I for one like to listen to his antic minstrelsy.

For downright playfulness I doubt if there is a living thing that is the equal of the otter—that obscure and fascinating creature, aristocratic, valiant—and truly the playboy of Nature. On several occasions I have caught this shy animal frolicking. There was the solitary otter of Wambaw Reserve, a fine artificial lake in the Carolina woods; a romantic place where interesting wild-life observations can nearly always be made. Four or five times I saw this otter; in every case but one he would be seen swimming in his lithe graceful way; then, seeing me, he would hump himself like a jackknife diver, give his brown tail a wave, and vanish beneath the black waters.

One day in late October I was paddling alone up the mirroring waters of this solitary lake, trying to make no noise in order the nearer to approach the wild life abundant there. At several bends I flushed wood-ducks, regal of plumage. Turning at last from the main channel, I pushed my way far into the silent heart of a glimmering estuary, over the mystic waters of which great yellow pines loomed momentously, as if listening on those fairy verges. Ahead of me, as I made my way onward, I heard a quiet splash. It did not sound like the leaping of a black bass. There was something prolonged and slithering about it. From the nature of the sound I felt that it might be made by my otter.

Pushing my canoe to the shore, I got out on the damp pine needles carpeting the gentle slope. From pine to pine I stole forward. The soft splashing continued at intervals almost regular. At last I came actually within sight of the lone frolicker himself. Here was a solitary otter having a beautiful time romping all by himself.

From the friendly shelter of a myrtle bush I watched the glistening creature clamber up a low bluff that overhung the water. He seemed to be almost at home on land. At the top of the incline he paused to look about him, every feature expressing wild attentive grace. Then he took his position on his slide, and in a moment was gliding swiftly downward, head-first. When the impact came, the water was jettled violently forward in a rainbow arch, beneath which the otter was momentarily hidden. When he reappeared, he was just lazing there luxuriously in the dark waters studded with snowy bubbles. Along the shore line near which I stood tiny sibilant whispers ran musically into the fringing sedge of pine needles. These were the little waves from the otter's private festival! For some time I watched this beautiful and harmless creature at his innocent pastime—as refreshing a spectacle as it had ever been my privilege to enjoy.

Perhaps the most appealing playing of wild things that I ever watch is the romping of the wild whitetail deer at twilight. This merry game I have repeatedly seen in the heart of the greenwood during the mystic half hour between sundown and dark. I used to go down the edges of a splendid water course called Montgomery Branch to watch for the deer as they emerged at dusk from the Ocean, a tremendous jungle into the inviolate fastness of which they had retired for their daytime rest.

Let us say that it is a still evening in late December, which, in the Southern woods, may be balmy and fragrant. Fading now from the happy forest are the brilliant lights of day; but they fade gorgeously; and if the world is wistful, it is with a golden regret. The bold radiances of day are succeeded by the enchanting lights of evening. I have come about a mile through the woods without having seen anything bigger than a squirrel, though in the rosy air immense flocks of blackbirds are thronging toward the river marshes where they spend the night. The flocks give the sense of power that large creatures or accumulated small creatures always afford. Just as I am entering the borders of Montgomery Branch, where I am brushed by aromatic myrtles, I walk full into a stag coming out of that darksome tangle of innocent wild beauty. The buck behaves as he would on no other occasion; for at twilight deer are frolicsome. He doesn't dodge back into the thicket. He looks at me with undetermined big eyes; he gives a loud coughing snort; then he takes a prodigious leap over a small bush. Here he stops, his tail still held high. Suddenly, putting his head on one side, he peers round the bush at me. Down into the dewy grass goes his black nose, snuffing. Then he simply tears loose. He just runs as if he were showing off. His gait is sky-prancing. I can see him, even in his flight, with his snowy tail astonishingly large and high, turn his splendid head from right to left. A hundred yards away he stops again, suspiring a scornful snort, precisely like a high-spirited horse that has been tearing around in a meadow. When last I see him, he is waltzing away under the pines, gamboling in the twilight.

Farther down the branch, and near the ocean, I take a stand, perched in a low fork of a tree bay. The forest now shows here and there fairy risings of mist. The west displays incredible beauty of lilac, amethyst, rose, topaz, jacinth, emerald. The earth and sky are blissful with a joy born of peace. It is all so beautiful and so spiritual that I am sure God loves us to make it so. He made us divinely vulnerable to His love. In equipping us for life's battle He gave us no armor against love. Only those meet ruin who arm themselves against love.

As I watch the magic forest, I see coming toward me through the breast-high broomgrass and the cool gallberries three deer—a buck, a doe, and a yearling. They do not come trooping out like cattle. They pause often, with graceful heads held high. They separate suddenly, as if provoked. Then with all the charm of swift relenting they come skipping together again. I say "skipping," for how else shall one describe the gait of a deer in a whimsical twilight mood? Now I see the buck leave the tiny woodpath he has been following. He is heading for a hurricane-thrown log. Twenty feet from it he pauses, eyes the obstruction, then races for it with his superb native vigor, and, with a great show of his snowy flag, jumps three times as high as he needs to in order to clear this self-imposed barrier! The yearling, not to be outdone, at sight of the buck's performance does a little Virginia reel all by herself; and the doe, not caring to have even her own daughter surpass her in agility and in joy's abandon, pretends to be frightened, dashes down toward the thicket where I am, turns, curvets lithely over low bushes, and after a few fascinating ballet steps, comes up naïvely face to face with the lordly stag. After the long day of drowsing in the hushed emerald thickets, these wild children come forth to roam the dim and solitary country of the night. But before they begin to feed or to travel far, they love their little innocent frolics under the waking stars.

Wild children at play! Their innocent merrymaking draws us closer to them, increases the capacity of our hearts for affectionate appreciation, gives us a feeling of family fellowship.

While it is true that, of all created things, man alone appears capable of living in opposition to his physical instincts—man alone who seems to feel and to act as if he were immortal—nevertheless there are remarkable ties of blood comradeship between us and the lower orders of creation; and to acknowledge these and to learn what we can from them is to have that deep quality of heart-wisdom that we call sympathy. Watching the fun and the downright skylarking of wild things is likely to help us immensely, if for no other reason than that it serves to remind us that our own happiness depends far more upon our love for others than upon the love of others for us. There seems to be an eternal law of exquisite beauty and final power that the hearts spent are the hearts joyous.

XI FEMININE TRAITS IN WILD
THINGS

IF COMRADESHIP manifests affection, what shall we say
of motherhood? And the capacity for motherhood confers certain powers which show themselves almost as
clearly and appealingly among the wild children of
Nature as among human beings.

Science may tell us that mother-love is a mere mechanical device for insuring the continuance of the species.
Well, when did science ever say the *last* word about
anything? Is it not always the *latest* word? Science,
that will not speak to God to-day, will probably kneel
to Him to-morrow.

Shall we look at some of the feminine traits in wild
things to find, even here, the touch of the Hand Divine?
Without consciousness of that touch, or of the power
of it, or of the infallible precision and sagacity of it,
no mortal will ever discover peace.

The thing happened at a place called Fox Bay, deep
in the wild and fragrant heart of the romantic Santee
country; and though at the time I was only about ten

years old, the impression left with me was so vivid—probably because of the pathetic beauty and charm of it—that I have always treasured it among my fondest woodland recollections. I was riding the woods with my father—a pastime in which I delighted as a boy—rounding up stray stock, particularly the mothers that had wandered away from the plantation to give birth to their young in the fastness of the solitary greenwood. It was in late May, and the foliage everywhere was dense and lustrous. Giant ferns of an incredible tender green drooped regally in the dim savannas; jasmines rioted everywhere, blowing their golden trumpets from the massive pines that they wreathed, the white-barked hollies, the aromatic sweet bays. The air was still save for the droning of bees, and the faint chanting of the pines, and the delicate singing of a parula warbler. It was a magic scene, and magic affairs were about to begin.

At the head of Fox Bay my father and I separated, each one of us riding one side of the misty swamp, from the lambent bosom of which odors as out of a dewy dreamland were delicately exhaled. I rode down a little wood path through the green broomsedge bordering the swamp. I could now and then hear my father's horse, beyond the wall of greenery; but once, as I drew rein to listen, I heard another sound. Something was stealthily walking in the shallow water of the swamp. It might be some of our strayed stock. I waited where I was, behind a clump of green bays. Presently there stepped, or, more accurately, there stole with elfin grace, palpitant and beautiful, a mother doe, behind her a tiny fawn. My father had evidently disturbed them where they had been couched in the dim swamp, and she had led her baby across the swamp to avoid the danger. Now the two were in full view of me: a wild mother and her little one. The keen awareness of the doe was extraordinary to watch; she did not even move her head without a certain tremulous wariness. One ear was turned back toward the swamp whence she had come, the other forward toward the open pinelands. The fawn, apparently imagining that all this was a morning frolic arranged for his especial entertainment, was inclined to frisk. Several times he made cunning little starts and jumps. To these the mother made no objection until my horse happened to stamp his foot. We were hidden from view, and the wind was from the deer to us, so that they could not get our scent. But the doe had heard the sound, and she knew that danger might be near. Then followed what I have always loved to recall.

At a faint bleat from his mother, the fawn came and stood a little ahead of her, on the right, facing ahead. I have no doubt that she told him where to stand. Her beautiful head was now high, her body tense. Had she been alone, she probably would have stolen off; but she had a charge to keep. The fawn didn't enjoy standing still. He began to fidget. My horse stamped his foot softly. At that the doe raised her right forefoot gracefully, set the hoof on the fawn's back, at the withers, and gently pressed down. Into the dewy covert of the broomsedge the tiny creature sank, deftly hidden by his mother, while she never for a moment relaxed her vigil of love. . . . I thought (or at least have come to think since then) : here is a wild heart of the wasteland, brimming with mother-love. Defenseless, she is approached by unknown danger. Her first thought is for her baby. In the few days that he has been at her side, she has trained him well to listen, to obey, to trust. Peril menaces; she is afraid that the marauder will see her fawn, and, realizing its helplessness, will attack it. So she hides it, shields it; with the grace that wild beauty alone possesses, she finds a covert and a hiding place for her little one. . . . Surely, the genuine mother heart is in these wild things—wondrous affection, watchful devotion, tireless sacrifice!

The incident just recorded, and many others like it, have long since led me to ask two questions: first, do the females in wild life have definite traits which distinguish them from the males? Second, if they do, how are these traits manifested in behavior? The longer I observe these creatures of the wastelands, the more human they appear; many of their domestic problems are identical with some of ours, and their modes of solving them are sometimes similar, sometimes vastly superior. I am a little puzzled to distinguish what we are to call a purely feminine trait; but I shall do the best I can, not going beyond inferences that are drawn from what I myself have observed, and asking the reader's considerate judgment on a matter that must needs have somewhat shadowy boundaries.

In wild life the bringing into the world and the caring for the young is a consideration that appears to be left almost wholly to the mothers. It is therefore perfectly normal in them to develop traits peculiar to them. The doe was concerned for her fawn; her thought was not for herself. Where, at this time, we may ask, was the buck? The answer is simple: the buck has nothing whatsoever to do with the rearing of the fawn. Indeed, there are naturalists who believe that by a marvelous provision of Nature the stag carries soft tender antlers when the fawn is young, else he might, with the truculence that is almost habitually his, attack his own young. The great things that concern him in life are his own welfare, his own physical supremacy, his own safety. But in her meek, wise heart the doe carries those deep hopes and fears that are concerned with the continuance of a race. With birth and mothering she is absorbed; with the great elemental essential things that shall not change so long as life endures on the earth. I think I have detected in does a delicacy of perception, a sensitiveness about others, with the art of shielding them, and a concern over the epic matters of existence that I have not discovered in the big burly manful stags, selfish, self-conscious, powerful, vain. A buck looks out for himself, but a doe mothers the race.

In much the same way, it appears to me, despite man's wars and tumults, despite his superb assumptions and thrilling achievements, after all, upon the meek almighty shoulders of woman rests the burden of the world. Often impatient with all but the gravest and most beautiful things in life, she is the warden and the savior of humanity. The Creator dowered her with the irresistible quality of insistence, knowing full well that no mere physical strength can cope with the other quality; that no rock, however tenoned and mortised and grim of visage, can resist the ceaseless, gentle dropping of water.

I have been wondering whether the maternal instinct, which is essentially sacrificial, does not carry with it a kind of spiritual fiber that is peculiar to feminine nature. I realize that I am on the boundaries of a shadowy land when I begin to talk about things spiritual; yet in motherhood is a recognizable quality of divinity; without the depth and quality of her devotion, no species could survive. I have seen wild mothers display traits of daring, of affection, of sacrifice that I have never seen in members of the opposite sex. Not long ago, for example, I was walking under a young maple, not quite out in full leaf. Suddenly at my very feet, with much commotion and with strange cries of distress, a dove fell. It struck the ground with sickening force; then it began to beat its wings impotently, at the same time retreating. Poor pitiful fugitive! What but mother-love could make her so valiantly, so perfectly feign distress? Glancing upward I saw her two young, hardly feathered, side by side on a low limb. I followed the retreating mother, and she led me more than a hundred yards—attracting to herself the danger that had menaced her babies. I have yet to see a male dove display such intelligence of courage. He will flute his mournful whistle, he will sail proudly in the mating season, but out of his nature has been left that mystic love which finds its joy in giving, not in receiving; not in glorifying self, but in sacrificing self.

One cannot make many such observations without

coming to the conclusion that, at least in wild life, the male has a different kind of temperament, perhaps a different heart; certainly a different outlook upon life. Lord Byron claimed (upon I know not what reasonable assumption of authority) that love is a woman's whole existence, whereas a man can find and enjoy a score of other interests. It seems to me fairer to say that women are more intent upon essentially great things, the greatest of which is love. Men usually act from motives relative to their interest; women from motives relative to the preservation of the human family. Man loves the triumphs of to-day, woman, the integrity of the soul's to-morrow.

That, in natural life, females are more thoughtful and wise than males there can be small doubt. Males spend much of their time in sleeping, fighting, curiously investigating, idling, bullying. Their mates are modest, retiring, industrious, infallibly occupied in some essential task. I recall watching the behavior of two black ducks that had nested in the lush grass of a small meadow through which ran a trout brook. The grass there was tall and wavy; the swift narrow stream brimmed its low banks, forming all sorts of delightful tiny estuaries and bays, retired mistily among the reeds and grasses. In the marsh edges beside a miniature bayou I found the nest, with eleven eggs. The hen was on it; upon my approach, she slipped away into the water, her bright eyes fixed on me. The stealth of her escape was prompted by the desire to prevent my detecting the treasures that she was leaving. The old drake I flushed in the sedges a hundred yards away.

. . . Two weeks later, near the same place, I came on the mother with her elfin babies. She had them in a little bay, into the still waters of which dripped silvery grasses. The drake was nowhere in sight. When I made myself known, the mother, uttering lamentable cries, flapped her way *toward* me—then off to one side, desperately, devotedly trying to "draw my fire." The tiny ducklings meanwhile dived, or innocently hid in plain sight beside tussocks of swamp grass. Two of the little adventurers came my way underwater, and as it had the pearly clearness of a spring-fed stream, I could discern them easily. They had gone under, but they did not seem to know that they need not keep on swimming, especially since their fairylike bodies, mere balls of down, were exceedingly hard to keep down. One elf, swimming valiantly, came close to me; completely played out, and irresistibly buoyed by his own lightness, he bobbed up beside me, his beady eyes glistening. Gallant infant! He did not see me; and there beside a marsh stem he sat, enigmatic, obedient to the mother's warning. . . . In wild life there are few liars; and the guardian does not need to call "Wolf" more than once.

I retreated from the scene, but hid behind a heavy haw tree in the near-by meadow. Soon the lamenting mother ceased her cries, swam toward her scattered family, calling them softly and reassuringly; and ere long, reunited, they moved silently off into the misty fastness of the deeper marsh. . . . Where, meanwhile, had the father of the family been? I could find him nowhere in the meadow, though a day later I saw him there. As far as he was concerned, the whole brood might have perished. It is true that with certain birds and animals the domestic cares are sometimes shared. That is, the males assist in a more or less clumsy and inefficient fashion. Yet I repeat what I believe is nearly always true: that the burden for the rearing and care and protection of the children devolves upon the female. It is the mother upon whom rests the safety and the continuance of a species. Nor is this so much a wild-life fact as it is a feminine fact. Unless most of my observations have been wrong, or unless from them I am drawing false conclusions, it is the mother who, from the time that the young first appear in the world, protects, guides, comforts, shields them with her life.

As I think of this subject of comparing the feminine in the natural world with the masculine, the more I realize that care must be exercised in making generalizations. There are certain modern authors who are supposed to be experts in the matter of analyzing the characters and the motives of women; but the more I read of these writers, the less convinced am I that they really know much. They and their publishers are very insistent upon the fact of their omniscience, yet the business appears to me so essentially mysterious as to be likely to yield less to smart investigators than to patient observers. The subject is naturally of profound and eternal interest. Kipling, with his customary discernment, has sung that the female is more deadly than the male; but he stopped too short. There assuredly are traits far more attractive and vital than deadliness that distinguish the feminine from the masculine nature.

It has seemed to me, in years of watching wild life

in waste places, that the females are not only a little keener in alertness, persistent in having their vital ways, unselfish, and valiant-for-others than the males, but they appear possessed of a self-sustaining joy that is lacking in their lordly consorts. They give evidence of being more satisfied with life as it is than are the restless, roaming males. Perhaps it is because into their keeping are given the almighty issues of life and death. They have a far deeper patience and a calmer acceptance of life than have their mates. I remember with what curious interest I watched, not long since, in the mountains of southern Pennsylvania, the contrasted behavior of two wild turkeys, male and female. It was in early May, and the sexes had separated, the male to roam the wild glens and the solitary ridges in lonely self-interest; the female to find a nesting place to lay her eggs, to hatch them, and then to rear her young amid a thousand imminent dangers.

Far be it from me to animadvert upon the grand system of Nature; yet it does appear that life is incalculably more interesting, dangerous, noble and glorious for a mother than for a father. Certainly it is so in wild life. . . . The big gobbler that I came upon was raking the leaves thoughtfully under a wild-grape vine. I had heard his noise in the leaves, and had crept up to him by getting above him on a ridge and looking down at him at work in a shadowy hollow. He was all alone. He was hunting food to satisfy his own hunger. I suppose he had no thought for any other living thing. After a few moments he walked from beneath the heavy vines, and into the full dreamy sunlight his lordship stepped. I never saw a more stately wild creature; regal, superb, the sheen on his neck and shoulders glinting soft iridescence. Monarch of the dim kingdom of the mountains, matchless in speed and in sagacity, yet his rôle was an inferior one: grubbing in the woods earth for food for himself. He may lead the flock in the autumn and the winter, but after the mating season, Nature directs that he take a very diminished seat. And his glamour is still more seriously abated when we look upon his modest mate.

I found her perhaps a mile away, stealing in a silent, self-effacing way along the pine-bordered edges of an old upland pasture. I think no wild creature of equal size is capable of moving with more caution than the turkey hen going to her nest. She was close on me before I saw her; and she was as silent as an apparition. Moreover, about her was an air of dread secrecy, as if she were the bearer of great and mortal tidings. She did not see me; and by a little cautious maneuvering I was able to follow her unobserved. Whereas in normal times wild turkeys usually travel with their heads high, in going to her nest the hen is likely to travel with her whole body low, an indescribable meekness and modesty about her. By following her at a great distance, I at last discovered her nest, but did not attempt to approach it until, on another day, she had left it for her few minutes of rest and relaxation. Yet a wild turkey will not readily quit her nest if she suspects danger; and so closely does she sit, especially as the time approaches for the eggs to hatch, that it is not impossible to catch her on her nest. Wild mother, with the wary palpitant heart and the mighty urge of love! The whole process of motherhood apparently has a transfiguring effect upon the soul; and it is only the feminine spirit that has the privilege so to be glorified.

During a long month this wild mother managed to protect her nest and eggs, though in those same woods dwelt wildcat and fox, weasel and skunk, and a score of other natural enemies. Nature probably helped her a little; for it is said that when a bird is incubating, she gives off less scent than she does at other times. On this point I have no authentic information; yet if it were not so, I hardly see how a wild turkey or a quail could ever hatch a brood in wild country. At any rate, this nest beside the old pine log, dewily overhung by a thin tangle of fox grapes and broomsedge, remained safe.

When the brood came out, I watched them. The mother would lead them slowly and gently down the thickety margin of the woods, being especially partial to an old ditch-bank that had both shelter and sunshine. I used to see her walking ahead of her querulously piping brood, always alert, always anxious; her head now very high, watching; now, very low, clucking and calling softly to her little ones. Though I had this wild mother under observation about six weeks, I never saw the gobbler but once, and he was then intent upon himself. More than likely he had left the neighborhood. It is customary, during the season when the turkey hens are doing the difficult and dangerous work of rearing the young, for the gobblers to roam away together. They range far by themselves, and only rejoin the flocks in autumn, or not at all. I have known solitary gobblers, and others that went in pairs, until the mating season.

The mere fact that a work of utter sacrifice and unselfishness devolves upon the wild mother accounts, it seems to me, for the development in her of a spiritual superiority; we develop physically, I take it, by acquiring for ourselves; but spiritually we develop by giving to others. The truly great of heart are those who spend their souls. I think this law holds in the natural world as well as it does in humanity's realm. Feminine nature in wild life appears to have a divination, a delicacy and a celestial felicity that is, in its sphere, identical with that spiritual grace inherent in womankind.

But wild mothers also have feminine faults. I remember one day seeing a mother fox and three little cubs coming down a woodland path. I was on a log, concealed by a clump of myrtles. Just to see what would happen, when the foxes were quite close, with the wind blowing from them to me, I tossed a little ball of earth at the mother. It struck her in the flank; and as she had not seen whence it had come, she imagined that one of her babies had played a senseless trick on her. Turning sharply, she gave the nearest cub a sharp cuff that sent him sprawling. Meanwhile she growled and glared at the two others that cowered before her anger. . . .

Was this behavior of hers feminine? Well, perhaps. The nervous tension under which a mother lives sometimes makes the human nerves give way. But, while her hands may punish, her heart never does. Was her behavior forgivable? Well, the chill austerity of unctuous

175

goodness is often redeemed by a little display of human weakness; and those imperfections that reason discerns may be among those very qualities which provoke love by the frailty that mortality thereby confesses.

To me the greenwood has always offered that kind of magic that has upon it the bloom of wonder: the blue above the towering trees; the hush that is a little stiller than silence; the hale odors awaft from shy thickets; the little leaves glinting in the lustrous gloom; the wildflower's immaculate grace; the veery's song, that is full of green shadows and dew and halcyon love. And the other wild things—they teach me much about life, telling me not to use its oar too clumsily; telling me that not only human life but that all life is sacred; and that in feminine character at least, here in the deepest wildwood, are discoverable traits that have in them the quality of divinity.

XII   STRANGE PLACES OF WORSHIP

WE HAVE now come far together into the country of flowers, and warbling streams, and fascinating wild folk. Lost angels from the ruined paradise of civilization, we are recovering somewhat our sanity, poise and joy. We are discovering in the reading of the First Gospel a panacea for *ennui*. To us is coming the peace that can come only from a realization of adequate resources. And what spiritual resource can be greater than the awareness of God's presence and His love? Since He is with us, our foes are already defeated.

It is time for thanksgiving. And, fortunately, we do not necessarily have to repair to a builded shrine to worship. Strange places of adoration are there; secret sanctuaries. Wherever the mortal worships the Immortal, there is a shrine.

When I asked my genial host where George Washington Alexander Burnsides Green was sleeping, he said, "With the hounds." Naturally, my curiosity was aroused, and, perhaps, better feelings also.

As soon as opportunity offered, I left the wide hearth before which a lot of us had been swapping hunting yarns, and strolled out into the starry Southern night. We were hunting deer on a remote plantation, so inaccessible that the only sound of really blatant civilization to reach us was occasionally the faint whistle of a locomotive, twelve miles, six swamps, and two rivers away.

Under great oaks I walked, toward a curious little brick building that I knew had been given over to housing the hounds—a yowling, restless crew, indispensable, melodious, but difficult to manage. Their control had been given to Wash Green, a negro as humble as he was efficient. On that same day I had been given cause to marvel at the occult finesse with which he had handled the swarming pack. But now the nature of his sleeping quarters troubled me.

Nearing the tiny quaint building, not larger than an ordinary smokehouse, I saw through its open windows the shadows made by firelight dancing and running on its walls. I did not want to open the door, for fear that some of the hounds would slip out; I did not want to knock, for old Wash might be asleep, and there was really no need to awaken him. I just went to the nearest window and looked in. What met my gaze was one of the most memorable scenes that my eyes have ever looked upon. It was such a picture as the heart carries for the rest of life.

I looked into a tiny brick-walled room with a dirt floor. The only bit of furniture in the place was an ancient bench, sagging crazily at one end because there it had but one leg. A cheerful fire of pine and oak burned in the black chimney. Ranged in front of the fire in a variety of thoughtful poses were about fifteen hounds. Some of them looked unutterable things into the flames. Some drowsed with paws outstretched on their extended front legs. A few hung back from the mystic semicircle, as if they had not yet undergone the awful rites which would admit them to so august a council. But, while the dogs were interesting, the man was fascinating.

In front of the fire, with the lolling hounds all about, old Wash was down on his knees. He seemed looking into the fire, yet far beyond it. His hands were clasped in front of him with unmistakable fervor. Down in the dirt and dust he was, literally among the dogs. And he was praying. A strange place for worship! A singular shrine! Yet adoration, I thought, is of the heart; and the soul's meeting with its Maker may be effected in all kinds of odd places.

I left old gray-haired Wash praying; and unless my judgment in such things is badly at fault, his petitions went as straight Home as those offered in cathedrals.

This subject of strange places of worship has long held a special interest for me; and I have tried to be on the alert to discover peculiar places of devotion and adoration. I have often asked myself, for example, what were the exact conditions under which a writer produced a masterpiece? In other words, what was the environment which afforded an author's spirit a chance to do his very best work?

The answer, of course, must come from the writer

himself. One day, when I was trout fishing with Henry van Dyke, I asked him where he was when he wrote "God of the Open Air," the poem that is generally conceded to be his best. I can remember how his face brightened at the query.

"It was in the winter," he said, "and I was staying in a tiny vine-covered cottage near Augusta, Georgia. I was close to the beautiful quiet heart of Nature. It was therefore easy for me to write of the God of Nature. The airs were gentle; there were bird songs, and fragrances of flowers, and elemental beauty everywhere. Perhaps in no other environment could I have written that poem."

He who reads that noble poem will find it a hymn of worship, of thanksgiving, a song of adoration of the Creator. In a genuine sense, worship always means just that—the heart's spontaneous and primitive reverence for God, its childlike gladness in God. Therefore, true worship is a far greater thing and a far more frequent act than mere going to church or saying one's prayers. For example, in its broadest sense, worship is often associated with work, either in the thoughtful preparation for it, or in its actual performance, and this alleged sinful world of ours has far more unfeigned worshipers than the pessimists imagine.

But the human heart has a quaint and appealing tendency toward being individual, toward choosing, therefore, odd places for worship, and perhaps unusual forms of worship. The savage Pawnee Indian from the brow of some beetling cliff pouring out his wild chant to the Great Spirit is, essentially, as true a worshipper as the chanter of Psalms in some gorgeous church.

An understanding of some of these strange places and ways of worship, with a due appreciation of their significance, is one of the most heartening things I know about these strange, lovable, wayward yet winsome mortal natures of ours. Hearts don't like to be herded. Christ told his followers to be sure to pray in secret. He practically advised them to pray in odd and obscure places. He himself repaired to the lonely wilderness to restore his spirit.

Recurring for a moment to the proper environment for a literary worker, we shall find that almost every writer has an especial preference. Sinclair Lewis declares that he can do his best work on an ocean liner. Joan Sutherland, the gifted English novelist, has lately engaged a private airplane, and is making excursions several thousand feet in the air to gain a certain pitch of inspiration for her work. Clemence Dane says that she finds it practically impossible to work on her country estate in Devon, declaring that the cackling of the chickens and the other rustic noises disturb her so much that she has to flee to her London home in Holland Park when she wants to do serious literary work. When Compton Mackenzie wishes to start a new book, he seeks the quaint seclusion of one of the isolated Channel Islands.

Sheila Kaye-Smith says that she finds a hotel room a most excellent place for work, as the impersonal character of her surroundings enables her to concentrate without any desire to rearrange the furniture or to change the hangings! Du Bose Heyward, the author of *Porgy* and of *Angel,* had built for himself a small cabin on a lonely hillside overlooking a peaceful valley in the mountains of western North Carolina. There he does his work, far from the tumult of civilization, hearing only the mountain winds in the hemlocks, the song of the stream in the glen.

All these places are really places of worship, for they are scenes of high thought, toil, and achievement. All life seems to be a struggle for some kind of self-expression, the utterance of aspiration in some form that aims to be permanent; and in this scheme of existence we apparently praise God best, not when we read the longest chapters in the Bible, or say the greatest number of prayers, but when we do our work most honestly, with the highest degree of quiet and loving fervor.

I remember an experience I had in the hills of southern Pennsylvania a few years ago. I was hunting for a nest of the ruffed grouse, one of the shyest and most romantic of birds, and my quest took me through swarthy thickets of rock pines, through sunny glades, deep into the heart of the wilds. After a long ramble I decided to climb to the crest of a high hill, where a great cairn of rocks afforded an admirable site from which to view the surrounding country. I wanted to locate myself. But what was my surprise when, after a long climb, I reached the rocks to find that I was not alone. A grizzled mountaineer was sitting on a huge boulder, gazing out over the miles of beautiful wild country. I could not imagine what he could be doing there. He would not be hunting the nest of anything, and the hunting season for big game was far off. Yet, as most men do when they meet in the woods, we greeted each other as friends, and for a long time we sat together on the cliff.

I told him the object of my quest, but he did not tell me his until I was about to leave. After having directed me to where he said he thought I might find the nest of a grouse, he said, with a certain manly shyness, "I reckon you wouldn't know why I come here?"

I told him I did not know, and paused to hear.

"I believe you'll understand," he said. "I like this place because it's here that I come on God."

He waved his hand in a gesture that took in the rolling sea of hills, stretching beyond the vision, and, to the east, the far-shining valley.

"I can't get the feeling at home somehow," he said, "nor yet always at the meeting house; but it never fails me here."

Down through the woods I went, "Here I come on God" making music in my heart. A strange place of worship—that rugged hilltop! But about the memory of it there is something sacred to me.

Shrines for worship, the world over, testify to the turning of the human spirit to God; but in reverencing these places we ought to remember that in the heart of each one of us God has a secret fane to which He especially loves to repair. He fashioned the place with wistful and tender care and He visits it often, to discover whether the music there is sweet, the prayer unfeigned, the lights shining upon the altar. A cathedral is truly a grand achievement; but I doubt whether God is much impressed by it. He who reared the firmament alone will hardly marvel at man's magnificence. What is the beauty that we build, to Him whose mansion is the dwelling place of light? I mean that we should not imagine that the splendor of an edifice can atone for our sins. If the shrine of the heart is dark and cold, vain are any temple's myriad lights, gorgeous windows, rolling music, and solemn hymns.

It appears that a man can worship most truly in that place in which he comes into harmony with the scheme of things. I have a friend who, when he is disgruntled with the world and all that is therein, goes out and cuts down a tree; then he sits on a log, rests, and peace comes stealing back to his soul. Another friend, when a hard rain is falling, loves to go to his woodshed, open at two ends, and there do his meditating. The rain is all around, and the hale smell of it, and the good odor of the wet earth, but he is dry. And there is for him in that strange setting a mystic spell cast over life. Rain is a living thing; it speaks to us of elemental forces of the world. This friend tells me that there is no place in which he can think straighter, and meditate and worship more genuinely than in this humble woodshed, with bark and chips littering the floor, and with the streamers of the rain hanging silver curtains at the doors.

And how great is this provision of God! To give us a chance to worship in strange places! He wants us to be happy, and to approach Him naturally. Fearfully and wonderfully He has made us; and not least wonderfully in this: that peace can come to us in the oddest places imaginable.

I once knew a very beautiful woman named Rosalie. She was happily married, and one little daughter made the joy of the household complete. I used to pass their little cottage in the pine lands; a vine-covered place it was, with roses rambling on the tiny porch, with the child's toys in the front yard, with everywhere the evidence that the man was a consistent and an intelligent worker.

Then came a sudden boom in Florida. The man decided to go there to investigate conditions, with a view to moving if the outlook was favorable. Drawing most of his savings from the bank, he left home. He never came back. A few days after he left there was a fearful train wreck in Florida, and there were some unidentified dead. Probably he was one. But, at any rate, Rosalie and the little girl never saw him again; and the little home that he had builded with his own hands started almost at once to go to decay. His loss was as a blight upon it.

I used to see the bereaved woman often, and the little girl and I were great friends. Every time I saw her she used to ask me if I knew how soon her dad would be home.

Not far from the cottage was the river, a lordly stream flowing between high bluffs, from the tops of which one might see for several miles up and down the great watercourse. As the road that I traveled ran near the tallest of these bluffs, I could see the trees that fringed its edge; and I noticed that Rosalie often went with her little girl, or alone, to a fallen oak overlooking the river.

There was no need for her to expect her husband from that direction, for the road from Florida lay in the other direction. But there she would go to drink into her heart the beauty and stillness of the vast delta country lying below her; to watch the dappled, dusky radiance of the sunlight falling on the mighty pines; to see the little waves scramble laughingly on the glimmering beach far below her. I know that there she came, after her trial, to some degree of peace once more. She told me so one day when I stopped to leave a few little gifts for her child.

"I am going to be all right," she said. "I go down every day to look at the river. For a long time I couldn't say my prayers. My faith seemed gone. But God has given it back to me again. I thought I could not love God any more; but I can adore Him, I can worship Him—down there by the river."

Often, indeed, our sorest need is for a change of environment, even though slight and temporary, which will afford us an opportunity for worship, a chance for the souls to search in freedom for the light. Our human joy is pain-surrounded; but beyond the pain is God, I believe. In our worst extremity He never forsakes us. To save us He made our hearts divinely insecure against the entreaties of love, the appeals of innocence and beauty. He makes us feel that something in us was not born, and cannot die. He makes us aware of His love; and we worship Him spontaneously, in many varying ways, because we know how merciful and wistful-tender He is toward us. If Rosalie could worship again, all the rest of us surely can.

Worship, it seems to me, is a natural part of human inclination; it is not an elaborate function conducted under circumstances of pomp and awe. After all, the question of where one worships is paltry compared to the vital question of how one worships and if not with the whole heart, in an outpouring of joy and reconcilement, then not at all. I know that there must be millions who feel precisely as I do when I see the primitive, inevitable beauty of the rising sun, or the silvery somnambulism of the moon; the emotion to worship is as natural as the appeal of the heroic to a man, or the appeal of compassion to a woman.

I recall going to church one cloudy May morning, when the world was shrouded in fog. The minister preached a rather severe sermon from an Old Testament narrative, a story full of anger and sin and punishment. He had said that he was going to read to us "the Word of God." I confess that the services somewhat depressed me; and when they were over I was glad to reach the open air again. As I left the church, the sun broke through the mists, and set all the jeweled trees glittering; the birds began to sing; the flowers— I could almost hear them open! "The Word of God," I thought; "is it not a much greater and a much more heart-reaching thing than the Bible, great as is that wonderful library of human experience that we call a book? Is not virtuous beauty everywhere the Word of God? God's writings—are they not the gleaming flowers and the lustral stars? The universe is a Holy

Scripture; there are Psalms of the forest trees, and Isaiahs in the voice of the sea. And he is a reader of God's Word, who, apprehending the wonder and the loveliness of the world, knows that these things reveal the Maker. And he is the true worshiper whose spirit is joyous because it apprehends God."

I love that ancient word "worshipful." It means, I believe, "worthy of worship." And wherever we turn in the world we find those evidences of God's power and mercy that make Him worshipful to us. No wonder is it that there are many strange places of worship— there is so much to make us reverent and adoring.

There is an especial time when a flood of adoration fills my heart, a strange shrine, where I can worship as naturaly and joyfully as a robin can sing above his new nest on an April twilight. It is in the wild pinelands in mid-March, when the long savannas glitter with the rain water through which the grasses are springing; when the air of early spring has a tinge of wood smoke in it; when from the margin of a sunny lagoon the first frogs begin their flutelike pipings; when the wind in the tall pines has in it the songs of hope and love.

To me, being in the pinelands at such a time, with azure clouds of bluebirds warbling like aërial rivulets; with everywhere the poignant, nameless promise that precedes the coming of beauty; with the heart welling with unreflected joy—glad of life, of Creation, adoring the Creator, loving my fellow man, hoping for his happiness—such is true worship.

And such an inclination comes to me, and to all of us, far from creeds and churches. We are God's chil-

dren, wherever we be; we are in His hands. The world
is His sanctuary; and while the superb modern highway
of the church will, no doubt, take us Home, there are
some who know dewy by-paths to the same City; who
follow flower-scented lanes of the spirit, pausing to
wonder and adore in secret Him who, on the highway,
is proclaimed with pomp and ceremony. To love God,
we have only to apprehend Him; and we ought always
to be very patient and tolerant toward those who find
Him in their own way.

I take it that God designedly provided myriads of
avenues of approach to Him; and those of us on one
road should expect and rejoice in many serene arrivals
by other paths, unseen of us, and totally different from
the way we travel. If any one thing is right in this life,
it is that every heart should be free to take its own way
to God. Every soul knows at least one way to heaven.
Some hearts reach home by the way of the wild flowers;
some are led by the frail, unerring hands of little children; some "meditate on Him in the night-watches,"
and ascend homeward by the silvery stairway of the
stars.

I recall going one pitchy night through a wild wood,
so dark that, against so swarthy a background, a black
bear would have resembled his polar cousin. Some days
before there had been a small fire in the woods near this
place, and I noticed now and then a smoldering gleam
from a charring stump, and once a strange mild flame
burning almost as steadily as a candle. But these lights
were stationary, and they were quickly passed, to be
seen no more.

As I drove, however, what really guided me was a great star that, though often hid behind towering trees, would emerge blazingly—always in the same relative position. Vanishing and then coming gloriously to view again, it guided me and kept up my heart until I came at last to the end of forest—to open fields and houses. There was my star. I could not follow those other lights, but I could follow this. The one afforded fitful luminance; the other, eternal radiance. The thought made me want to worship: the thought that, despite the paltry, spluttering blazes of this life, stationary and unreliable, we do have great stars of truth and beauty to guide us out of the darkest forest of trouble.

Whatever makes us rejoice, makes us want to worship. We seem to want to tell God all about it, just as a child will take a new-found joy to its father and mother. Sorrow, too, should make us want to worship. If we tell God, we are better for the telling. In all the Bible I know nothing finer or more affecting than the attitude of Job when, as we are told, the full extent of his calamities had been made known to him, he "rent his mantle, . . fell down upon the ground, and *worshipped*." In the agony of his sorrow he blessed God, worshipping Him in the dust, and from the ashes of appalling grief. A strange time and place for worship!

As a boy, I went to a school conducted by a private family; and often at recess, because water has always exercised a certain fascination over me, I used to go down to the river that flowed by the end of the ample old yard, where I could watch flocks of wild ducks deploying over the delta, the sun rays prancing on the river waves, and the romantic far shores stretching dreamily toward the distant sea.

A tiny river tug used often to be anchored near my favorite rendezvous, and through my frequent visits to the river I came to know quite well the negro engineer. He was a most unusual character; and now that, as a man, I remember him, he looms much larger as a significant human being than he did when I, as a barefoot boy, used to listen to stories of his adventures on the great river.

Several things about this man, Hacklus Manigo, impressed me. The one that never failed to fascinate me was the immaculate condition of the crude little engine of which he was the overlord. All the steel parts shone glossily; all the brass parts beamed and glistened and winked. Yet the engine crouched in the most dingy of holds, and the windows of the engine room were grimed and battered.

The province of Hacklus terminated with the engine itself; and in this miniature kingdom there was always the beauty of order and the order of beauty. Nor did this strange negro like to leave his humble throne. For hours he would perch on the window sill of the engine room, a little copy of the New Testament in his hands. He never tired of reading this, the most profound book in the world.

There are many people who think of a negro only as a minstrel; but it is only justice for me to testify that I have learned the meaning of religion and of worship even from this humble source. I asked Hacklus one day where he went to church. His answer was remarkable;

and it is one of the things I have treasured all these years. As it was given me, it was as free from self-righteousness as the prayer of the Publican.

"I try to live in God's sight," he said simply. "I think that's going to church."

There is a shrine at which I can worship most readily. It is the shrine of memory. I think of those who loved me, and are gone. And I can truly worship the remembrance of them, not alone because they loved me, but because I can feel the goodness of God even through bereavement. The human tie may be severed; but only to make a bond that no fate shall ever break. The mortal rose is gathered, only to lend aid to the amaranth to rise. Death divorces, but he unites. He comes at first to steal away, but at last he shall restore forever what he has taken. I count this thought full of joy and wonder and hope: that they who are joined by death are never parted. It is easy to discover that I believe in personal immortality. I do, with all my heart. No human soul that feels that God is Love could reasonably take any other view. Indeed, it is the only view that makes and keeps life sweet and rational.

Strange places of worship! A woodshed in the rain, with a robin's song mingling musically with the drip from the eaves; Job in the dust with his fresh sorrows; Wash Green on his knees before the dying fire, an immortal soul communing, among hounds, with his God; Rosalie—gentle, beautiful, heartbroken Rosalie—coming again to worship because she found peace by the river; Hacklus, keeping in God's sight, and therefore always worshipping. Strange places, true worshipers!

We worship when we love best "all things both great and small," as Coleridge reminds us. We worship best when we spend our hearts' best. And it seems that they were given us for such spending.

XIII SOLITUDE

WE HAVE seen how it is possible to worship God in unpremeditated and lonely shrines. This fact leads us to inquire into the character of solitude itself. If out of silence come music and a sense of God, shall we not find that solitude also has its especial gifts and graces?

I once knew with a considerable degree of intimacy a wild stag that I presumed to christen Old Clubfoot. His identity was not difficult to establish, for his horns were decidedly freakish in the form of their architecture, and he walked and ran with a limp. His right hind foot had in some way been injured—possibly in a steel trap—and the track made by that particular foot was like a hole punched in the ground. As sagacious as any buck I ever encountered, he could be depended upon to do the unexpected. He positively refused to run to regular stands and crossings.

But what rendered Old Clubfoot truly fascinating to me was the fact that this great wildwood personality was solitary. I never saw him with another deer, and his track showed that he always traveled alone. Repeatedly, in the woods where he roamed, I started small groups of other deer—sometimes as many as seven in a drove. But this stag selected himself for company. Here, then, was a wild creature that had become solitary.

Without feeling certain of the real cause of his self-imposed isolation, I conjectured that because he had been injured while in the society of others of his kind, he associated his misfortune with the business of traveling in a crowd. It seems undoubtedly true that one deer is more truly alert than a herd of deer; for an individual, having all the looking and listening to do, does them to perfection.

Old Clubfoot appealed to me as a genuine personality, chiefly because of his apparently deliberate choice of solitude. Indeed, such expressions as "the lone eagle," "the lone wolf," and others of similar import have their origin in Nature and in truth; and a correct understanding of what they connote leads us to consider thoughtfully the whole matter of solitude, both as it concerns wild creatures and as it concerns human beings.

The great house of life has many rooms, many halls, many corridors, many secret stairways. To me, solitude seems that other room into which we can retire whenever we radically need a change from present company. It is a bourne of solace and reflection.

We human beings love to steal away into solitude for no other purpose sometimes than to rest; designedly to relax; luxuriously to do nothing. It is a sanctuary, spacious, silent; or if there be music, the airs are of

Nature's own ancient motherly making. When the Master said, "Come unto me, all ye who are weary and heavy laden, for I will give you rest," surely He must have known that as we retire to solitude, to us may come stealing unaware spiritual insight as well as the more obvious physical refreshment.

One of my friends is a delightful companion, partly because he has a humble, self-mocking estimate of himself, and partly because his view of life is as refreshing as a sea breeze to a Kansan. Not long ago, eyeing me with his whimsical and affectionate glance, he said, "Well, I've found it at last."

"What?" I asked, mistaking his mood; "the Lost Chord or the Missing Link?"

But his tone had an almost wistful tenderness as he replied:

"I'm serious this time. I've discovered the highest social circle in the whole universe. It isn't at Newport, nor yet at St. James's Square, nor anywhere along the Riviera, nor in any proud city. It's in solitude. You see, the only people there are oneself and God. Solitude is a mystic association of souls. Anyone may belong, but each communes with God alone. I know nothing that would bring more people more swiftly to God than the habit of cultivating the romantic and fascinating society of Solitude."

Yet there are many people who fear solitude, confusing it, no doubt, with loneliness. But in solitude, as nowhere else, there is always, or there can be, divine companionship. To be solitary is to be in communion with God. Solitude is an escape from life's wild noises,

196

wild lights, wild shadows; it is a refuge where silence dwells, and quiet luminance, and spiritual radiance; it is a rendezvous with Love Eternal.

Of my solitary friends who have taught me much by their views of life, their opinions of human nature and of human destiny not the least remarkable is Richard Manigo, a negro of the aboriginal type, who for many years has been the watchman of a wild sea island, which, though a most regal game preserve, is seldom visited by its owner. There Richard lives alone; there, when I have visited the island to study its wild life, I have walked and talked with him. To begin with, he is as religious as the peasants with the bowed heads in The Angelus. Belief is to him as easy as breathing. I asked him how he could live in that offshore wilderness, far away from his kind. He said:

"Livin' one place is just the same as livin' another if a man loves God. And He's been good to me."

"Do you read the Bible, Richard?" I asked.

"I can't read," he confessed; "but it don't seem to make no difference to my Maker. He takes care of me just the same. I like to visit the mainland, but I like to stay here too."

Then he said something that gave me the kind of thrill that comes only when my mind, or the mind of another, manages to pierce with a ray of perception the far depths of life's shadows:

"On the island here, 'ceptin' the deer and things, ain't nobody but me and God. If I walk on the beach, or down in the woods, or go fishin' at the inlet, He's gwine be there too. So I never does get lonely, seein'

as how I got somebody to look out for me, and somebody to tell all my troubles to."

Solitude has brought me to a certain way of regarding Nature; a certain philosophy of the Creation and
the continuance of things. To me it appears that the
natural world, spiritually discerned, has so much of the
supernatural about it that we perceive in it immediately
the hand of God. Moreover, the beauty and the wonder
of the world cannot, I believe, be a mere matter of
chance; nor yet can it be the result of the operation of
blind mechanical laws. There is something more behind it.

I affirm, chiefly because my entire reason and my
instinct reject any other explanation, that this beauty
and this wonder were deliberately *premeditated*. And
if there are many things in the vast, momentous scheme
that we mortals do not yet comprehend; if apparently
there are irreconcilable elements; if sometimes the
shadow seems more than the sunshine, I believe the
hour will come when barriers shall fall, and we shall
stand as in a world of light. Through long years, assailed by grievous doubt, acquainted with sorrow, I
have come at last to feel with all my heart the immediate presence of God; I know that He predetermined
every physical and spiritual blessing that we enjoy;
and I am certain that He finds through the medium of
solitude access to these wayward hearts of ours that
He loves so long and so well.

I recall walking one sundown on an old upland road
that ran over the ridge of a long-deserted mountain
orchard. It was a place I was very fond of visiting,

partly because of the fine view to be had there of the far-shining valley; partly because of its solitude; partly because of the manner in which, from that coign of vantage, the watcher can see how the stars march up the great dome of heaven, as if they were angels in procession, carrying tapers, joyously climbing a mighty hill. I reached the pasture just at the right moment. The dark-blue flower of twilight was opening wide. The sky showed lilac lanes, wan gulfs, sea breakers of misty red.

In that high pasture I thought myself alone; but presently, as I sat on the roots of a gnarled and ancient apple tree, two cows with tinkling bells came by. They were followed by a tiny mountain girl, not more than five years old. I knew her well, but I hardly had expected to see her so far away from home at such an hour. She recognized me at once and stopped to talk with me; and the cows, no longer urged, buried their broad noses in the dewy grasses of the hilltop.

"What you doin' out here so late?" she asked, with womanly directness. She, of course, had her work to do; but why should I be loafing around?

"I like to watch the stars come out," I told her, "and I like to see the valley down yonder in the mist."

"Do you like them things too?" she asked, in a tone more kindly than that in which her initial question had been put. "I nearly allus stops here when it ain't rainin'. I don't get lonely when the stars come out."

"Why do you love to watch the stars?" I asked my tiny comrade.

"I talk with them," said the child. "And they lights me home."

In a moment she was gone over the fading hill, leaving me with another treasured memory about solitude. And I never look at the spangled heavens without recalling what that baby said of the stars—"They lights me home."

In our modern day, with the pace that our civilization tries to establish and to maintain, a great many people are made nervous by peace and solitude. Our speed of life is such that usually, when we seek repose, we make a mad dash for it. Solitude has a hand to still the pulse's leap, a voice to calm and to reassure.

I remember going late one afternoon to see old Sambo Boykin, an ancient negro who lived as a solitary on a deserted plantation. All his kith and kin were gone. It would seem that there was little left for him to live for. Yet, despite his dusky skin, despite the apparent desolateness of his situation, he was a grave and charming philosopher, made what he was, I think, by living close to Nature, by watching, with dim eyes but a discerning heart, the stupendous mystical ways of life.

The old negro was sitting on the wooden bench before his doorstep. He greeted me with affection and that easy courtesy that not many people realize a negro possesses. I gave him the little basket of things I had brought, and his gratitude was touching.

"Sambo," I said, after we had talked about many other matters, "you must not mind being all alone like this."

He looked far over the fading country, his eyes seeing

more than the saffron sedge field and the towering pines beyond.

"Cap'n, I ain't 'xactly alone. I miss all who are gone, but I ain't alone."

It is not infrequent for a plantation negro to utter simply the great truths of existence. He lives so much with the infinite patience of Nature, and he feels so keenly the mystery of life and the presence of God that it is natural for him both to think and to speak with the thoughtfulness of an Oriental.

"Somebody else has been to see you then," I ventured crudely. "I am mighty glad to hear it."

"Cap'n," he said, and he laid his gnarled black hand on my knee for emphasis, "you know Who I mean. He was my first friend in this life, and He will be my last —same as He is to you. God don't come to see me; He stays with me all the time. I ain't lonely."

A masterly work of any kind, whether it be natural or produced by man, can seldom be sincerely enjoyed save in some kind of spiritual isolation or solitude. I remember going into an art museum where there was a famous little masterpiece. It was in a room by itself. Before it was a single chair. And the guard at the door permitted only one person at a time to enter. When asked the reason for this practice, he said: "Everyone can get it for himself; but when several people go in together, each is liable to spoil the picture for the others by trying to explain it. We think really fine things don't have to be explained."

I remember going to visit one morning an expert woodworker by the name of Hulon Padgett. He and I were on intimate terms, so that as I went into his sawdust-smelling workshop that morning I did not even speak to him when I saw him perched on a high stool, his head in his hands, bowed over some problem of construction on the table before him. One flaming maple actually hung into one of Hulon's open windows. It's a pretty thing to have a tree look into a house. At last my friend straightened himself, slipped from his stool, and turned to face me. He was smiling.

"I knew you were here," he said, "but I had to stay by myself until I got this thing."

He then showed me the design for an interlocking splice for the broken back of a hickory chair.

"All day yesterday," he went on, "there were people here. I had time to do this, but I hadn't the quiet. I don't exactly have to be alone to think, but I love to be alone to finish thinking—to do that last bit of it that completes the job." He smiled reminiscently. "The very best work I ever got done," he said, "was during the summer when we had a smallpox scare over at the next farm. Nobody would come near this place. I had a chance to think our designs entirely new, and to work them out in wood."

For a good many years I used to take my youngest boy hunting with me, and of course together we learned much about game birds and animals. Yet I always felt that he was depending on me; and his own ideas simply echoed mine. Then came the great day when I gave him the old setter and told him to go out alone. That night he could hardly eat his dinner for telling me about the things that he had seen for himself.

Once I watched a white chip whirled madly down the wild waters of a rain-filled trout stream. It raced toward me frantically; but a backwater eddy caught it, and quietly it floated into a little sheltered bay. We, too, ought to leave the mad current sometimes, to rest our hearts, and, ere it is too late, to muse upon the innocent beauty gleaming on the banks. If we do not so retire, how shall we ever be thrillingly pierced by the music of silence? How shall we hear the lustral music of tall, rustling corn? How shall we ever feel the pure, inevitable charm of the woods?

It takes solitude for these great and humble pleasures to be enjoyed. And it takes solitude, under the stars, for us to be reminded of our eternal origin and our far destiny.

BUT if solitude has its solaces, what shall be said of comradeship? I have already told of my affection for my humble and faithful Prince. I shall now try to tell how much peace of heart and how much gratitude for life my beloved Colonel brought. True love brings us into the sweet wildwood of quiet contentment; and my Colonel it was who opened for me those vistas in the wood of life that have never since failed to fascinate me.

The fact that Colonel Henry Middleton Rutledge was my father need not, I think, with discerning and considerate readers, convict me of immodesty in telling this story. It is not as if I were claiming anything for myself. I had nothing to do with his creation. Here was a real man, the personification of a great era in American life. Why should I not give what I know to be an authentic picture of him, one that I trust will be convincing? That he was six feet tall; that one shoulder drooped because of two wounds, one from Malvern Hill and one from Antietam; that his fine head was regal in its carriage, with its thin aquiline nose, its eyes the color of the blue early-morning sky, its strong and tender mouth, half hidden under the white mustache; that the cast of his countenance was gentle, yet with nobility and pride and honor suffusing it softly—all these matters are in a way descriptive. But it was by behavior that I came to know the real character of this picturesque personality.

I used very often to drive in a buggy with my Colonel from his plantation on the river to the seacoast village, ten miles away, where he had his summer home. Such a journey reveals the character of one's companion.

Born a woodsman, the Colonel, to his last day, took the keenest interest in all forms of wild life, and spoke of game birds and animals with an accuracy that is attained by observation alone, and with a gravity which gauged his feeling. He would stop to show me the very spot where two years before, in the mist of morning, he had seen a huge stag walk across the road. He would point out to me on the sandy highway the track of a deer or of a fox, a raccoon or a wildcat.

I recall his showing me late one afternoon a broad, straight, shallow gully that had just been made across the road. "That's the track of a diamond-back rattlesnake," he said; "a lordly serpent like that never does so ignominious a thing as to wriggle. He travels straight. That's more than some men do; yet I don't consider him a proper associate for any man."

The Colonel had a certain spiritual delicacy in his appreciation of all things beautiful. This awareness of his to loveliness often made him totally unconscious of the

somewhat significant detail of time. A wild rose, blush-
ing alone by the dusty roadside; a wild flag flower,
standing like a blue banner beside some woodland pool;
the naïve beauty of a tiny green fern, the dream song
of the parula warbler, or the wild, sweet chant of the
mocking bird—all these waylaid his soul, deliciously
ambushed him, so that, through much lingering, he
was often long after dark in reaching home.

But his human contacts were most revealing. The
road we traveled was a lonely one, through heavy forest; yet here and there were humble homes, standing
in small fields; in some of these lived whites, in others
negroes. With all of them the Colonel's relations were
the same in affectionate solicitude. I recall counting one
day the requisitions that were made on him by his many
and importuning friends, who knew well that his buggy
was always loaded with produce from the plantation.

As a matter of fact, when the ordinary planter drove
by, these pinelanders paid no attention to him; but when
my Colonel's old sorrel horse hove in sight, and the
familiar identifying squeaks of his buggy wheels were
heard in the land, work came practically to a stand-
still, and people walked out to their front yards and
actually into the road to hail him, to wave to him, to
give him commissions to the village store, and literally
to rob him in friendly fashion of everything he had in
his buggy. The first hold-up on this particular day came
in front of the cabin of Old Ephraim, an aboriginal
black, to whom the Colonel was very devoted.

Battered hat in his hand, and ancient affection in his
eyes, Ephraim stood beside the buggy while the man

whom he revered as his lord and master bestowed upon him his only cigar. There was also between them a little subtle badinage, that can occur, I think, only between two such old cronies. And there was a promise on the part of the Colonel to bring to Ephraim on the morrow some medicine for a vague ailment that he described as "plain worriment and misery in the back."

At the next house, the abode of a mendicant pine-lander, a man of small means but of huge family, the Colonel stopped to inquire about little Winnie, one of the children. The other children—it seemed to me that there were scores—were eagerly draped on the staggering fence, their eyes fixed on the Colonel and on his buggy. They had seen good things come before from beneath that friendly buggy seat.

"Colonel," said the mother, a gaunt, sweet-faced woman, "Winnie ain't so good. 'Pears that she won't eat anything."

Under the buggy seat the old gentleman reached—he could always reach something for someone else!—drew forth the family pail of fresh milk, and handed it to the grateful mother, who thanked him almost tearfully. There was a small basket of peaches, too, that the Colonel had intended for his Sunday dessert; but he couldn't resist the bright appeal in the eyes of the little children. As we drove off, I overheard the mother say to herself thankfully, "That man's almost raised my children."

Farther down the road there were further distributions to many others, especially to the old, the sick, little children. The last quart of wild whortleberries, the

Colonel's favorite fruit, he bestowed on a crippled oar-maker who lived on the outskirts of the village. . . . Long after nightfall, whistling an old love tune, his buggy empty, his waiting supper cold, the Colonel drove into his yard. . . .

What a man's worth is in this world depends on the kind of wake he leaves behind him as he passes. If my Colonel came home empty-handed in a material way, it was because he had "bestowed all his goods to feed the poor." His riches consisted not on what he brought with him but on what he left behind him. He had the superb gift of making other people happy, a power that makes all others appear insignificant. His compassion was sensitive, restless, constructive.

Of his many charities, all of which were bestowed as obscurely and as surreptitiously as possible, the most remarkable that ever came to my attention was that which he showed to poor Amos Brown, a negro who was taken down with a virulent case of smallpox. The local medical authorities had him removed to a deserted cabin far away in the heart of the lost pinewood, sending to nurse him another negro who, having recently recovered from the dread plague, was considered immune. I was told that a physician paid one or two perfunctory visits; but the plight of the stricken man was desolate in the extreme. It would probably have been hopeless had not my Colonel daily, in secret, turned off the plantation road to drive down the grass-grown cattle track toward the cabin in the woods. Nearly a mile from it, he would have to leave his buggy, simply because there was no more road. The rest of the way he would walk through the humid, snake-haunted woods. One day he would take broth to the patient, then pieces of ice carefully wrapped in newspaper to keep from melting in the fierce midsummer sun, now fruit that he had bought with the quarter which was supposed to purchase his own week's supply of cheroots. Quite frequently he left with Amos the luncheon that had been packed for himself.

After a few cheering words with the sick man, and after certain quiet admonitions to the caretaker, admonitions rendered tenfold strong by the accompanying gift of the old gentleman's very last dime, utterly oblivious to the downright beauty and valor of all this behavior, the Colonel would retrace his steps to the waiting buggy, climb in, a little tired, and drive on to the plantation, where his negro workmen, never sure when he would come, would be making the best of a chance to rest.

That my Colonel made these perilous visits to the afflicted negro no one would ever have known, save for Amos Brown himself, who said to me one day, in a good negro's humble and direct fashion, "If de Colonel had not 'membered Amos in his trouble, dere wouldn't be no Amos to-day."

Another negro, Joe Vandross by name, had been friends with the Colonel since boyhood days. They were of the same age; and by one of those chances of human nature that must ever remain for us more or less mysterious, they were just born congenial. Their affectionate comradeship grew during more than seventy years. I saw it come beautifully into flower during those last months, when both Joe and the Colonel began to fail very fast. Joe lived about a mile away, making his home with a son, a negro minister, and a good minister too. It was a long walk for Joe in those last weeks, and a long ride for the old Colonel. But, as if aware of a parting soon to come, they let no day go by without seeing each other.

The Colonel always scrupulously gave Joe half the medicine that the doctor had prescribed for his white patient, showing a quaint and impatient disregard of the fact that their ailments were of entirely different natures. He seemed to take the attitude that medicine, affectionately bestowed, will be certain to work a cure. How often I used to see these old friends sitting together, talking, walking together, lingering together at the gateway!

Down to the very last Gate these old comrades went hand in hand. When Joe was buried in the plantation graveyard, my Colonel read out of the Prayer Book the stately service over the dead.

During this painful ceremony, his voice never faltered; but I saw him blink suspiciously once or twice, and when he turned away as it was over, he blew his nose rather loudly, although he had no cold.

Many things about life I learned from my Colonel, not the least of which was this: That the deepest and truest affection and comradeship may exist between an aboriginal African and the proud yet humble descendant of English Cavaliers and French Huguenots; between the son of a slave, the grandson of a savage, and the grandson of a Signer of the Declaration of Independence. Father taught me, by his behavior, that, while equality is often impossible, brotherhood never is.

A great lover of children, the Colonel was also, in a most inoffensive way, a keen matchmaker; and there was hardly a real romance in his community in which his genial and serene influence had not been felt. But he was at his best in conciliating young couples who had quarreled. I have heard happily married people, with homes established now for more than thirty years, say, "If the Colonel had not *made* us settle that quarrel, we never could have made it up."

This wholesome interference on the part of the Colonel had a profound effect on the whole community. To bring about one happy marriage is really a triumph, and he achieved scores. Nor was the least detail beneath his attention. I remember what he said one day to a beautiful Titian-haired girl out in the woods who stopped him to ask him please to bring her from the store a red ribbon. "The same kind you got me last winter," she added.

"Margaret," he said, with becoming gravity, "if you don't mind, I'll bring you blue. It's more becoming to you; besides," he added, his eyes twinkling with understanding and affection, "I happen to know that Jack likes blue better."

Who could resist his charm?

Once or twice I knew him to exert himself slightly to disinterest young people in each other. "But a man has to be very careful about that sort of business," he told me; "the trouble is, you never really know how the thing will turn out. Some of the supposedly worst marriages have turned out to be the happiest. Marriage is largely a matter of adjustment; and the fact is that some unpromising people are uncommonly good adjusters, whereas some of the finest people you ever saw aren't adjustable at all. And the dickens of it is that you can't always tell the degree of adjustability until marriage, which is the test supreme and irrevocable. I like to help matches along, but I hate to break them up. Besides, young people have a certain wisdom in these matters, a certain intuition perhaps, that moves in an orbit just a little outside our own sagacity, old as we are."

A lover of the wild greenwood, my Colonel drew many deep and permanent truths from the earth. He found God in Nature because he found Him in truth and beauty everywhere. The Colonel always seemed aware of the lavish life-giving power of the serene mother of us all; and, loving her, he came to love all ancient, elemental, enduring things. I remember one day when we were riding the springtime woods together, and had paused to marvel over certain miraculously tall and deep-purple wood violets. He said, "I used to see these violets here when I was a boy. They die; but, in their way, they rise again. Do you know the only thing we have which defies the years? There's a kind of love that takes, even from the fatal touch of time, which corrodes all else, a new and beautiful luster. That there should be this affection in our mortal world is a miracle of major importance. Indeed, I think it a proof of the spark of divinity in our natures."

Owning a vast place, he had every reason to expect

that trespassers and poachers would visit his property. But really he was not much troubled. The negroes of a considerable district he permitted to trap foxes, wild-cats and raccoons, and to gather what firewood they wanted.

But such was the peculiar hold that he had on the hearts of hunters of the pinelands through his humanity to them and to their families that, year after year, they paid him the incredibly affectionate tribute of not killing his deer.

But there came a winter when strange guns began to sound in his beloved woods. The first time the Colonel heard the shots blaring, he was inclined to overlook the trespass; but the second and third times that the offense was committed, though he rode valiantly out after the offenders, he could not apprehend them. Yet they had done sore damage, and had done it in a way to touch the Colonel nearest his heart: they had shot a deer and crippled it. He saw the poor thing limp into the unavailing shelter of a myrtle thicket. The very next day, sounding out brazenly on the wide stillness of the sleeping plantation, he heard the guns again.

This time he was thoroughly aroused. As he left the house, the servants heard him mutter in just provocation that somebody would pay for this. My mother tried to catch him, to ask him to wait until after dinner, which was then almost ready. The Colonel shared with most country husbands the disconcerting habit of vanishing just as a meal was about to be served. But, righteous resentment giving him speed, he was on his horse and away before anyone could stay him. The manner in which he sat his horse and the martial air of his advance boded ill for wrongdoers. It was with this same direct and fearless spirit that he had helped to rally his men on that field of carnage before Burnside's Bridge, and had led them desperately on the slopes of Mary's Heights. If now his heart would only continue as stern as his bearing, all would be well!

The second act of our little comedy opens a half hour later. The scene is the noble live-oak avenue, through the vista of which the visitor sees the glimmering white pillars of the Colonel's ancient ancestral home. Down the avenue four men are now walking toward the house. The Colonel is leading his sorrel horse, which had not greatly shared in the warlike excitement of his master. Beside the Colonel are three poachers, and the four of them are chatting gayly. At a certain bent oak along the avenue the old gentleman halts them and points out a deer crossing of uncommon fame, since there he has made five double shots on stags.

Now they come onward toward the house; the Colonel deftly drops his bridle rein over a post beside the mounting block, and the four walk up the wide steps to the spacious and beautiful veranda. Here, courteously excusing himself for a moment, telling his guests to mark how high the yellow jasmine vine has climbed one of the pillars, the Colonel hurries into the house.

"My dear," he says to his wife, "I've brought these gentlemen home to dinner with us; there are three of them. Hadn't we better use the silver coffee service? Why," he explains, when his wife asks him if these are the poachers, "we could hardly call them that. They are gentlemen, you see. I knew it the minute I saw them. They did happen to get across my line; but they are from the North, and all this is new country to them. But they were most polite. Besides, we can hardly call guests poachers. I am quite charmed with them, and I know that they will be with you. Yes, they are the same men who have been hunting here for the past week, but they are members of the Oakwood Club. We must be hospitable to them."

Gallant, tender heart! You were never made for stern reprisals. You gestured at being severe with those who wronged you, but your arm, raised to strike, yielded to the nobler instinct to embrace!

I do not know whether those of painfully worldly mind would approve the Colonel's manner of disciplining offenders. Probably not. But, though utterly naïve and ingenuous, his plan of entertaining the very men he had sworn to punish bore gracious fruits. In the long run, a man cannot lose by courtesy. After that day, those three hunters would rather have died the death than have hunted without permission on the Rutledge property; and the Colonel himself became a frequent and a beloved guest at the famous Oakwood Club.

There's an ancient Cavalier lyric which tells us that, under mountains, over rivers, and seas, through dark caves, over sheer and perilous barriers, love will find a way. It is the one true magic in life. It is the one force upon the constant use of which Christ insisted, with reiterated pleadings almost pathetic. And no one with any experience of life will be ready to deny that, compared to the supernal power of love, all other powers are mean and insignificant. It makes hate look paltry. Having all the dreadful might of gentleness, love has all the quiet conquering way of some living thing eternal. He who employs this force to effect his purposes, as Colonel Rutledge did without design, will have the stars and the sun with him. All beauty and all virtue will be for him. God will be ever at his side. I think the real secret of the charm of the Colonel's personality was a simple one: he had the priceless gift of a loving heart.

The main traffic of life is, after all, with one's own spirit; and if it be gentle and affectionate, how can the journey be aught but joyous?

The Colonel was wholly genuine. His title he had come by through four years of battle strife. With very little persuasion he would tell you about the war; and, of course, there was but one war to him. Though he bore two wounds, and though I treasure the gray home-spun coat that was his—a coat with that parch over the breast where the bullet tore its way through, and the ragged collar with half the stars shot away—he was totally free from any taint of bitterness or of self-pity. After all his fighting in Virginia, he returned home to a ruined estate and a collapsed civilization. Yet I never heard him speak of President Lincoln save with considerate and kindly judgment. "To the brave men on both sides," I used often to hear him say, lifting his glass for a toast, "to the brave men who fought, and to the braver women who waited." And to him Gettysburg was ever the greatest disaster in history.

Behind him was a depth and richness of background

216

utterly lacking to most men who bear his title. He had
known intimately both Lee and Jackson. He told me
that, one night of rain and fog, on the dreary and deadly
ramparts in front of the trenches at Petersburg, a
cloaked figure had suddenly appeared to him out of the
mist. It was General Lee. Together they stood talking
in the steady downpour; talking of the war, of the
coming battle, of those fallen, of those left behind. On
leaving, the general said: "I hope your men are well
sheltered, Colonel. Keep them dry if you can, and give
them extra rations." More than a mile back to his head-
quarters Lee walked in the rain.

The Colonel told me that he had seen Custer at
Appomattox: "A most romantic figure," he said, "with
fire and dash; extraordinary flowing curls; the most
picturesque man I ever saw, save only Pickett. Jackson,
if you did not know who he was, you might laugh at,
for he was awkward and looked far more like a preacher
than a soldier. But if you knew him, you'd worship
him. Lee, of course, was supreme. I do not know that
the war ruined the South; for it gave her Lee."

In 1918 he visited me in the North and I drove him
down to the battlefield of Antietam, which he had not
seen since those woeful September days of 1862. The
guide took us to the tower overlooking the historic
field, and pointed out to us the maneuvers of the troops
on both sides, naming the commanders, and describing
the fighting. "Just over yonder," he said at last, "the
Twenty-fifth North Carolina regiment was bloodily engaged. It was commanded by the gallant Colonel Henry

Middleton Rutledge, the youngest colonel in the Con-federate Army. He was badly wounded in this battle."

Father took off his hat and bowed to the guide: "Colonel Rutledge," he said, "and at your service, sir."

I might add that, after Antietam, upon Lee's re-crossing the Potomac under the fire of sharpshooters, the Colonel would undoubtedly have lost his life but for the intrepid devotion of his negro body servant, who attended him throughout the war. The negro had gone ahead, and had reached the Virginia shore, when Father, exhausted by his wound and by the onset of an attack of typhoid, fainted, and fell from his horse into the stream. Under the deadly fire of the Federals, the negro went back, lifted the Colonel's senseless form, and bore him in safety to the friendly shore. Whenever I hear anyone speak disparagingly of negro character, I remember that incident.

That same body servant, within a few years, became the fortunate recipient of a pension from the United States Government. An agent canvassed all the able-bodied negro men to discover whether any were eligible for pensions. As the agent worked on commission, he was not vitally interested in the legitimacy of the claimant's case. Father's body servant assured the investigator that he had been in the war, omitting only the slight detail of which army he had been in. The agent accepted the negro's "I been fightin' wid Mas' Henry" as sufficient proof of the man's eligibility to a stipend. Father was secretly delighted, and never told his faithful servitor of the dubious nature of the busi-ness. The pension came in regularly. At length the negro's wife died. He married a young mulatto; and she to-day, a widow, draws a pension from the United States Government because her husband served four years in the Confederate Army! Many a pension is fearfully and wonderfully made.

In the Battle of the Wilderness, the Colonel captured, after a strenuous personal encounter, a Federal officer—a giant of a man named Olaf Svenson, a Swede, with typical blue eyes and yellow hair. Captor and captive became friendly.

"Where is your home?" asked Father.

"Minnesota," Svenson responded.

The Colonel was astounded.

"Why, man," he exclaimed, incredulous, "we aren't fighting the Northwest!"

This incident has always seemed to me a most interesting illustration of the South's failure to comprehend that she was fighting, not New England alone but the whole of the vast region north of the Line.

My Colonel kept open house for travelers; and as his home was near one of the ancient parish highways, there was seldom a time when he was not entertaining someone. "I like to have somebody to look after," he would say.

We children in time became established in life; but one or two always managed to be visiting in the old home. After a long absence, I returned for a visit. Father always called me "Benjamin," because I was the youngest son. From repeated experiences, I was fully prepared to have the Colonel give me the ancestral watch, which, as long as I could remember, had been presented to me every time I came home, and always again on the eve of my departure. And, as often as I received it, I would carefully and secretly lay it back in the little top drawer of Father's mahogany dresser, knowing quite well how sorely the good old gentleman would really miss it if it were gone; knowing, also, that the ancient timepiece, too old to run accurately, was truly invaluable as a gift that could be repeatedly presented, accepted with the solemn gratitude due the possession of an heirloom, and returned faithfully. This whole performance had taken on the grave precision of a religious rite.

On the evening of my arrival one Christmas, after supper was over and the family had gathered before the ample hearth for reminiscences, I saw my father disappear into the bedroom, with the air of one about to spring a joyous surprise. I of course thought that the familiar watch was forthcoming.

But when Father reëntered the room, carrying in his hands a somewhat dilapidated matchbox, I could not imagine what kind of heirloom would be so lightly regarded as to be made to repose in such a receptacle.

There is a type of momentous yet pleasing gravity which sportsmen assume when they discuss sports; and such was the seriousness with which the Colonel approached. With great solicitude, as if he were handling something very brittle, he slid off the cover and placed the matchbox tenderly in my hands. It was packed to the brim with damp white sand!

"Benjamin," said the Colonel, pulling up a chair close to me, adjusting his glasses, and laying one hand on my knee, "it was just like this: I simply could not bear not to have you see that track."

Then for the first time I noticed, in the center of the small block of wet sand, the track of a buck. Deeply the heavy stag had set the imprint of his hoof in the damp earth.

"I was driving home from the mail," the old gentleman explained, now fairly launched on his story, "when just this side of Bowman's Bank, where that little scrub-oak hill is, I saw this track in the road. It was so fresh that it was almost smoking. I don't think the deer could have been gone a half hour. As you know, I always put out every deer track that I see, not caring to have any of the pineland hunters take too deep an interest in them. But I just felt as if you had to have this track. Your mother had told me to buy a box of matches at the store. The Lord will provide! The thing came over me in a flash. Here was my chance to preserve the track for you! Emptying the matches on the floor of the buggy, I turned the opened box down over the track, ran my knife 'round the edges to give me the outline; then, lifting the box, I cut down deeply into the sand, and lifted the block intact. Isn't it the finest track you ever saw? And to think it was made by one of the deer of our home woods!"

The good old man's delight was so unfeigned, and his pride in his singular achievement was so refreshing and ingenuous that no real lover of humanity but would be irresistibly drawn to the ardent author of so quaint and whimsical a performance.

The Colonel was a great lover of flowers, as I have

said; and in his own woods Nature was lavish in beauty and abundance. I have seen him ride into a bay thicket and break a great fragrant cluster of snowy blooms for his wife. Of the flowers of the garden, he loved the red rose best; for half a century ago his mother used to wear one in her hair. He even went so far in sentiment once as to write a little verse about a rose; but he never showed it to anyone, and barely mentioned it to me, having a deep regard for the sanctity of personal emotions, and a reticence about his own feelings. As he used to ride about the plantation, he was forever reining in his horse to admire the beauty of the cloudy-purple pines, the dazzling fairy work of the humming birds, the misty-tender radiance of the blossoming fields. This close association with the loveliness of Nature kept him close to God.

Touching matters of a religious nature, he was reverent in a manner almost antique. He had nothing in common with those who say in their hearts that there is no God, for he had passed through many dark waters, and had found Him in their depths. He always said his prayers; though, as he confided to me with real contrition, on very cold nights he was shockingly liable to cut them a bit short. His favorite prayer was that of the Publican, and he often repeated it with comforting sadness.

I have mentioned certain incidents of the relationship of my Colonel Rutledge with the negroes. All of them in his part of the country knew and loved him; and whatever failings negroes may have they are among the most discriminating judges of character I know. At least three dusky families lived entirely on the Colonel's bounty. He built two cabins on his land and furnished them for two ancient negroes: Old Galboa and Old Morris, both of whom had been slaves. All their many descendants had deserted them, but their former master did not.

How often have I sat with my father and Old Galboa under the oaks and pines in front of the negro's cabin, listening fascinated to the talk of these two men, each one a sage in his own way, each devoted to the other. Galboa was both by nature and by circumstances a recluse, but to the Colonel he opened his heart. Formerly the plantation fisherman, he had an almost occult knowledge of wild creatures and their ways. Deep, primeval, was his philosophy, smacking of the very odors of the brown earth and of the forest. I remember him saying, "God is good enough to do anything." His descriptions of things had a certain poetic felicity, unlearned and therefore piquant. I recall his describing a hog as being of "a sort of a kind of brown-ashes color"; and one day, when the Colonel asked him if he had seen a certain wild heifer, Old Galboa said, "No, sah, but I will take a sly look for her."

I remember how amused I was over an appeal that a much baffled negro bridegroom made to the Colonel. This young man, Alec Jones by name, was a very gentle, respectful fellow; Father had almost reared him, and he had always come, in the most confiding manner, to the old gentleman for advice. About a week after the marriage of Alec to a most buxom and commanding woman, several years his senior and, as she let it be freely known, centuries his superior, the bridegroom, much crestfallen, appeared in the Colonel's back yard. Alec gave unmistakable signs of being in a most painful state of mind. The Colonel at once apprehended the young man's distress, but he had rather a difficult time ascertaining the real nature of the trouble. At last it came out:

"Mas' Henry," asked Alec, fathomless faith in his troubled eyes, "is you know any way for a man to head-off a woman?"

Alec's old friend and benefactor was obliged to confess that even his long experience of life had not enabled him to discover a single method by which a mere man can prevent a woman from having her own way. But he attempted to console Alec by adding, "We men must remember, Alec, that women are generally right."

Nor was this opinion delivered without profound conviction on the Colonel's part. He reverenced women as no other man of my acquaintance has ever done. I might hazard the conjecture that the high estimate he put upon womankind might account in no small measure for his serenity of spirit and for his popularity.

On one occasion a young negro man was rather disrespectful to the Colonel—a thing so unheard-of that it caused a considerable stir on the plantation, and rumors of it ominously traveled for miles. The negro in question was one Mingo, the son of old Isaac McCoy.

Many were the scathing personal remarks passed on Mingo by the members of his own race, the attacks ranging from animadversions concerning his morals to ridicule of his indubitably peculiar head. But it was reserved for old Isaac, the chagrined father, to make what I have always considered to be the most amusing and unique apology I ever heard. Approaching the Colonel with a certain air of deference yet of ancient wisdom, he said, "I done come for tell you 'bout Mingo. Mas' Henry, you ain't 'zackly understan' my son."

This beginning did not promise an apology, and the Colonel did not look pleased.

"Mas' Henry," old Isaac explained, as if such manners should really be understood by a man of the Colonel's intellectual ascendency, "ain't you know, sah, if eber you see a nigger wid a raccoon head, he ain't got no sense?"

The Colonel melted; old Isaac chuckled. Peace and order were completely restored by this original and magnificent apology.

Father was the only man living who could give a negro in that part of the country his genealogy. I always used to get a thrill of genuine pathos when some black man or woman, in perfect trust and confidence, having walked miles out of nowhere, would come to the Colonel, and plead, with appealing and devastating blankness, "Mas' Henry, please, sah, tell me who I is."

"Why," the Colonel would say, "your people, William, came from the old Ormond Hall place. You are the son of Charlie Washington, who died when you were just a little boy. Your mother was Sarah Colleton, and your grandmother was Mamie Weston, who nursed my mother. They were all fine people; you come from the very best stock."

My Colonel's utter humanity was by no means lim-

ited by his relations with his fellowmen; it included all
living things, especially horses and dogs. On a hot day
I have known him to dismount and walk in the sun beside his horse, just to give the poor creature a respite.
He was never more boyishly happy than when someone
made him a present of a puppy; and as his acquaintance
was large, gifts of dogs were so frequent as to come
near dislocating the domestic machinery of his home.
I can see him now, seated in his favorite rocking chair
on his spacious veranda, his right hand hanging down,
playing with the prodigious drooping ears of a hound
puppy, regaling me with tales of woods and waters. At
such times the gentle affection with which his bronzed
hand played with the pup was as indicative of his character as the genial light in his clear blue eyes.

One cold January day, when Father and I were deer
hunting, I left my stand in the woods and joined him
on his, to suggest that we make a little fire, it being
better to let a deer escape than to freeze one's self. I
found him on a pine log, somewhat huddled by the cold.
Seated very close to him was Blue, his favorite old
hound, who had apparently wearied of the chase and
had rejoined his master. The hound saw my approach,
but the good old man did not. Singular indeed was the
performance that I beheld, and of a nature so whimsical
that I can never recall it without a smile.

The Colonel had carefully unwrapped on the log
before him the one precious sandwich that he had for
luncheon. This he had scrupulously cut into little squares.
In his hand was a tiny silver flask, a few drops of the
priceless brandy from which, with the grave precision

of a connoisseur, he would pour on the bread. Then he would give old Blue a square, and would take one himself, share and share alike. The hound, looking unfathomable things at me, resented, I think, in his stately fashion, my intrusion upon so personal and solemn an occasion. As I came up, the Colonel said, with a smile:

"Benjamin, an old dog, you know, has to have a little stimulant as well as an old man."

That the singular remedy he gave Blue was efficacious, I am certain; for the hound, rejuvenated, soon rejoined the pack. But the more I think of his secretly leaving his companions, the more I am convinced that not weariness but sweet recollection and anticipation had prompted him. This same performance that I had witnessed had doubtless happened many times before!

Such was the man I knew and loved. He is gone. But the memory of him gives life for me—and I believe for many others—an aspect of nobility and grace. My Colonel helps to redeem humanity. They throng back to me—the memories he created; they mingle, they brighten. And in the moonlit, shadowy land of the past I see my beloved Colonel greeting affectionately his roadside neighbors; talking with Old Galboa; visiting the stricken Amos Brown; feeding his luncheon to an old hound; walking with his black friend, Joe Vandross, even to the very grave; giving his son a treasured deer track; rejoicing in Nature's beauty and abundance; ascertaining artfully a somewhat lagging lover's preference for color, and then, with naïve charm, telling the sweet girl in the wild pinelands to buy a blue ribbon instead of a red one!

XV AUTUMN

THE story of my Colonel that I tried to tell you brought us to the autumn of his life. But just as my memories of him can never be sad, so autumn has always been to me a joyous season. Even in fadings and declinings one may discover reasons for peace of heart if one will be spiritually aware. Autumn eventually confers spring; and I believe death confers immortality.

One of my first really graphic impressions of autumn was not half so dramatically impressed upon me as it was upon the negro with me, old Cæsar Moultrie, who, when I was a plantation boy, used to be frequently commissioned to accompany me on some of my expeditions into the forest wilds. He was a good comrade, was tolerant of my boyish views, was wise in an ancient Nature-taught way, and left me many a happy memory.

That day in late September we were sitting together under a big hickory nut tree, a few resplendent leaves from which glided to the placid waters of the creek before us, and rested there, sumptuously, royal barges

for the Cleopatras of the fairy world. The utterly peaceful reverie that comes over fishermen who are good
companions and are having no especial luck was upon us.

Old Cæsar had laid his battered cap on the grass beside him. His bald head glistened amiably. I was half
asleep. The universe seemed to be in a joyous trance.
When I heard a slight sound in the hickory tree overhead, I just thought that another big gold leaf had
started down. But this was no drifter. In a second, with
a resounding crack, a heavy hickory nut landed squarely
on the top of Cæsar's head. The nut, clipped from its
twig by a foraging gray squirrel, was still in its outer
green shell, and therefore doubly heavy. The blow was
enough to knock out an ordinary man. But Cæsar, after
an initial blink at the moment of contact, reached over,
picked up the nut, looked at me, and chuckled.

"De fall o' de year done come," he said.

The fall of the year! It is a magic expression, ancestral, poetic, universal. It is like nightfall, like dayspring,
like evenfall. The year ripens like an indolent misty
peach—and falls. Sundown is the fall of the sun—his
gorgeous foundering in the blazing vortex of the west.
Those critics of language who insist that we always say
"autumn" overlook the appropriateness and the beauty
of connotation of "fall." The fact that dictionaries do
not always give it is perhaps one reason why it should
be treasured.

I recall another incident of the declining year which
perhaps well illustrates one of the elements of this
fascinating season's character. We generally associate
autumn with the ripeness and the richness of age, with

life's promises fulfilled, with the infallible wisdom that comes like the growth of a mighty oak out of the very heart of Nature—out of the soil and the sun, the starlight and the rain, with the beautiful slow passage of the years.

This old wisdom is almost cosmic in its sagacity, having in it the human spirit's fathomless far reach to the heart of God. I came upon this example of it in this way: I was talking with old Anthony Lee about the little negro church that he and the other negroes on the plantation had started to build, and I was lamenting the fact that the steeple of the humble edifice had never been completed. Anthony listened to me kindly enough, but I could tell from the light deep in his brooding eyes that he had reservations to make to my criticism. When I was through, he said gently, touching his ragged shirt over his heart:

"Cap'n, here de Temple."

Was there ever a sermon more eloquent? Was there ever a keener rebuke of worldliness in religion? Anthony was thinking of the only true altar, the shrine of the heart, builded by the Almighty, and visited by Him. And this humble negro was telling me that God cares only for the offerings upon that sacred altar, for the music welling from the virtuous soul, for the unfeigned worship of the human spirit.

Children are usually, I think, far wiser about many essential things than we are. They know instinctively that all of us live in a world made sacred by the very wonder of it. Spiritually aware of the mystery of existence, they see a million miracles, and they have the grace of heart to acknowledge their true character. Children have an artless and disarming honesty of soul that we are always in danger of outgrowing. Naïve to the point of indiscretion, their thoughts, their celestial reflections, their talk—all these seem to be spiritually extemporaneous. Often they converse truly like Children of Light. The supposed errors they make are commonly to be laid to their fortunate ignorance of our complex, dubious, and disingenuous civilization.

Christ, who understood everything, said that Heaven is made of children; that is, of people as refreshing, as native, and as fragrant-hearted as children. Now, in this festal season of autumn, all of us take a childlike joy in the winy air, in the resplendent colors, in the beauty and abundance in garden, field, and orchard. It is then that all of us rake leaves together, talk honestly, abandon our cumbrous dignity, love one another, and are as serenely happy as little children.

Here a great maple is softly burning like a vast yellow primrose. The water-oak by the winding creek is some mysterious jewel, glimmering with dewy flames of topaz, amethyst, and rose. The old sassafras tree on top of the pasture ridge looks like a miniature sunset, all saffron and ruby. About all this beauty there is something communicable. All of us feel it; and we have to see as much of it as we possibly can. Yet we do not like our neighbors to imagine that we can afford not to be busy. We therefore pretend to rake leaves; but in reality we are steeping our very souls in the glory of autumn, ruddy autumn, fruitful, fragrant, generous, and gorgeously fading.

When the leaves begin to fall, we slip back into happy childhood; and literally from sea to sea every man, woman or child who has a rake, and who has a yard to rake, is now busily raking leaves. What pastime is more harmless, childish, delightful, and futile? It would be far better for our lawns if the leaves were left where they fell, for they are Nature's blanket for the winter. But Molly is out in her yard raking leaves and Annie is sweeping them from her tiny pavement; and the Taylor boys are carrying great baskets of red and yellow leaves from the lawn to the chicken yard. People rake leaves as they do everything else—characteristically.

Now the good housewife is down on her knees to get that sly leaf that has hidden under the hedge. She'll not have it said that she sweeps dust under her carpets! Now the village Rip Van Winkle, who really ought to be hunting in the hills, is raking leaves as a sportsman does who wants to be after the real business of his existence; but the vigilant eye of his wife, and her tongue, the tone of which seems somehow to lack the general mellowness of the season, keep him at his task. Yet with Rip raking, leaves have a chance.

There is something universal about this spirit of raking leaves. All of us have a lingering ancestral feeling that we must be getting ready for winter. Doubtless the cave man gathered leaves for his bedding in his dusky cavern. Then in the autumn we are alert to Nature's changes. Life becomes more of a game. Every move that Nature makes we interpret as a signal to us to bestir ourselves. She scatters her leaves, and we rake them up. It is a tremendous racial gesture that we are aware of the coming of our annual fight with winter.

Besides, when we rake leaves we have a very soothing feeling of respectability. There is a real community interest in this activity. I may not have a cent in the bank, but if people see me going after leaves energetically they feel that I am in the common cause, and that I am a man of thrifty ways. It is an innocent outdoor sport, this raking of leaves. It brings millions of people out to do the same thing; and all of them draw close to the ancient hearthstone, to the humble yet matchless beauty of earth. Autumn and the raking of leaves draws us close in some immemorial democracy. I believe we think long thoughts when we rake leaves. For one thing, it is very easy then for us to see that, while all our lives we strive and struggle to produce beauty (occasionally achieving a somewhat sorry imitation), the creation of beauty is natural, is spontaneous with God.

And when we think of Him, we think of each other kindly; for all of us are in His big back yard raking leaves.

Beautifully the leaves are falling, with an impartiality directed by a justice divine, radiantly on the lovers strolling in the twilight, brightly under the dancing feet of little children, gently upon the old, tenderly on the hallowed graves in the village churchyard.

There is about autumn the golden glamour of a memorable farewell; but if it is sad, its sadness is visionary. In reality, the parting is happy. It is not permanent. The voyage is not one into blank space. It is a circumnavigation. All this beauty is fading, not so much because it is dying as because it is going on a journey. Other lands shall see her loveliness and rejoice in her charms, and soon she will be with us again. The ancients with their mythology really did very little intellectual clowning, they usually had things right. In autumn, they said, Persephone has to go back to Hades to visit her husband; but within a few months she will once more return to the old home where Mother Ceres lives.

That idea is a beautiful one, and more just than Bryant's, that:

The melancholy days are come, the saddest of the year. . . .

Though a great poet, he there suffered a spiritual backsliding. Trivially viewed, autumn may be sad; but in a broad and general sense it is the most gorgeous, the most opulent, the most enamoring of all seasons. The time of harvest, of mellow fruitfulness, of strangely renewed vigor and strength, of the sumptuous funeral of foliage old, of the splendor of the mighty southward migration of the birds, of the smoke from burning leaves and from cleared gardens, of Indian Summer, of matchless days when the earth seems hardly to breathe under her canopy of golden mist, of piles of yellow corn, of rows of corn shocks like Indian wigwams, of heaps of ruddy apples, of bubbling cider presses, of aromatic odors from the fields, the woods, the roadside—such is autumn.

Nature has yielded her all; she is a little tired but triumphant, fading but beautiful. She is the proud mother. Her beauty has the noble effulgence of maturity. The fragile flowering of maidenly spring has at last borne its fruits and its grains.

Autumn is Nature's joyous wistful pause to look with benignant smiles upon her handiwork and upon her happy children. Autumn is the long afterglow of summer, a time in which the heart may well rejoice, reflect, be calm, be radiantly grateful to God. It used to be called St. Martin's Summer, and it was a favorite season with lovers. Beloved also of artists, of it many a masterpiece has been painted. Yet the originals of these masterpieces are ours, for nothing; and the artist is the Almighty. Paintings are copies. All the originals of all pictures of Nature belong to the lover of Nature. Nature's beauty, autumn's loveliness, these belong forever to the hearts that delight and rejoice in them.

I remember how autumn came to me one day when I was fishing for bass. Most people imagine that fishing consists in catching fish; but the name of the sport describes the effort. Much fishing is a fine gesture toward being busy when the soul languishes to loaf. It is one of those harmless human deceits which help to keep our appearance respectable. To make the bluff complete (as all wives know) a man's preparations for fishing are artificially elaborate; it is as if he had discovered that he had been trifling long enough, and must now get down to the real work of life. Moreover, a certain solemnity attends the preparations.

But when the genial and beloved hypocrite is once planted by his favorite pool, he becomes so enamored of his peaceful surroundings, so secure in the delusion that his wife imagines him laboring hard for her throughout the livelong day, perhaps braving perils for her dear sake, toiling in deep waters that she may enjoy the fruits of her hero's efforts, that he drowses blissfully; he grows careless of life and of time; careless of fish and the supposed vital object of his coming to this remote bank overhanging the lonely, placid creek.

He puts in the day loafing incessantly, vigilantly, virtuously; and when at sundown he takes home a few infant chubs instead of a dozen five-pound bass, his wife manifests both her mental and her spiritual superiority by praising with charming innocence his extraordinary ability as a sportsman. Light is by no means the swiftest thing in the universe: the swiftest thing is the way in which a wife gets onto the curves of a fishing husband. Fishing is one of my favorite vices.

That day in late September I was at a famous stretch of bass water of one of the tributaries of the Potomac. From shore to shore the wide creek lay dreaming. The silvery sycamores, the massive white oaks, the plumed and graceful elms, the stalwart shagbarks—all these lay mirrored in the silent water. They seemed like music, and the images like its echoes. Down the still tide floated gaudy leaves, many of them curled into tiny crafts, little *Pintas* and *Santa Marias* voyaging adventurously.

In the very center of the stream a belated dragonfly dipped his wide wings to the water, starting faint ripples as he performed some aërial stunts. In a patch of reedy marsh bordering the stream a flock of redwing blackbirds called incessantly. Far overhead I heard the faint "spink-spank" of migrating bobolinks. On the limb of a sycamore an imperious blue jay with an acorn in his bill was hammering it softly. I could see in the water every move he made. Of all bright-plumaged birds, none is more energetic than he.

Looking down the creek, I became aware of another fisherman. He was sitting on a rock that jutted into the stream; and rock and fisherman were dappled with sunlight. Setting my line, I strolled down to have a chat with him.

He proved to be an old farmer with gnarled hands, ruddy honest face, and piercing blue eyes. We fell easily into conversation, as fishermen and other idlers generally will. I asked him if he knew the stream well, and if fishing were what it used to be.

"I was born in that house on the bank over yonder," he said, pointing to an ancient stone structure overlooking the creek. "Sixty years ago, to this very day, I was sitting here on this same rock."

This, thought I, was the preliminary of an entirely new kind of fish story.

"The fall of the year was just beginning," he went on, "just like it is now, without a body's hardly knowing it. I was a little boy then, and I had played hooky from school. I was sitting right here when, away off yonder to the south, I heard what I thought was thunder. But it kept up too steady, and there wasn't a cloud in the sky. My conscience made me think that the devil was getting ready to come after a boy who'd stayed away from school. The thunder got worse and worse—just growlin' at me. At last I couldn't stand it any longer. I set my line and headed for the schoolhouse. I got there late, but in plenty of time to hear more than I could take in."

"But how about the thunder?" I asked, seeing him fall suddenly daydreaming about that ancient time.

"Those were the guns of the battle of Antietam," he said, "the guns of the opening day's fight—about twenty miles to the south of us here. And this creek looks to-day just like it looked that day; these same red leaves floating down, these same restless birds calling and heading to their winter home. And sixty years from now," he added, "things along this creek will not have changed much. Nature never does change much, does it?"

When I went home at twilight on that autumnal day, I had but the proverbial three small fishes; but I had acquired a quaint little chapter out of real history and out of the history of human nature. Beautiful it is to me to think that with each succeeding autumn the rolling guns of Antietam sound dimmer and farther away, hushed out of existence by the positive virtues of love and purposeful forgetting. Year after year the hatreds pass, having in them the seed of death; and love grows from more to more. Autumn is a time of memory, but of reconcilement. We then look toward the past, but see it only, as Timrod beautifully says, as

> A shadowy land where joy and sorrow kiss,
> Each unto each corrective and relief;
> Where dim delights are brightened into bliss,
> And nothing wholly perishes but grief;
>
> Ah, me, not dies! No more than Spirit dies,
> But in a change like death is clothed with wings;
> A serious angel with entranced eyes,
> Looking to far-off and celestial things.

AUTUMN

Autumn has always had for me a radiant charm. Well can I recall, even at this distant day, how autumn used to come to me in the little Carolina seacoast village where I was born. As a barefoot lad, trudging a mile to school up a bush-bordered village lane, I used completely to forget the importance of a classroom education in studying the things in creation's vast and fascinating schoolhouse, especially alluring on a fragrant morning in the early fall.

I felt the certain glamour of the season, though I never tried to define it; but it compelled me to stay outdoors as long as possible. A migrated catbird lurking fussily in a clump of pokeberry bushes, slyly and ravenously devouring the succulent black fruit, would hold me like an enchantment. I loved to listen to the telltale rustle and the soft sunny whistling of the white-throated sparrows under the wild hedges. Thrilling to me were the mellow human flutings of the long-billed curlews as they wheeled in the golden haze of the tranced autumn sky, or streamed in long lines gracefully toward the lonely sea-beaches.

In those far early years the strange beauty of autumn haunted me like a passion; and I have never lost a certain romantic unrestrained rapture over it—an emotion that is native, I think, to our whole race. I remember the radiant bronzing of the water-oaks; and the shining buckeyes that we used to gather; and the glistening black live-oak acorns.

In the great pine forest just across the tidal creek near where the schoolhouse stood there was, at the wane of the year, a glimmering world of tawny wild

239

beauty; and one of my very clearest recollections of boyhood is of my inability to get to school on time because I had to pass through a world that the season had turned into a sumptuous daffodil field. And now, when I see children lagging their way wistfully on an autumn morning, eagerly and joyously delaying, I know how they feel. Their sensitive and reflective hearts cannot resist the fabulous splendor of the year's gorgeous pageant of the Field of the Cloth of Gold.

Despite the glamour of the fall there are those who find the autumn depressing, because, discovering in it what they believe to be the sign and signal of our own time of departure, they have brought home to them a sense of the transiency of life.

But the autumn, to those who understand it aright, is a premonition of spring, a pledge of immortality. Because of its nameless glamour we feel a certain nearness to a spirit world. Hallowe'en we have paganized, for it was really All Hallows Eve, the night before All Saints' Day. It is a sacred time, and somewhat more significant than a mere religious festival. I have often wondered whether the belief that on that night spirits walk the earth had not some explanation in the fact that the migration of many birds and of some animals is then in full swing: we come upon beautiful wild strangers in our streets and back yards, and the nights are filled with the beat of mysterious wings, with weird sweet cries from invisible voyagers.

Amid such real sorcery and honest necromancy we feel that autumn has really come, though the almanac tells us that it is at any time between the sun's south ward passage across the equator and its northward passage, three months later. O. Henry says when women with no fur coats grow kind to their husbands, then the fall of the year is at hand. But we can recognize its coming in ways far less sophisticated.

One day before the serene spell of summer had broken I went far back in the lonely mountains to see if I could find some fringed gentians; among wild flowers they are comparatively rare in our part of the country, and they are always of exquisite beauty. Driving twelve miles up Path Valley, I left my car in an old sumac-bordered lane, where goldenrod gleamed and dusty daisies nodded. Two miles back into the woods I walked, into the wild and fragrant heart of the solitary greenwood, into a veritable sanctuary of Nature called by the Tuscarora Indians, long ago, Orquic Valley. Down the wooded glen of this vale bubbles a pure mountain stream.

I found one cluster of gentians, and they would have repaid me for my trip; but there were other rewards. As I sat on an old chestnut log that spanned the stream, autumn came to me through the suggestions of several beautiful reminders. First, from a huge old sugar maple rustling liquidly above me, a crimson leaf fell at my feet.

A little later I saw a gray squirrel burying a hickory nut in a pile of old dead leaves. He knew that the fall had come, and I knew it, though there had been no frost, and though all Nature was tranced in dreaming sunlight of a delicious quality. I thought of the dead of winter, with a deep snow over that hickory nut, and

I knew that that squirrel would come back for it and dig it out, though he would have no map to guide him to his hidden treasure. In the fragrant little dells away from the stream the air was silent, having the listening stillness of expectancy; here, where of late the wild wood warblers sang—the vireo, the towhee, the wood pewee, the veery, and the hooded warbler.

From the dew-drenching of the night before the woods were still and bright and aromatic. There was a richness about this quietness that told me autumn had come, and the hale odors from the hickory, the ash, and the oak mingled with the delicious fragrance from ripened wild grapes. I almost saw Autumn herself musing in her lovely garden of the world; she was wearing a little bunch of red berries in her hair. Thoughtful she stood while raying from her on all sides were the resplendent fruits of all her toil and love.

All the magic and mystery of those autumnal mountain woods were gathered for me into one sound that day when I heard, from a thicket far above me, the soft drumming of a ruffed grouse. There is no sound that has a more remote significance, a more fascinating unreality. Ordinary sounds break the spell of autumn, but here is an authentic voice of the woodland, ancient in origin, delicately golden in quality, as befits the season.

But there is one bird that chooses the fall of the year for a regular lyric festival. This is the mocking bird, perhaps our finest grand opera performer. Though he sings during the mating weeks in spring, and in a desultory manner throughout the summer, it is during the glamorous moonlit nights of October that he pours forth the full splendor of his song. There is a tone of richness, a contralto depth to this singing that is not heard at any other time. It is as if the bird were not rejoicing in his own personal happiness, as he does when he is in love, but rather as if he were trying to express to the world in gorgeous song the luxurious beauty of the autumnal days and nights. I hardly know what birds one should expect to hear in another world; but I hope the mocking bird will be there; and if he is, I know he will sing as he does during the full moon in October.

It is commonly accepted that autumn is an ending; but in a very real and vital sense it is a beginning. The law of the conservation of energy tells us that no force ever really has a termination. Autumn, while it is the wane of summer, is likewise the beginning of spring. It is astonishing what Nature knows about preparedness; she should be our ideal in all such matters.

Unhappily, we spend much of our time preparing for war, whereas Nature prepares for coming peace and happiness, for fruits and flowers, for beauty and abundance. She plans for life, not for death. There is not a tree that, in the autumn, does not hold in thousands of tiny tightly clenched gloved hands the leaves and flowers for the coming season, months away, across the bleak expanse of winter.

Deep down in the heart of the strawberry plant, snuggling close to the earth in mid-November, there are even now our strawberry shortcakes of next June. The peaches and the apples are always on the trees, either ripe, or to be held in safe keeping until spring weather

243

gives them a fair chance to develop. The hazel nut blossoms in the autumn. Nature is always ahead of us in having an early garden. Her little perennials curl up and go to sleep under the leaves, or under the waters of the quiet pond. The first balmy sun, the first genial persuasive rain will awake them. Nothing seems to be an end or to have an end. What seems an end is merely the beginning of something else.

We live and move amid a million evidences of eternity. Nor is there a season more full of reassurances for the human spirit than the fall of the year, which is only superficially a time of fading and of silence. It makes death seem incidental, for both are apparently final, yet both presage immortality.

XVI MAGIC TWILIGHTS

If we can discover peace in autumn, the twilight of the year, we ought to be able to find at least quiet entertainment and calm joy in the twin twilights that every day supplies—the dusk of daybreak and the dusk of evening. Dewy and mysterious are they, alluring the spirit to innocent delight. Glamour is in these magic twilights, and ancient infallible springs of youth. To roam the two dusks has been with me a passion since boyhood. Let us wander together through this secret country of dim loveliness and glimmering solitude.

The swarthy hemlocks drowsed; the tall grasses fringing the borders of the mountain pasture dreamed; already some of the little wild flowers had closed their brimming eyes; the soft lights of sundown slept against the quiet hills. I had been far back in a lonely uninhabited valley; and just before leaving the borders of this wilderness to return to the highway, and the smell of gasoline, and madly hurrying mortals, I had stopped in this old pasture to see what wild life the day's ending might bring forth. There is a brief period just after sunset when profound stillness may hold the world. There may not seem to be any retirers or any comersforth. Yet always there are those two classes of movers in the half lights of the faded day: those that have been abroad during the daylight hours, who now seek shelter and sleep; and those that are at home in the deep of night.

It was in late Maytime, and locust blooms were drifting down on the dewy evening air, shedding odors of magic sweetness. The world was tranced in quiet, suspended in a halcyon haze, breathing softly, exhaling delicate scents from damp hickory leaves, from dewy pines, from the dim water-course that rimmed the lower edge of the pasture.

Two rabbits were the first wild things I saw. He who would like to know the habits of deer will do well to watch the rabbit; for probably no two creatures so apparently unlike are so identical in their ways, especially in the details of that continuous strategy that wild creatures must adopt if they wish to make their lives safe. We hear of a rabbit's hopping, yet, if undisturbed, he far oftener stretches himself along the ground, literally elongating or measuring himself, his delicate ears turning tremulously to catch the slightest sound. I do not suppose that another thing of the same size makes less noise than a rabbit. His padded feet are shod with silence. He sits up on his haunches, looking, listening; he creeps forward; but I can detect no sound from him. And it is with eerie stillness that these two wild comrades steal forth into the twilit pasture.

Hemmed by the darksome wood, which is full of enemies, they must depend for their safety upon their craft and upon their speed. Yet, for all the perils that beset them, they are lovers of life; and I know that they are enamored of their beautiful solitary home, sequestered against the sweet bosom of these ancient hills.

My next visitor I hear but do not see: it is a Wilson's thrush, or veery, chanting his vespers in the fragrant glen below the pasture. I find in the song of this bird something of spiritual beauty that is lacking in the lyrics of ordinary singers. It is heard best when the incredible iris gardens of sunset are fading, like the glory of life passing away, and when the soul, viewing that paling pageant, has imperious need of sustaining, everlasting arms. It is then that the song of the veery comes with its mysterious comfort, having the very tone and the supernal beauty of the eternal and the spiritual. It is a triumphant song, despite the wan gulfs of evening that succeed "the golden vortex of the west over the foundered sun." Its music breathes the assurance of immortality, the love of God for His children, the peace beyond our understanding. It tells us that, when all the yearning is over, our spirits shall be joyous and free. It has told me that, as a child is born into the world naked, weeping, alone, unaware of the awaiting love of a mother, so, though we leave this life for an unknown country, a solace not less than love's shall be ours there.

All my life I have loved to be out during the two twilights—that of the morning and that of the evening.

Each has for a background the richness and the depth and the magic of the night. It is then that one is most likely to observe the shyest living things, and to hear music hushed by day and stilled in the deep of night. These twilights quiet the spirit; the one for the strife of the coming day, the other when the labor and the pain are done. Each one has often had upon me the same effect as going to church, or to an organ recital. God gives us a day and a night and two twilights, mysterious beautiful sisters, long-lashed and darksome-eyed, exquisite and divine with spiritual companionship. To be associated with them is like walking hand in hand with angels. They suggest God's infinite compassion, and man's right infinitely to hope and to trust.

I remember starting one morning long before daylight to hunt wild turkeys, only to find, when I was about three miles from home, that I had brought my gun but no shells. It was too late to return for them. I therefore decided to "make it a morning" anyhow, and repaired to the glimmering borders of a lagoon hidden mysteriously in the pine forest. It is really an artificial lake, formed more than two centuries ago by rice planters in that region of the Carolina seaboard. The growing of rice requires water, and this lagoon was made so that water could be drawn as required. Its massive bank is still intact, and the lagoon has become a paradise for wild life, for herons and egrets, for gallinules and nesting wood-ducks, for myriads of migrated wildfowl, for alligators and black bass, bream and jack, fish hawks, frogs of amazing size, and hundreds of wary land wanderers who come there to drink. I do not know another place where wild life may be more interestingly observed. I went out in the woods that morning to slay, but I remained to worship. That seems to be the best word to describe my state as I turned homeward after those few memorable hours.

The east was faintly paling as I reached the edge of the gleaming waters. A massive pine, hurled to earth by a cyclone, offered me a convenient perch from which to watch the mysterious country that surrounded me. For some moments after settling myself I could hear no sound save the sibilant, lustrous fall of heavy dewdrops slipping from the fragrant leaves of a sweet gum tree beside me. In the blue silence of the heavens the morning star burned blazingly in silver solitude. Though it was early January, the air was mild, and from the crest of a myrtle I caught the scent of a yellow jasmine, the first of the year, tossing its saffron showers delicately. The first bird note I heard was that of the phœbe, a timid yet rejoicing song, fluted down the silent forest aisles just at the breaking of day. Then from the lagoon came the soft converse of a flock of ducks, and these I soon made out, floating in dreamlike beauty upon the placid, mirroring waters. Mallards they were, the males almost spectacular in their brilliant casques of green. There were perhaps fifteen in the flock. So near shore were they that I could see their eyes gleam, and little sparkles were reflected from their wet bills. Suddenly an old drake stretched himself and gave what I should call a hilarious yawn: he struck his wings on the water and quacked shoutingly, with complete abandonment of caution and decorum. His jovial shout got an answer.

Beyond the languorous lagoon arose the mighty pine forest, misty and grand. It was there, I knew, that the wild turkeys roosted, and it was in that direction that I had been headed when I discovered that I had no ammunition. And now, at the sound of the old drake's call, there came from the deep heart of the wildwood the gobbling of a wild turkey. An old gobbler is prone to answer from his roost any sound that irritates him; and a little later in the year, when the mating season begins, he will answer belligerently almost any noise that he believes a possible rival may make. I have heard a wild gobbler answer for at least a half hour the weird, shrill cry of a redtailed hawk circling high above the pine forest.

Now behind the trees to eastward the red roses of dawn began to clamber upward, illumining with everchanging fires of bloom the oriel windows of those orient skies. A dawn wind, laden with woodsy fragrances, breathed through the pines and cypresses, swayed the long pennons of Spanish moss hanging from their still branches, and here and there upon the lagoon's limpid surface made the leaf of a water lily slide suddenly as the movement of air caught in the upturned edge of the leaf. Water lilies make me think of human beings: we see them, and we do not see them. Apparently they are floating on the surface, but what really gives them life comes from a profound and unseen source. As a water lily is invisibly anchored to the earth, beyond the power of mortal eyes to discern, so are we somehow anchored to the Eternal. Sometimes, caught by the winds of chance, we seem to leave our place; we skim away; but always we are drawn back to that which is our source and our bourne.

Behind me is a thicket of young pines so dense that a man cannot come through without a hard struggle. Yet I heard something coming, and I knew from its stealthiness that it must be some shadow-footed wild thing. A buck it was, that all night long had been roaming the woods and the edges of the plantation fields. Now, in the dreamy twilight of morning, he was hunting a place to spend the day. If my observation is correct, a stag does not like to lie down in a thick place. I have startled them countless times, and I have found them to prefer edges of thickets, thin copses, or positively open places in which to couch themselves for the day. A stag is usually careful also to lie down so that he faces the direction whence he has come; he watches his own trail. With an easy grace that was almost eerie in its deft precision the buck insinuated himself through the dense tangle. I saw his snowy throat; I caught the gleam of tall antlers. A moment later he stepped into a little glade between the pines and the water. In any sense he was superb, and as a wild-life picture he was matchless. A deer is a great aristocrat. I never saw one in his native haunts look mean or haggard or disheveled. This stag, his regal head high, winded the fragrance of the morning breathed to him through the dewy mosses and over the gleaming beds of water lily and wampee. I have found the twilight of the morning the best time to watch deer. It is better than in the evening, for then the light is fading fast. Yet in a real sense twilight is the proper setting for a deer; for he himself is shadowy, evanishing, an almost magic creature of forest dreams; a master of the subtle arts of dim avoidances, of silence, of delicate secrecy. Turning his beautiful head toward me, he must have made me out, more likely by scent than by sight. At any rate he whirled, flashingly stooped under the low-sweeping pine limbs, and was lost in the fragrant, hushed depths of the thicket.

Now the sky was all pink and ivory, saffron, flame-breasted. Little clouds the color of azaleas burned iridescently. I caught the sound of wings. Then came shrill, sweet voices, sad and strange. A flock of wood-ducks that had spent the night among the old rice fields of the vast Santee delta sped overhead, made a half circle, and alighted in the lagoon in plain view. The lagoon has all sorts of interesting little arms that stretch mistily away into the forest fastness, and up one of these estuaries the wood-ducks swam. If there is a more beautiful bird than a male wood-duck on placid water, I do not know it. There are birds of far more gaudy and elaborate coloring, but the size of the wood-duck and his plumage are in a taste so exquisite that Nature must have been in her best artistic mood when she made him. I never cease to marvel at the rainbow play of colors on his head and neck, and over his back and wings. The prismatic, soft lights that glint and gleam from him as if he were a great jewel, and as if his breathing liberated a hundred soft fires that flame momently, are quenched, and flame with occult radiance again.

Suddenly, through the awakening forest, came the first real song of the daybreak: it is the rollicking carol of the Carolina wren. In this sweet and piercing call there is no shadow of hesitancy or doubt; all is assured joy, an outburst from a heart full of strength and gladness. I tried to estimate the distance that the bird is away from me. It could not have been less than a quarter of a mile, far down near the bank of the river. Yet the buoyant lyric sounded as if the singer might be within reach of my hand. For a day's beginning, for a sweet memory to keep after the twilight of morning has passed, I do not know a more joyful and soul-stirring song than this frolicsome, delicious hymn, almost swaggering in its brimming certainty of love and gladness. This marvelous carol, heard in the quiet cathedral of the morning woods, has power to lift the human heart into ethereal light, into lands of the spirit. It has always seemed to me that if the departing morning star could be vocal, its glorious canticle would have the magic and the beauty of the dawn-song of the Carolina wren.

When I left the lagoon that morning and walked home through the balmy sunshine of early day, I really felt richer than if I had had a twenty-pound gobbler slung over my shoulder. I have hunted much, and it is good for a man in a physical and perhaps also in a mental way; but I confess that it lacks the spiritual enjoyment afforded by affectionate observation. And, if I may be permitted to suggest it, I believe there is a type of the observation of Nature that is superior to the purely scientific. The scientist searches for facts, for knowledge. His function ends when he has discovered that a thing is so, or is not so. But there is another kind of observer who goes beyond the scientist, for he asks:

"What does this mean in terms of the spirit? What does all this beauty and intelligence suggest to the heart? What can I learn of my own soul by surveying in thoughtful love the souls of God's wild children?" I have no quarrel with science, for it is splendid and indispensable; but its province is circumscribed. Where it ends, true religion begins; for religion is of faith, and with faith science refuses to deal—which is, from a scientific viewpoint, perfectly just. The scientist says that the Carolina wren is *thryothorus ludovicianus*. I can't curse him by calling him that. To me he is one of God's choristers who has with felicitous accuracy the wave length of the human heart.

There is a place about two miles from home that is rather remarkable as the scene of activity in the magic twilights. The artificial damming of a spring has overflowed a huge meadow, forming a pond some twelve acres in area. Here goldfish are raised. It is a fascinating industry, but not nearly so interesting as watching the wild life visible at the pond as soon as the sun has burned his way down through the pines fringing the western hills. I go to this place often, especially in the early autumn, when to the resident wild creatures are added the migrants moving southward toward their winter homes. One afternoon during the first week in October I spent the last hour of waning daylight on the banks of this extraordinary pond. It was a still evening, with odors in the air of sumac and ripened shellbarks and frosted fox grapes. Down the placid stream behind the pond bright-colored fallen leaves drifted idly—tiny argosies of faërie charm. The sky was blue and gold.

Peace was everywhere, as if Summer had finished her work and was resting quietly.

The first thing of interest I saw was a mink; and this is one of the most difficult of all wild creatures to observe. I saw him for several minutes before I recognized him. Bolt upright he was, sitting on a vividly green bank of grass edging the still water. He looked like a little brown stump. A wild thing, it appears to me, is quick to detect when it is seen; for I know that such a creature has often remained motionless, quite close to me, until I saw it, whereupon it would make off instantly. The mink afforded me the privilege of watching him for a moment. Then he slid with amazing dispatch into the water, which hid him on the instant. But so shallow is the water that I could watch for some distance the path of his progress by the little wave that rolled along the pond's surface. What interested me chiefly was the speed of the wave. As an underwater swimmer, I doubt if the mink has a superior among animals, though the otter would be no mean rival for aquatic honors.

And now the sky was fading; and silhouetted against its gorgeous gloom myriads of blackbirds came streaming, like long, dusky pennons, into the reedy margins of the pond to roost. Many of these birds, I knew, must have summered far north of this place and were really on the beginning of their migration. Following them came, in rather ponderous but stately flight, the night hunters of this quiet lake: three great blue herons, and at least a dozen black-crowned night-herons. Most of these alighted on low trees or in shallow water. I heard the thin, sweet music of wings, and overhead passed a flock of at least twenty green-winged teal. As if magic springs had been released, they dropped from their level flight and in a moment had glided joyously into the gleaming water. They were silent and motionless for a few minutes, turning their heads, making sure that all was well, getting their bearings. It seems characteristic of birds, especially of those that are hunted by man, to take time to look craftily about when they alight amid new and strange surroundings. I have had a ruffed grouse, come from a flight of possibly a half mile, alight within three feet of me. He came to earth behind a big stump, I was on another. It was at least ten minutes before he took a single step, yet it is hardly possible that he knew I was near.

Still lies the pond, and in its mystic waters the dying colors of sunset flame and fade. The myriads of black-birds are now quietly settled. The herons make no sound. The teal are swimming off in their dainty, noise-less way. But I hear a voice that must be, to nearly all these wild children, the voice of an ogre. Two hundred yards down the stream there is a high bluff on which some hemlocks of virgin growth are standing dark-somely. From their shadows comes the melancholy "hoot-a-loot, hoot-a-loot," of the great horned owl (*bubo maximus*). Weird and enchanting it is, soft and ventriloquistic, a voice of the waning twilight, occult, haunting, dim, remote. I never hear this great bird with-out a startling thrill. Death's eternal hush is in his tone, yet mystery too, as if he were telling us that the things unseen are the abiding ones.

It is with reluctance that I leave a place so fascinating as this twilight fishpond. Nature may seem to have regions of desolate quietude; but the wastes and the wildernesses are full of life, and in the two twilights some of its most secretive and beautiful forms are to be observed.

One April morning, down on the plantation, I had a curious daybreak encounter. I was going along a dewy pineland glade near the river when I met unexpectedly a rather forbidding stranger of the general family with which Eve, so long ago, appeared to be on rather friendly terms. This was none other than a huge reptile, a female alligator, come out of the river in the twilight of morning to deposit her eggs in the warm sand under the lonely pines. She had already accomplished her mission and was eager to regain her natural element. As I was weaponless, and as she was not unwilling to defend herself, I did not molest her, but stood watching her with amusement as she charlestoned down to the deep waters that glimmered between the trunks of the cypresses and the burly tupelos.

Eggs that are incubated by any mother will hatch within a given period, for the warmth that they receive is constant; those that hatch in the sand hatch at periods fixed by the degree of urgency of the sun's heat. As these eggs had been laid in a favorable place, I expected the young alligators out in rather speedy time; and that I might see their elfish parade from the nest to the water, I managed to visit the place pretty frequently for two weeks. Altogether I was near the nest for thirteen days, and never once, save on that first

day, had I seen the mother. For all I knew, she might
be miles away, having gone wherever the tidal waters
might have taken her. But then came *the* day. I was out
early after some cattle, and rode by the alligator nest.
A mist hung over the river and, creeping forestward,
"put forth an arm and shrank from pine to pine." To
my delight I found the tiny black dragons crawling
from their bed of sand; and to my amazement, the old
mother was on hand to witness the glad arrival. The
watchful parent evidently recognized me as an intruder
into this domestic scene, but this time she made no effort
to escape me. She was there to guard her little ones;
the primal mother-instinct was awake in her savage old
heart, touching it with the glamour of tenderness, the
fire of courage. As the last of the little 'gators emerged
from the sand, the mother led her strange brood down
toward the big river, each little fellow imitating in
ridiculous fashion the cumbrous crawling of its mother.
As I approached the water after this strange procession, I saw, lying like a lurking submarine, a giant bull
alligator straight in the pathway of the oncoming crowd
of mother-fed youngsters. I do not mean that he was
on shore. Some ten yards from the bank he lay in the
river, grimly expectant. Knowing the true nature of a
bull alligator, I know that he will not hesitate to devour
his own young.

A thought came to me then that served to inject mystery into the whole odd performance. How did the dim-
brained old mother know exactly when her eggs would
hatch? She had left them because she was not needed;
but as soon as she knew that her little ones were due

258

to arrive, she was on hand. Perhaps she was well aware
of the menace of the bull. At any rate, like a true
mother, at the critical moment she interposed herself
between her children and the danger that menaced
them. Yet, deep in the monstrous waters of that gloomy
river, how did she know when that strange pile of leaves,
so precious to her, would begin to stir with the life that
she loved? It is a mystery to me—magic of the morning
twilight—a part of the profounder and more sacred
mystery of all motherhood. I must add that when I
say that one alligator will destroy another, I am positive, for I have seen the thing happen.

The great river that I have mentioned divides some
fourteen miles from its mouth, the two branches flowing
parallel, a mile apart. Between them is a wild delta
wondrous in its wealth of natural life. From boyhood
I have roamed the delta, but particularly at twilight
have I visited it, because it is then that the myriads of
wild ducks that have spent the day drowsing in the
warm waters and on the sunny sandbars at the mouth
of the river begin to pour in countless thousands into
the old abandoned rice fields. For years I used to be
on the delta two or three times a week throughout the
winter, from a time an hour before sunset until darkness had folded the world. I saw much wild life, certain
of the forms of which impressed me as picturesque and
memorable. It is at twilight that the marsh-hawk does
a great deal of his most effective hunting. On wide and
tireless wings he beats his way slowly just above the
marsh, poising, veering swiftly, dropping from sight,
rising without apparent effort. The flight of no bird is

more enigmatic than that of a cruising marsh-hawk. So intent is he upon his business that he often runs almost into me where I stand on the desolate rice field bank, when he flares away; but he does not go two rods before he is back at his hunting again. Just at that time of day I believe the rodents that he so loves are a little unwary, and the relaxation of their vigilance gives him his chance.

The ducks come up the river in varying forms of flight. Sometimes solitaries will beat by, with heads far outstretched, and turning to look downward for a favorable place to stop. Sometimes huge flocks that almost darken the heavens stream northward like gigantic black arrows, speeding for the river swamps where acorns abound. As the twilight deepens, the onlooker is bewildered by the incredible numbers of the arriving hosts: these have come to light on the delta, and guns will not deter them. Big mallards and black ducks, pintails, wood-ducks calling shrilly, widgeons, teal, and shovelers—the sky rains them. Those that are down call to those in the sky, and receive glad comrade answers. The vast delta seems to seethe with ducks, and the clamor of their coming drowns out every other sound. At such a time they are partly off their guard, and they seem to shout joyously and without restraint. Ducks in the daytime are far more secretive and self-effacing.

To the westward the sky is ablaze with a wide-winged sunset poised above the velvet-purple wall of the pine forest. Then the ruby wings droop, fading to pearly pink, then to emerald, then to amethyst that blends

with the deep blue of the pines. Against that sky I see
what is the lordliest of all birds powerfully beating his
way homeward through the twilight. It is a splendid
bald eagle that all day long has been foraging northward over the delta. But he must sleep on Cedar Island,
which is at its southern tip. Onward he sweeps, solitary
and superb, the very magic of twilight's beauty about
him. Far, far through the rosy afterglow the lone, illustrious eagle pursues his glorious flight until he is lost
to the vision of man in the liberty of God's sky.

XVII   CHILDREN OF THE NIGHT

SINCE we have been watching together the children of the twilight, why should we not "make a regular night of it"? At least we can stay out long enough to drink deep of the sparkling wine of darkness. How strange is the superstition that night air is unhealthful! Rich in elemental fragrances, it is buoyantly life-giving, pungent, virginal.

The afterglow had been so brilliant that its suffused radiance of color did not seem to die, but softly to merge with the mellow light of the moon, streaming goldenly through the lonely stretches of pine forest. After a long delightful day in the woods I had started home about sundown; but the glamour of the evening forest stayed me, and I was still two miles from the plantation gateway when the iridescent afterglow and the serene moonlight performed their mystical rite of marriage. Twilight was soon passed. The "dead vast and middle of the night" had not yet come. Should I not stay out for a few hours in this silvery silent country? Was not all this beauty about me tangible romance? Out of dusky sweet thickets were deliciously exhaled aromas from sweetbay and myrtle, ilex and gallberry; while from the long sleeping savannas, wearing the mist like raiment, there breathed an odorous cool wind that set the tall golden broomsedge whispering elfinly. Surely these were the alluring aromas of Eden itself. And through all this beauty and mystery, I knew, there would soon be journeying those Children of the Night —those shadowy creatures that hide themselves by day, and come forth delicately under the pale career of moon and stars to roam the dim and lovely forests of darkness and silence. For when one half of creation sleeps, another half wakens; and it is an eerie, obscure, fascinating half. I shall try in simple fashion to tell of the behavior of some of the wild creatures I have seen and heard in the deep of night.

Candor compels me to admit that such observations often lack that degree of completeness and accuracy that it is possible to attain when observing by daylight. Some allowance must be made for the dimness of the light, and some for the natural difficulty that the human vision has with the moonlight. But I shall recount in good faith what I believe I saw; then I shall at least be telling a moral, if not a downright physical, truth.

Of the more savage roamers of the night, I have not the acquaintance that I have with the gentler and the more timid creatures; yet I have heard and seen some of the former; and while I realized that there could hardly be any genuine peril from them, nevertheless they afforded a most decided thrill. On this same evening that I was describing I turned off the road and went down to the dim, dewy borders of a wild and winding watercourse known as Montgomery Branch. Here and there piles of drifted trash and leaves had made miniature natural dams, and over these the water fell musically. I found that greenwood music deepening as the darkness set in. When the very last light was tingeing the tops of the tallest swamp tupelos, I saw doves fleeting to roost in a swarthy pine thicket. I saw and heard woodcock speeding eerily in enigmatic flight through the glimmering thicket; and after I could no longer see them, I could hear them, for woodcock apparently prefer to move by night, and experience no difficulty in flying through the darkest forest. In the lonely swamp I heard the owls, the veritable oracles of the night, begin their weird intoning. Phantom huntsmen of the dark, they were starting their wild soft whooping. Ere long over the woods deep silence fell. Even the murmuring pines ceased to chant their vespers. Suddenly, out of a yellow canebrake some sixty yards from me, a place all misty and spectral, there came the savage snarling cry of a wildcat; and had I not known what it was, it would have chilled my blood. We are familiar with the many curious cries and calls given by the domestic cat. This vague yowling is a habit also of the wildcat; but his cries have a definite boldness and wildness in them that are quite distinct. Before this icily cruel cry came I thought that the forest had settled to stillness; but at the sound of that dread menace, a deeper silence came; a crouching, palpitating, breath-holding silence, the trembling stillness of terror. For the wildcat is the ancient, wise, implacable enemy of practically all wild life that is inferior to him in size, and to many forms that are larger but not so strong. I did not see this wildcat. The moonlight in the little glade was bright enough to make discernment of him possible. But he did not appear. Yet to this day I can hear that rasping snarl, defiant as only a feline cry can be, perfectly interpreting, too, the nature of the beast. Unlike a great many people, a wildcat has a voice that goes admirably with his character and his temperament. He belongs essentially to an age of savagery; perhaps to the Age of Monsters.

Not far from the glen where I heard the wildcat I had built in some young pines a platform from which I used often to watch deer. Not only was this place a famous crossing, but my stand overlooked what had once been a big churchyard. But the church had been burned, so that now nothing remained save a blank space of white sand—a curiously inviolate area on which the bushes and grass did not seem to care to encroach. In this white arena deer could be seen admirably, not only because of the high visibility afforded but because to such a place deer are naturally attracted. After brushing through the woods, they appear to delight in open places. Besides, I had put some rock salt on one of the charred sills of the ancient church. A deer will barter his soul for salt.

In country in which they are not much hunted, deer may walk about rather freely in the daytime; and they do this in any case when there are sharp changes in the weather, as, for example, when a heavy snowstorm sets in. But in North America, where the wild deer is hunted in practically every locality, it has become a creature of the night. To me it appears that there is a rather remarkable resemblance between the deer and the rabbit —and the similarity does not end with the possession by each of a white tail. They come forth at about the same hour. They feed during the same period; they eat practically the same things. The manner in which they take their food is almost ludicrously similar. A rabbit frequently rears up to reach his food; so does a deer. And it is a startling thing to see a ten-point buck apparently in the act of climbing a tree; I have measured croppings that a stag had made from a young birch seven and a half feet from the ground. In the manner in which they bed down for the day, crouch warily upon the approach of an enemy, and bound away when the suspense can be stood no longer, the deer and the rabbit are alike. So too are their maneuvers when pursued. Like a cottontail, a whitetail will make an explosive, an amazing break for liberty; then shortly thereafter will stop to listen, will skulk into cover, will steal along craftily a few yards farther, will stand in a palpitant listening posture; and, if long pursued, will always have a tendency to return at length to the place whence it had been started. In every one of these particulars the rabbit acts precisely like the deer. A buck rabbit is a miniature stag.

Watching for deer at night is truly a fascinating business. I used to see many other creatures from my platform, but the deer were by far the most interesting. Let us say that it is eleven o'clock. The white moon is now high above the purple pines, flooding the sandy arena before me with pearly radiance. Occasionally, from the distant plantation settlements I can hear the bark of a dog; now a barrel owl hoots from the river-bank; a wandering flock of teal speeds by over the forest, their wings making thin music. But the deer, though they are so comparatively larger, and though they are coming through the brush, are far less noisy than the teal. From observations made scores of times, I am rather sure that, under ordinary conditions, a wild turkey makes as much noise as a deer in moving about; indeed, a flock of turkeys can be exceedingly boisterous. But a deer, unless crashing away from a pursuer, is perhaps the most quiet animal in all the world for his size. Though five deer are about to emerge from the forest greenery into the amphitheater below my look-out post, I am not sure of their coming. I think I hear a halting sedulous brushing aside of the dewy myrtles; possibly the slight cracking of a dry twig that has been stepped upon. Of course, these deer are traveling in an ancient animal path, with a wet sandy bottom; and doubtless they know every foot of it. Nevertheless their approach is characteristic: they softly reconnoiter, doing as much pausing as advancing. What is it they so dread in these woods whence their natural enemies, panthers and wolves, have been removed at least a century ago? It is Man they fear.

Here they come. Out of the misty shadows into the celestial moonlight they steal, almost like pilgrims arriving, after a darksome journey, at some bright and blessed place. Two does are leading the band; then comes the hart royal, a magnificent full-antlered stag; then two yearlings follow. Their pace is slow and wary; their heads are alternately held high, and then low to the ground. Once or twice I see one of the deer extend its head straight out, with the ears forward. Not infrequently I have detected the presence of a deer by the movement of its ears. Upon the sense of smell the deer depends chiefly for safety; then upon hearing; last, upon sight; for the eyesight of a deer is not strong. It can detect movement, but its power of vision is not great.

Here before me in the mysterious moonlight are five vividly wild creatures; yet gentle, timid, asking no boon save that of life itself. I know where they are going: a mile behind my platform there is a dense pine thicket where mushrooms grow; it is toward there that these deer are headed. Perhaps, ere the night is gone, they will visit my patch of sweet potatoes, on the succulent vines of which they voraciously feed; last year black Gabriel lost all of his half-ripe peaches from marauding deer. Possibly they will call on him to-night.

I noticed that as one of these deer stood head-on to me I could hardly distinguish it, so eerily did the moonlight and the sand and its own coloring blend. But as soon as one would turn sideways, its complete shape came out clearly. For full five minutes they stayed in the clearing, walking about, listening, looking, apparently enjoying the openness and the serenity of it all. Why should not wild creatures enjoy scenes and odors and beauty as we do? Have we not failed utterly to give them credit for a capacity to enjoy?

Once, at the far-off howl of a dog, the old stag

stamped the ground nervously, his head rose regally high, and I heard him suspire uneasily. Now they are going. Almost under my tree they troop, falling silently into a shadowy line—stealing wraithlike through the forest aisles, vanishing like visions. To watch a deer by moonlight is to see something ethereal.

Among the great mountains of western North Carolina, where I spent sixteen summers, of all the wild life that I saw or heard, including one memorable encounter with a timber rattler, the finding of the nest of an albino quail, and hearing one night from a lonely gorge the mournful scream of a panther—nothing really engaged my interest as much as the flying squirrels. On our place, which consisted of two big wooded knolls and a tract of valley land—the whole being far removed from the highway, nestling eerie-like against Couch Mountain, there were a great many big oaks and chestnuts with hollows in them. Tall awkward sourwoods were there also, which never grew very large, and which seemed to have some affliction of the joints, for all of them were crooked, and all seemed to have hollows. Most of these holes were the homes of flying squirrels—those elfin gray acrobats of the dusk—those daring voyageurs of the twilight and of the mysterious night. For hours, both after sunset and in the later night, I used to enjoy these graceful aeronauts, of the truly remarkable character of which far too little has been said.

Here, halfway down the grassy slope of the hill in front of the house, an ancient black oak towered fifty feet to the first limb. At this crotch there was a hole; and in the dark abyss beneath there was apparently a regular ancestral home for flying squirrels. One evening I counted eleven squirrels emerging from that old homestead.

Let us say that the sun has now foundered behind the hero wave of Mt. Pisgah, rising grandly among the mountain breakers' sea of flaming heliotrope. Rayed gigantic spears of light slant blazingly to the zenith. Remotely the outline of the Great Smokies can be seen, the outer combers of that mighty ocean of hills, the white horses of that magic sea and of that fabulous shore. Swiftly the incredible pageant fades. The earth and the sky darken, though a violet radiance lingers. In the Cane Creek Valley the Clans of the Mist hold one of their eerie and silent meetings. The stars begin to blink out. A stillness born of shadows and of dew is on the world. But on this wooded knoll there is great activity. I can both see and hear flying squirrels.

Here is one on the big dying chestnut; he has just sailed to it from the patriarch black oak. I can hear the squirrel travel scratchingly up the rough corrugated bark. Light enough lingers for me to see him. On he goes, looking down frequently to discover how high he is. From the time when his last movement is made and the moment when he takes his thrilling leap into space, several seconds may elapse. The squirrel, although he had a parachute that never fails to open, is carefully estimating the whole situation: his own position, whether favorable or not for the sheer plunge; the distance to the desired goal; the lay of the land— for even the slightest slope or roll of the country beneath must be taken scrupulously into consideration.

Having watched these eerie acrobats on scores of occasions in the afterglow when the light had a certain suffused vividness, I am sure that I never saw one make a false leap. Once I did see a baby fall short—a pathetic little gray aeronaut. But the hard bump that he got did not deter him from taking another and a higher leap a few moments later.

The flying squirrel knows with nice exactness what his height from the ground should be in order to accomplish a certain glide. I have often watched one, poised for a leap, change his mind, climb higher, get a better stance, and then spring confidently out into space. In this leap, the four legs are violently extended, stretching wide the strange thin membrane on either side of the body. The landing after this extraordinary flight is almost invariably made on the side of a tree, low down; and immediately upon alighting, the squirrel begins to climb; and almost before the observer is aware of what is happening, the climber has attained sufficient altitude for another leap.

Many a night, in its deepest hours, I have listened to the methodical telltale sounds that showed me, as clearly as if I could see the authors, that the flying squirrels were at their usual aërial performances, undeterred by the immense darkness that shrouded the world. These are true children of the night, gray nymphs of the shadows, winged voyageurs of the dewy heavens under the light of stars.

In most legend and story there are but two birds that are supposed to haunt the night—the owl and the bat; and the latter is no bird at all, but a mammal! Yet there are a good many other birds that are often active after dark—some systematically, others occasionally.

One evening, after fishing late for trout, I stopped by the edges of a big breeding pond for goldfish, situated in a wild meadow. It was in April, when some of the wild ducks which are supposed to be migrating are still lingering in alluring places; and I hoped to see some of them dropping into the pond at dusk. The west was still roseate when the first fleeting visitors came—five green-winged teal rushing out of the vastness and silence of nowhere. They dipped steeply to the water, flared wildly and yet in perfect unison, turned dizzily, and then glided to the glimmering water with little cries of delight. There they were softly mirrored in the fading lake. . . . Just as dark set in I heard the wings of other ducks; and from the resounding splash that soon came I was certain that a pair of either mallards or black-ducks had settled. There were gallinules lurking in the cattails, and these called to one another in their strange excited fashion. As most aquatic birds do much of their feeding at night, and are excessively fond of drowsing and of preening themselves by day, I am sure that they have a remarkable power of seeing in the dark. Certainly it is infinitely better than man's. At night, in waste fields frequented by wildfowl, I have always been surprised to find that ducks were apparently more wary at night than in the daytime; for frequently, in trying to stalk them, in a canoe drifting noiselessly down the moving waters of a canal or a small creek, I have had the birds flushed as far away as if I had been after them in full sunlight. And every hunter knows that if he stands unshielded in an old rice field at twilight, expecting that ducks will not notice him, he is sure to be observed, however motionless he may be.

Besides the gallinules and the wild ducks, other visitors came into the goldfish sanctuary; chief of these were arrant marauders, great blue herons and black-crowned night-herons. There were three of the former and at least seven of the latter. I could barely make them out by starlight; but they were easily identified by their raucous voices. I suppose in all Nature there is not a more unlovely sound than that made by the great blue heron; nor is that of the night-heron much more melodious. Both these waders are night feeders; and so obscure are the habits of the night-heron that a large colony can exist near a town without its presence being known. To their feeding grounds they journey at dusk, returning at dawn; and during the day they secrete themselves in evergreens. Despite the full darkness now settled over the misty pond I could see several of these grim pirates, standing spectrally in the faintly gleaming tide. Save for the occasional splash of a muskrat and the outraged cry of a blackbird that something had startled from his roost in the marsh, all was silent. Yet a deceptive stillness it was, for the course of life had not ceased because of the coming of night. It had merely changed. Nor were the creatures awake the denizens of the fenland alone; for far in the lonely sky I heard the human sweet whistle of the upland plover, flying in restless delight above the clover field where he had his nest.

When one lives on a remote plantation, as I have

done, he is likely to form the habit, before he goes to bed, of taking a last look out into the night to make sure that all is quiet among the stock; that there is no forest fire approaching; to listen, perhaps, to the mysterious voices of the night. I used to linger on the porch, or in the big yard under the huge live-oaks, or far down the road on the borders of the pine forest, drinking deep the dark wine of night, sparkling with stars. Lovers of the darkness are probably conscious that they are more spiritually aware than they can be in daytime. Perhaps, too, our physical senses are more keen. Night, with her loneliness and her beauty, takes us back into the ancient childhood of the race. Upon that dewy bosom our spirits delightedly rest.

One moonlit night in late October I heard a great outcry among the hounds; and supposing intruders to be about, I dressed and went into the yard. There was no need for a lantern, for the moonlight was blanching the tall magnolias, the dreamful oaks, the wide fields. Even the thickets, dark by day, had an eerie brightness. No sooner was I down the steps than a screech owl, dropping on muted wings out of the shadows of an oak, clapped his bill at me, cried out in his ghostly querulous way, veered upward, and, with his head on one side, perched on a dead walnut limb. This sort of performance on the part of this bird is the kind to send a plantation negro flying homeward full of tales of hants and other horrors. And, though we know that the screech owl is only bird, it is nevertheless a most uncanny, fussy, resentful-of-intrusion creature. Hardly real, it is like a drifting dead leaf come to life, a shadow vitalized; and it comes into being spectrally, when the white fingers of the dusk close softly the curtains of the night.

Going down to their pen to quiet the hounds, I heard a regular owl chorus across the river; a curious stentorian medley—voicing with weird felicity the strange and solitary beauty of the sleeping world. But in the virgin timber that stands in the ancient negro graveyard I heard my favorite owl note: that of the great horned owl. Could any sound be more remote, melancholy, supernal? It is one of the supreme spiritual voices of all Nature. One of the most impressive of all the feathered kingdom, the horned owl always appears to me regal, splendid. His face shows aboriginal sagacity. His brows are thunderous. And I can listen fascinated to his lonely calls, mournful, soft, and beautiful.

What disturbed the hounds I never discovered. But I believe that the wave lengths of their souls had been stirred by the voices of the owls; indeed, the nature of their singing made me sure of this; for the voice of a hound whose spirit is grieved is of a pathetic quality very different from the timbre of his ordinary note.

XVIII   WHY I ENVY WILD THINGS

The buck and the doe were coming daintily through the bronzed huckleberry bushes under the giant pines. I saw them from a crotch in a bay tree, into which I had climbed to watch for wild life. About me for miles stretched a green country, beautiful with spiritual springtime.

The deer came tripping forward, pausing now and then to browse upon the tips of green shoots. Coming to an obstruction of myrtles in their pathway, the buck, just like any man showing off his strength before his best girl, bowed his antlers and tore through the bush— bucked the line, I suppose! But just then the two got the scare of their lives. They ran almost into my hitched horse; and he snorted and tried to break away. A horse hates to be tied when anything unusual approaches him.

The deer, that but a moment before had imagined themselves remote and secure in their deepest forest haunt, sequestered by the falling twilight, now suddenly discovered that they had unaware encountered

Man. A deer probably would not mind a horse but for the fact that it associates the danger from man with a horse. The two must have got my scent as well. It all meant murder to them. No wonder these deer jumped desperately, bolted, tore through the greenery, crashed through the young cypresses and bays, and vanished running.

Had I been in their place, miles would swiftly have separated me from such danger as they had met. But wild things are different. It happened that from my perch I could see into an adjoining glade, not more than two hundred yards off—a lovely open place now suffused with the warm colors of sunset. I distinctly saw the two deer quietly enter the calm vale; they were walking. Moreover, they had started to browse again, apparently entirely forgetful of their late peril.

If the Thing which had menaced them had menaced a man, he would have run for a week, would have called in the police, would have been haunted day and night by the experience. Perhaps all his life he would have been shadowed by its memory. But wild creatures appear to have the fortunate power suddenly to recover their poise, swiftly to regain their equanimity, without delay to shake off the fears that beset them. And I profoundly envy them this virtue. What's past with them is past—immediately, definitely. I wish I were like them in this—and that all of us were.

Many a time I have watched wild things display this quality. Roosevelt remarked the same speedy return to normal among the frightened herds of African game animals. They run the gantlet, escape (sometimes), and then forget all about it—unchanged by the experience save, perhaps, by a heightening of general alertness, a development of keenest shrewdness. If poise is one of the finest traits of character, then surely the swift recovery of it is another.

There are many other qualities in natural life that appeal to me as well worth trading for some that we possess; and I shall try to explain what I mean by telling stories that illustrate the traits rather than by trying merely to describe the traits themselves.

In our South Carolina plantation house we had a rustic basket hanging in the hall; in it we used to keep gloves. One year we were delighted to find a wren building in the basket, and the next year she reared another brood in the same place. From her home to the front door the distance was only a few feet. The third year the house was closed—every door and every window. Yet when I went there one April day and unlocked the front door, the wren darted down the long hallway ahead of me. She passed through two rooms, and I saw her apparently fly through a window pane, at least eighty feet from her nest.

Investigating, I found in the glass of the window a small hole made by the passage of a bullet. I remembered then that some careless boy on a picnic had let a revolver go off, and had drilled the glass with a bullet. The hole was not bigger than my thumb, and its edges were jagged in places.

The tiny brown bird, finding her home shut and barred against her, had searched (with infinite patience and intelligence, I believe) until she at last found this singular mode of access. Through this minute, sharp-edged hole she had carried fresh sticks and lining for her nest. She had showed an affectionate persistence that any human being might well envy. I often think of that busy, caroling songster, of her quaint, confiding home in the dark hallway, of her devotion to it. "Love will find a way," says the old song. Even so. It will, when all else fails.

All observers of Nature have marked the patient persistence of wild creatures. There is a species of wasp commonly called the "mud-dauber," from its habit of making its house of wet earth, plastered neatly against a wall, always out of reach of the weather. I know that our plantation porch used to be disfigured every year by these curious habitations. The insect knows that the nest must be put where the rain cannot reach it; for it is not a house built upon the sand, but of sand.

I tried one day, more, I hope, out of a spirit of scientific investigation than out of one of mere torment of an inferior thing, to discover how often one of these wasps would begin a nest if what had been started was destroyed. I just sat on the front steps with a long cane, with my eye on the beginning of a particular house.

The river is about a hundred yards from the house, and I knew that the wasp went there for his hodful of mud. It took him about four minutes to make the round trip—most of his time probably being spent in gathering his load. As soon as he had laid the foundation of his house and had flown away, I pushed the flimsy thing down with the end of the cane. In a few minutes, back he would come with another burden; and, though clearly anxious, would begin again to construct his dwelling.

To me it appeared that he must have thought that he was bringing the wrong material—stuff that would not hold up; for I noticed, as I pushed down each succeeding foundation, that the *color* of the earth the wasp was using had changed. There was more and more clay in it. Doubtless he was saying to himself: "This is a funny thing. I thought I knew exactly how to build a house. But everything collapses. It must be that I am using too much sand. From now on I am going to make a mixture that is mighty strong in clay."

In all, I demolished the poor thing's house twenty-one times. Then I had to have a heart. He never once weakened, or showed any sign of giving up. Two days later, when I happened to look toward the place under the eaves where a half dozen of these wasps had built, I noticed one nest made almost wholly of red clay.

That was long ago; but the scene is vivid to me now, and I never think of it but I say: "That wasp had the kind of virtues which make some men stand before kings; that wasp had wholesome self-examination, the ability to criticize his own work, endless patience against the most frightful discouragements, a cheerful courage sufficient to see to completion the most baffling task. I envy those virtues, and I wish that through life they might be mine."

Supporting that same front porch were certain giant cypress pillars, hewn out of the swamp two centuries ago. In these a few bumblebees had drilled holes; and, as these were both weakening to the posts and unsightly,

I decided to stop up the holes with putty, thinking, of course, that the bees would go elsewhere. But the day after the putty was applied I found all of it neatly piled in powdered form beneath the holes! Then I tried successively plaster of Paris, wooden pegs, and tough clay, painted over. It was all the same. I hardly had the heart to kill the bees; and, as a result, their descendants are there to this day.

I think I would call this virtue the virtue of stubborn attack. Here an insect meets an obstruction to its home. It does not ask who put it there; it does not question whether it is worth while trying to remove it; it does not say hesitatingly, like Hamlet, "This should be scanned." It immediately makes a furious frontal attack —laying aside every consideration save this big thing of vital moment. With a pertinacity not to be denied, with a certain wild hardihood not to be gainsaid, and with intelligence sufficient for the occasion, this creature that we disdainfully call an insect goes right manfully to work.

Of the amazing, innocent, all-sufficing beauty and beneficence of Nature, I feel that wild creatures must be fully aware. At least, I envy them their apparent utter contentment—and this in the face of imminent and deadly perils.

I do not believe that they are contented because they are not aware of these dangers, but rather because they have come calmly to accept them as a part of the general system of their lives. They take the matter of existence as it comes. Moreover, they do not languish for some other land, some other life, some far-off and different mode of being. What they find here and now satisfies them very well. They achieve present happiness.

Nor can this feat be attributed to mere insensibility —"brute nature," as some would call it. Wild things have a grave beauty and rejoicing looks, as if their spirits were at peace. I do not think they feel like wanderers here. This earth is truly their home. They love it, and they love the life it offers. May we not justly envy them their serenity: a calm of heart that condemns our feverish activity, our restless longings, our vain, wild yearnings? They are happy with what is given, and question not what is withheld.

One day I happened to find the nest and eggs of a marsh hen (clapper rail) hidden in the green sedges that bordered a tidal creek on the coast. The nest was anchored to the marsh stems, and in it when I discovered it were three eggs. That was a time when I was a fisherman, so that every day, going and coming from the fishing grounds, I passed the nest. The second time I saw the nest, the eggs were gone, tipped from the structure by the tide that flooded the marsh regularly. I found the eggs in the mud under the nest where the waters had left them when they subsided.

The next day the mother had straightened the nest and had laid another egg. But on the morrow the same accident happened: The tide tipped the nest until the egg rolled out. I wondered what the wild mother would do. Within a week, a full complement of five eggs had been laid, and apparently they were safe.

It happened that the tide, at that time, was up to

the bottom of the nest, and as I waited I saw the waters lift it gently and float it upward. The bird had evidently released a tie on the nest, so that now, while it was still anchored to two stout marsh stems, the loops that held it were sliding ones, permitting the nest to move gently upward with the tide and then to move downward to its normal resting place on a bundle of broken marsh tops.

I am not saying that marsh hens build sliding nests, but here certainly was one that did. Think of it! a frail, tiny home in the heart of the vast, waste sea marsh, visited daily by the monstrous sea tides; and the bright-eyed mother, dismayed but resolute, finding a way out of her distress. She made one of the mightiest forces in all Nature work for her; what would ruin her, she, by a little deft precision of judgment, by a delicate adjustment of circumstances, made safe for her what was most precious to her.

I watched with no little fascination that sliding nest until the young were fledged. I frankly envied the lone bird with wit enough to handle a sea tide. I had never thought to find a marsh hen harnessing the main. But there it was.

A German scientist, after years of scholarly experiment in laboratories, came to the conclusion that wild things cannot reason. Well, they get along remarkably in a world in which reasoning men have a pretty hard struggle to succeed.

In the matter of the keenness of all their physical senses, wild things are infinitely our superiors. I have tried through many years to keep careful watch on wild creatures for the purpose of ascertaining just how far ahead of us they are in this matter of their senses. Their awareness is amazing. But not all the senses of all wild things are by any means equally developed. Birds in general see much better than animals; the animals I know seem to hear farther than birds, but perhaps not more keenly. I recall testing one day the hearing power of a wild gobbler.

It was in mid-March, the mating season for the wild turkey; and at that time the males are belligerent, seeming to take every noise as a challenge. It is quite possible to go into turkey country at such a time and make one bird gobble merely by giving a shrill whistle, whereas to call one up by imitating the note of the hen is ridiculously easy.

I located a big bird near the river by hearing him gobble defiantly when a rooster crowed in the yard of a negro cabin hidden away in the forest. I approached within two hundred yards and whistled loudly, and was answered by a perfect torrent of proud abuse. Far up over the dreamy pines I saw a red-tailed hawk soaring. As it was away from the river, it must have been at least twice as far from the turkey as from me.

Faintly I heard it give a scream, so faintly that I hardly distinguished it; yet the gobbler heard it, and the hawk promptly received a defiant berating. I stole along quietly through the thicket until I reached an old rail fence, beyond which was a clearing bordering the placid, wide river.

Full in view, some eighty yards off, I saw the gobbler strutting, his mighty fantail spread, his wattles crimson, his aspect regal, yet so overbearing as to be ludicrous. I think there is nothing more pompous in wild life than a strutting turkeycock.

Now was my chance to test his ears. I was close hidden behind a dense fall of jasmine vines that draped a wild orange tree. It was necessary for me not to make any sounds that the turkey might detect as human. Carefully, therefore, I imitated the notes of certain birds, the cries of certain beasts. The gobbler, remember, was full eighty yards off. Yet so keen was his sense of hearing that my most diminished notes and calls were heard. It seemed to me that I could utter no sound at all that he did not detect. If it was audible to me, it was to him.

Of course, it is difficult to be exact in estimates of this kind; but to me it appeared that the gobbler could hear a noise as clearly at eighty yards as a man could at a few feet. Finally, almost under my breath, I said a few natural words. Instantly, the huge bird, a moment before all fluffed out and full of abounding pride, shrank, glistened with swift stealth, became, under my very eyes, a trim racer, and in a moment was gone into the friendly depths of the sheltering forest. He had not only heard keenly but discriminatingly.

I used to have a horse named Redbird; and though certainly not wild, he had senses that used to put mine to shame. One night, I remember, I was riding him down a lonely road, and, just as we were dipping into a hollow, he suddenly snorted and came to a stand. I coaxed, gently, then with spur and whip, for turning back would mean a ride of six miles farther. We had to cross the swamp at this place or not cross it at all.

But Redbird had evidently made up his mind. I could feel him tremble and shiver under me. I knew then that he had the wind of something perilous. After a few moments more of useless urging on my part, we turned back. For an hour after that he was fidgety, and the least thing made him shy violently.

Next day a negro brought to the plantation a diamond-back rattlesnake that he had killed.

"Where did you meet it?" I asked.

"By Pinckney Run," he answered, referring to the swamp that Redbird had refused to cross.

"When?"

"Yesterday morning," he told me.

It must have been twelve hours later that my horse had caught the scent of the snake. Of course, the place where the snake was killed was deeply impregnated with its scent; nevertheless, Redbird's nose had been good; and I found it easy to forgive his behavior when I saw the thing whose scent he had feared.

I do not say that I covet his ability to smell a rattlesnake, for I have but meager personal ambitions in that direction. But I do covet his power to wind a scent infallibly. A human nose is a very degenerate organ. If we get, at a few yards, the scent of a rose bed or of a petunia plot, we are fortunate. I have seen a bird dog halt, lift his head to a damp breeze, and stand statuesque ninety yards from a covey of quail. I think we must completely miss, especially in the woods, many of the more delicate aromas, many of the more shyly wafted dim sweetnesses, less of the earth than of the air, sidereal and evasive.

Except, of course, in the sense that the Creator made some creatures to prey on others, wild things are singularly independent. They do not spend their lives trying to reform other creatures. They live fully and freely, untormented by the envy and malice that distress our lives. Depending utterly on Nature and on themselves, they have a certain tawny ruggedness of spirit reserved to those into whose lives the artificial never enters. They possess that fortitude that we always associate with trees and rocks and rivers; finding the unfailing source of their strength in the fathomless serenity of earth's bosom.

Matthew Arnold, in his great "Rugby Chapel," praised his father for having been the kind of man who made the gapped ranks close, who praised the brave, who encouraged the weak, who restored order when demoralization among those in his care was imminent. I have noticed a tendency among wild things to stand together—to call up the stragglers, to shelter the weak. There is a concert of action, a community morale that is remarkable.

Even a person who has never before taken any interest in observing wild things will be persuaded of their extraordinary tribal spirit if he will spend an hour watching a hill of ants, or a flock of crows, or a school of fish, or a hive of bees. Of course, among the larger animals, as civilization scatters the herds they live a more solitary and individual existence, yet always they are, in pairs or in groups of hundreds, able to execute, perfectly, mass maneuvers. To this day I get a thrill out of watching wild ducks coming into their feeding fields at sundown.

Here, for example, will come a flock of forty green-winged teal. A charge of shot could hardly be swifter. The speed of this arrowhead of flight had been carefully measured at a hundred and twenty miles an hour. When they are within fifty yards of me, I show myself from behind a marsh tussock. The flock makes a thrilling veer, whirls in the track like a racing car that is being wrecked; but this racing machine never skids.

The teal had been flying only twenty feet above the marsh, and I was close to them. When they passed above me they were more than a hundred feet up. To flare swiftly, enigmatically, yet with precision, is to them a business that they have long since mastered. It is not so much their speed that saves them, but their bewildering power to execute, as a body, at the proper second, without warning, and while going at cyclone speed, the exact maneuver fit for the occasion.

I am not saying that their beautiful swift dress parades in the sky, gallant and breathless and dashing, always insure their safety. But I am envying their ability for such speed; and, in such speed, their capacity to manifest a coördination and a control that must ever be the despair of a blundering mortal.

Patient wasp, buck and doe swift to recover your peace of mind, timid marsh hen bitting the sea-tide—I know you and love you. And when I say I envy you, I mean I am jealous for some of your clear virtues.

XIX MY CHRISTMAS WOODS

THERE is a great contrast between a Southern delta and a Northern wood; but the vast system of Nature embraces them both.

We are now coming in our ramblings to the end of the year. The last autumnal migration is over; all the deciduous trees are bare save some of the oaks that prefer sear garments to none at all; the abundant patient earth seems ready now for sleep. Can you not feel, on these first winter days, the infinite repose, divinely ordered, stealing over the world?

My way homeward lies through a pine wood; and because of the nature of my duties, often, before I reach that miniature forest, the "dead vast and middle of the night" has come. So it was on that memorable evening when the wildwood awoke my spirit. It may have been the splendor of the flaming planet setting in glory behind the dark mountain; it may have been the dewy fragrance of the white-pine boughs against which I brushed; perhaps it was the cathedral majesty of the night itself, profound with intimations of God and of immortality. But whatever it was which caused the feeling, I suddenly became joyously aware that Christmas had come. In the solitary wood, under the light of stars, in a silence that was lyric with unuttered music, it came to my heart before the calendar indicated its arrival.

I felt with the certainty of spiritual clairvoyance what it has always been easier for me to feel in a wood than anywhere else: that God is near, that all the trembling beauty of the earth and the sky was conceived, was fashioned, and is preserved by Him; that Christ is truly His son; and that Christmas is no vain worldly festival, but the time for spontaneous rejoicing by all human hearts over the birth of their Redeemer. Here in the wood the deep pure joy of the thought mastered me. A love of Nature makes faith not only natural, but inevitable: a lover of the trees, the stars, the flowers can never leave God out of it all. I find Him in the woodland, and that is why I especially love the forest at Christmas.

On the very next morning, which was the day before Christmas, when I saw a mountaineer in the little town in which I live selling Christmas greens on the streets, I thought me of a place far back in the lonely mountains where ground pine grew. Only a month before, I had been hunting grouse in Path Valley; and in tramping through the foothills of that remote and romantic country, once a favorite hunting place of the red man, I had come upon a fragrant dewy thicket deeply carpeted with trailing pine, making beneath the mighty oaks and hemlocks a fairy forest of delicate beauty.

A drive of fourteen miles up a solitary mountain vale that became more lone and beautiful with every mile took me at length into my Christmas woods. Leaving my car in what had once been a lane, but which was now only a thinly grown stretch in a general tawny wild sea of sumac and raspberry vines, I made my way across an old mountain field to the edge of the shimmering woods. All human habitations being miles away, there were no sounds that one associates with farm life. There was a virginal wild stillness like magic upon the world. Even when I heard a ruffed grouse drumming softly halfway up the mountain, the dim music did not interrupt, but rather supplemented the mountain silence. The mysterious sound seemed the very voice of blue distances, wildwood glamour, enchanted wilds. This bird seems the spirit of all that wanders and is wild, the genius of hushed seraphic places, the child of Nature's radiant solitude.

So still are the woods, so gleamingly misty the sleeping hills, so fragrant the hemlocks and pines, that any other sound at this season save that of the princely grouse would be a desecration of this wild and lovely shrine. Here in this solitary wood I was alone with Nature, with the God of Creation, and of the equally superb continuance of Nature, with the God of the powerful, matchless rhythm of the seasons. And this is the Christmas season, a time sacred, I believe, to Him as well as to us. A festival of childhood, of love, and of the grace of the heart, Christmas should have an ingenuous, elemental simplicity about its spirit; and for this spirit we can draw infallibly upon Nature. Every wood is a sanctuary. Every tree is a shrine. Every star is a Star of Bethlehem.

Into the aromatic wood I walked, over a carpet of fresh snow. Here were rock pines, sane and swarthy and stalwart; here were glimmering birch trees, their delicate branches sweeping like long tresses to the ground; here were patches of cool, gleaming mountain laurel, lustrous in the snow. I saw where rabbits had been hopping about—those shadow-footed elves; where a gray squirrel had been digging in the snow to recapture a hidden hoard of acorns and shellbarks; and in the tangled top of a fallen oak I found, by following a thrilling track, a fresh deer bed. Laying my hand in it, I discovered it to be still warm. Either he had heard me coming and had stolen forth in his eerie way from his fragrant covert, or else, as it was late in the afternoon, he had come forth to browse and to roam delicately the fairy land of evening.

All about me the woods withdrew magically. On every hand were gleaming aisles, dim corridors, mystic arras, lordly transepts, wondrous vistas into the abodes of beauty. All was as hushed as in some mighty cathedral just before the beginning of a splendid burst of music. And damp fragrances there were from dewy pine, from late hickory leaves just fallen, from the burly bark of the leafless trees themselves. Down one of the scented aisles before me I saw the luxurious bed of trailing pine for which I had been searching.

Long since, it has seemed to me that we do not get enough of the outdoors into our Christmas spirit; and sometimes, alas, our festivals at that mystic and sacred time, lacking the poise and the sanity that we should learn from the virtuous course of Nature, often resemble orgies. The breath of the woods is ever the breath of continence, of wholesome joy, of childlike gladness, of temperance, of happy worship. Somehow Christmas appears to be more of an outdoor festival than we are commonly in the habit of regarding it and celebrating it. Surely it had distinctly rural origins; the shepherds, the Star, the angelic song out of the beauteous lonely sky, "no room at the inn." We do, indeed, make merry with greens and with a tree; but some part of our Christmas Day should be spent in the open, resting upon the ample bosom of the all-mother, conscious through every sense of the loving and affluent generosity of God.

Besides, the human spirit is a curiously sensitive thing, and perhaps its most frequent experience is to be wounded. To be healed in spirit, therefore, is what all of us most constantly need. Christmas is the best season for heart healing, for all forgiveness and reconcilements; and the fragrance, the silence, the beauty of the woods supply the environment for deep and pure compassion. I know that I should be a far worse sinner than I am were it not for the December wildwoods that have often renewed "a right spirit within me."

Having found my patch of trailing pine, I gathered a basket of it negligently, deliberately delaying to do what I had hastened to accomplish. Who would not be half regretful over breaking the living ties of so much innocent beauty? Taking hold of a stout green tuft and gently lifting it, I soon made an inch, then a foot, then a yard of the lustrous greenery start up out of the smothering snow. Readily, as if its nature were gentle, the delicate pine yielded its tenuous hold on the soft, black soil beneath the white blanket. Here was a miniature forest, strung on an emerald string; with the string apparently raveled into elfin green tufts on either side of the main line. As I filled my basket, I could think of but one thing—the matchless planning of God, the massive solidarity of His work, with the light of His tireless love effulgent upon it everywhere. I do not worship Nature; but the beauty and the utility of the things of Nature convince me, past the possibility of any doubt, of the immediate presence of God, and of His infinite capacity and yearning to love us and to care for us.

As I emerged a little while later from those mountain woods, with my Christmas basket of trailing pine, to which I had added some branches of laurel and some sprays of teaberry, the sun had gone down behind the hills, leaving the world in a rosy trance. Sunset, like a maned sea breaker, was gorgeously rolling up in the west. All the beautiful lonely vale was suffused with ruby lights that tinged even the tattered broomsedge with a soft and joyous radiance. A sense of brooding love, of the infinite compassion of which the human spirit at Christmas time is likely to be peculiarly aware, held all the earth in the tremulous loveliness of an immortal dream. Other than this sense, in pitying Nature, of the boundless mercy of God, His sympathy, His love for His children, however erring their hearts may be, we do not have apparently, save in the Master, a nearer approach to Him. Little children, indeed, with their "trailing clouds of glory," make us keenly aware of the presence of God; but children are so close to Nature as to be a part of it, true fairies of the wildwoods and the dewy greenswards of the ancient mother.

Here about me in these gently fading sunset fields, far from man, but close, I believe, to God, I seemed to find the spirit of Christmas; here, and in the scented darkening wood behind me; in the effulgent valley blossoming with light as with flowers; and yonder in that matchless pageant of the sundown. Close to Nature one is close to the source of things. Surely, "through Nature to God" is not a phrase to be despised. These are His mountains, His valley; this is His trailing pine; and yonder comes a star. He made it.

In these old pastures and in the adjoining forests one sees, in elemental form, both life and death. Here are the green leaves and the brown, the standing trees and the fallen. If one is honest in answering the question, "What is it that perishes?" one will be obliged to say, "Whatsoever the eye sees." Close to Nature, especially in the mystic Christmas season, one comes to understand that if we are to hold to anything in this life—and there come times to all of us when we *must* have something to which we can cling—it must be to the unseen. For the strength that is permanent we have to lean on visions; for immortal hope we have to trust, not the things that we perceive, but the deep affirmations of the spirit. After all, what is it that we so greatly desire in life? What do we wish from this thing that seems lent us for noble purposes? Is it power? Is it fame? Is it sympathy? Perhaps it is a quiet mind, a contented heart, beauty of God's handicraft to look upon, music of His minstrels to charm us, the blue stillness of the sky's felicity to fill our hearts with grace. Without money and without price these are for us in the Christmas woods, pledges of the wistful, tender care of One for His children. In the wildwoods, and perhaps there alone, it is easy and natural to shed away the tawdry cap-and-bells of worldliness, and to don the simple humble garb of spiritual contentment. Pride, selfesteem, resentment for the general system of life—all these fade from one in the woods. A noble soil will not grow morbid and exotic weeds. But the human spirit blossoms there.

XX WILD BROTHER WINTERS THROUGH

WE HAVE wandered in the Christmas woods together, discovering peace there, finding reasons for quietness in the works of God. Perhaps you would like to study even more deeply the question of how the wild children of Nature provide, not only for their Thanksgiving and Christmas dinners, but for their sustenance throughout the bleak months of the year. Let us see how wild brother winters through.

Being a lover of handsome wood, I had long been envious of that huge, old, black walnut tree standing in the very center of the township road known as Hammond's Lane. Its burly dimensions were such that the roadmakers of half a century ago decided to make their thoroughfare pass on either side of the great tree; for undoubtedly it was a big walnut even then. Three feet from the base it now measures nearly fourteen feet in circumference. The ownership of it rests equally with the two farmers whose fields border the road. Here it has towered all these years, overlooking the peaceful valley, gazing at the violet-hued mountains standing in a far, friendly circle about it. A thousand storms it has withstood, taking from them nothing but greater strength; thousands of those aërial miracles that we call dawn and sunset it has watched; and after the enchanting lights of evening have gently faded from the fragrant valley, how often this beautiful Titan has watched the timorous young night approach, almost like a fugitive fawn, emerging from the pinewood yonder, lurking, approaching, always mystical with eternal beauty's shadowy avoidance! How often, in the deep of moonlit, summer nights, has this old tree heard the pensive fluting of the upland plover, high in the starry heavens, restless to begin his lone and splendid flight to the pampas of the Argentine! How often, in the green shadows of those mighty limbs, shy birds have rested! And now came a man to cast upon this majesty the eyes of cupidity!

One day I went out carefully to examine the tree, with a view to purchasing it. The heart wood from such a craggy old giant might be exceedingly valuable; and I had pleasing visions of tables, chests, bookcases, and radio cabinets made from that one massive trunk. The burl in such a stump might be gorgeous. But an examination showed me in only a few moments that my dreams were of an illusory order: the noble monster was hollow from base to crown. Moreover, wild brother had evidently used this hollow for many years as a winter granary and general commissary. I discovered this fact when, pushing a stick up into what seemed but a small hole at the base, just where it met the ground,

I broke through a mat of old leaves and grass and similar bedding, and down tumbled and rattled not less than two or three pecks of dry acorns, shagbarks, butternuts, walnuts, grains of corn, and ears of wheat. Some of these were mere husks, but all represented the foresight and toil of wild things, that, prescient of the certain coming of winter, had gathered their provender in this picturesque old natural barn, even as men hoard their corn, their apples, their wheat, and their potatoes in storehouses of their own building.

This incident of the old walnut tree serves to remind us of those curious and fascinating provisions made by Nature's children to meet the ancient cosmic enemy, Winter; and invites us to consider how they live in the bare, cold, grieving wood and along the frozen fence rows during those grim months when we are housed and warm.

Let us remember also that while man is constantly improving fortifications against the discomforting forces of Nature, wild things live now as they have always lived. The squirrel winters now as he did ten thousand years ago; whereas the man who formerly dwelt in the gloomy depths of a noisome cave now has learned so to use Nature that she ministers to his every want; he no longer has fearfully to stalk wild animals across the frozen waste in the hope of procuring a meal for his famishing family; he has warmth, heat, food—everything he wants in his own cozy home. The truth of man's amazing advance, while the animals have stood practically still, is recommended to the earnest consideration of those who regard man as merely a different sort of animal. The gulf between *homo sapiens* and the rest of the living world is so profound that I believe it would take far more than one missing link to bridge it. The only reasonable way to explain the widening chasm between man and the wild creatures is simply to admit that divinity within us which not only contributes exciting promise to life, celestial charm to beauty, and the blessed hope of immortality to our hearts, but keeps us ever conscious of the proximity and the compassionate character of God. Nature has many aspects, but God is behind them all; and He appears in this tremendous difference between us and our cousins of the woods and fields. I feel His hand also in the fact that we can love not only our own kind but also these appealing inferiors; and we can have an interest and a concern in their problems of facing the winter almost as much as if such problems were our own.

The mighty miracle of bird migration is remarkable in many ways, and not least in this one: that there are stay-at-homes who have every facility to spend the winter in Florida, in Mexico, in the West Indies, or in the lonely and beautiful forests of Brazil. But they just do not choose to fly. Thus, while the fragile humming bird leaves us, mounting fearlessly on gossamer wings the blank height of the misty vault of glimmering darkness, the lordly ruffed grouse remains; the bluebird goes, but the redbird stays—or migrates only indifferently; the plover, the warblers, the wild ducks, the geese, the soras—all these go, but the bobwhite stays firmly fixed on his ancestral range. True, in the autumn,

when choice stubble fields are plowed up, and when
much of that friendly cover in which the quail had hoped
to spend the winter is destroyed or thinned badly by
the falling of foliage, quail may act in a migratory manner. They are hunting a winter home. They make short
flights of an erratic kind, which account for their sudden appearance in our backyards and in our village
streets early on magical October mornings, when the
air is winy and the trees are raining gold. The quail's
forced flights at this season explain also why many
bevies appear in fields where none had been seen all
summer. They move locally, in sesarch of suitable winter
quarters. But they never seem to join the general hegira.
For some inscrutable reason (but perhaps it is because
of this bird's remarkable self-dependence and his high
intelligence) the epic flight is reserved for others, and
in many cases for those far less ably equipped to achieve
it easily. For example, one of the rail family is about
as capable of sustained aërial activity as a feather dus-
ter; the same is true of the grebes. Yet these birds travel
safely prodigious distances.

One interesting exception of the disinclination of the
bobwhite to migrate and thus to escape the rigors of
winters is the behavior of the Mexican quail in our
Northern states. For many years the game departments
of various states have imported these fine birds to re-
stock their depleted supply of native birds. These two
varieties are practically identical, the Mexican being
a little brighter in coloring, a little smaller, and perhaps
more nervously inclined to elevate his topknot. I have
helped to liberate hundreds of these Mexican birds in

the stubble fields of Pennsylvania and Maryland. I have
found their nests and watched their young. In the late
summer I have seen full-grown coveys of these northern-
hatched birds. But I have never seen a Mexican quail
in the North during the winter. Occasionally they may
remain, but for them to do so is exceptional. As autumn
comes on, what goes through the mind of a Mexican
quail in a northern locality is probably something like
this:

"It has been fine to stay here during this past summer. But now all the bugs and flies are gone, and so
are all the little fruits. These nights are colder than any
we ever had at home. What if the fields get barer all
the time, and the days and nights keep getting more
frosty? We have a notion that we had better be going
where all these other birds are going. We can't tell
exactly what their destination is, but as for us, why
shouldn't we go home?"

That a keen and prescient sense of direction and a
genuine love of home are inherent in all wild things
must be apparent to anyone who has observed them
over a period of years. All of them have what we might
call place instinct, and they have domesticity as well. It
is touching to observe how even the wildest creature
will manifest many of those home-loving traits that we
associate with the gentlest natures.

So our bright-eyed Mexican friends depart for the
chaparral and the mesquite and the sunny, sandy wastes.
But the native bobwhite winters through. In preparing
to face the long, cold months he will always have, as
has already been suggested, some suitable location

chosen; a briared gully close to a cover field; a creek bank sloping southward, where the bushes are thick; an old wood lot where friendly piles of brush on the ground offer shelter; a swampy meadow where grow hawthorn trees and wild rose bushes, on the red fruits of which he can feed; a thickety fence row adjacent to patches of ragweed; and always, wherever possible, the mountains. This last resort is, as far as my observation extends, the favorite winter home for quail bred in the near-by valleys. He who wrote "Flee as a bird to yon mountain" was, whether he knew it or not, describing the bobwhite with great felicity.

For many years I accepted as fiction the stories told me by hunters and sawmill men of seeing in the mountains coveys of eighty and even a hundred birds. To a farmer who does not hunt, a covey always seems to have about forty birds in it; in reality, there are likely only about a dozen. I therefore thought that these rangers of the hills had probably walked up bevies of an ordinary size in the laurels and bush-huckleberry copses, and had determined the number of birds by the degree to which they had themselves been startled by the explosive rise of the fugitives. But one December day, in the wild mountains between the Big Cove, in Pennsylvania, and Hancock, Maryland, I walked up a prodigious covey of quail in the sunny mountain laurel near an old abandoned sawmill. I thought at first that the flock was of ordinary size, but the fleet-winged bombs kept on exploding under my feet incessantly. At last, realizing upon what I had come and estimating the number of birds already flown, I counted the others as they rose. My full tally came to sixty-seven, and I believe the estimate was a modest one.

On one or two other occasions I have encountered these huge coveys of the mountains. Undoubtedly these birds, bred in the valleys, had gathered in community fashion to winter in the adjacent protecting hills. No doubt, the persistent hunting that goes on in the lowlands drives them to these high shelters, but certainly that is not the only reason why they leave the fields. They know the meaning of those swarthy pines, of those still thickets into which the winter sunshine comes stealing in soft surprise, of those lonely but generous solitudes. When the deep snows cover the valleys, particularly if a hard crust forms, the food supply of bobwhite is cut off; but in the mountains the bird can always find both shelter and food. During an aftermath of a blizzard I once roused a big covey of quail from under a rock-overhang high on Twotop Mountain, from the very kind of place to which the Delaware Indians used to resort, long ago, under similar weather conditions.

On one occasion, on the plantation at home, I ran into a giant covey of quail. It was in flood time, when all the lowlands were submerged. I was guided to these by their continual sweet, excited calling. Four or five flocks must have come together during this period of general confusion and distress. It was a beautiful sight to see them rise, singly or in groups of two or three, from the brink of the yellow freshet tide and go curveting around the brimmed border of a sedgefield, toward a lilac sundown. This family reunion spent the night in a field of tall, golden broomgrass not far from the water's brink. For several days I kept them under observation. They stayed together. But as soon as the flood receded, this interesting community broke up into families again, and each covey trooped off dutifully to its own ancestral range.

Of all the birds that winter in the northern latitudes, perhaps these two illustrious mountain dwellers, the wild turkey and the ruffed grouse, are most deserving of special study. Excepting man himself, the wild turkey has few natural enemies. Barring the wildcat, the fox, and the golden eagle, he is practically safe, and so keen is he that he usually evades both wildcat and fox. The golden eagle rarely visits the North in the winter. The damage he commits is done chiefly during his two migrations. The largest wild gobbler is quite helpless before the tremendous attack of the king of the air. But in spite of enemies and in spite of winter, turkeys fare remarkably well. I have known several large flocks to come through the bleak months without the loss of a single member.

When the snow is deep on the hills, and its stay prolonged, artificial feeding helps greatly. Many a time I have taken wheat and corn to hungry wild turkeys back in the frozen heart of the hills. I usually feed corn on the ear, sharpening twigs two feet above the snow and sticking the ears on these. Without this precaution the corn would soon be lost to squirrels. Once I put an ear on a somewhat limber twig, and on revisiting the place I surprised a gray squirrel in the act of deftly bending down the twig to get the corn.

Rude shelters are built in the mountains for turkeys,

but as a rule they quickly detect any object with an air of artificiality about it, and they are wary of what looks like a trap. I once built a shelter out of a pile of old slabs at a deserted sawmill; the great birds, being accustomed to the general aspect of the place, came unafraid beneath the shelter of the old mossy boards. Wild turkeys are exceedingly intelligent birds, adapting themselves readily to unusual conditions. For example, I have known them, in flooded swamps, to pass at least two weeks in trees, feeding on buds and berries.

As these splendid birds commonly roost in deciduous trees, and high up, many lovers of wild life wonder how they can manage to hold on to their perches on those winter nights when wild storms are raging through the bleak mountains, when the snow shakes its tumultuous mane, when the bare world lies unshielded from the gloomy wrath of the tempest. I have seen roosting wild turkeys so tossed and rocked by a freezing gale that I could not understand why they were not blown inside out, let alone their ability to keep their dizzy, perilous perches. But by a marvelous provision of Nature, when the turkey's knees bend forward, his feet close tightly, through the delicate mechanism of an arrangement of tendons. As a result, when he settles on a limb, his feet automatically grip the perch with a grim tightness that is involuntary. Moreover, as the turkey subsides on the limb, he covers his feet, which are thus kept warm against his breast. Then, roar the wind ever so savagely, he will rock back and forth serenely, as much a part of the tree as the limb itself. I have never seen a wild turkey blown from a tree; such an accident might happen, but it would be of rare occurrence.

As a boy, I used to watch fascinated the going to roost of our huge flock of seventy-eight half-wild turkeys, led by the stately wild gobbler that we had raised from a tiny chick. They roosted in two great elms that could be seen from my window. As I had to get up early to help with the stock, I used to take notice that, even after a night of the wildest storm, all the turkeys high up in the great trees had stayed put through all the roaring darkness of the long winter's night.

When the food supply is constant, wild turkeys, like all other living creatures that do not hibernate or migrate, suffer little from the cold. Repeatedly I have known them to stand a temperature of ten below zero without apparent discomfort. In Colonial days, turkeys roamed New England without suffering particularly from the arctic conditions in winter. But if their vitality is impaired by too long a period of fasting, they become weakened, and then they are liable to succumb either to natural enemies or to disease. For more than twenty years I have, every winter, observed wild turkeys in the snow. It does not appear that they mind it particularly. As in the case of all wild things, while snow has the effect of revealing them by obliterating their natural cover, it likewise makes conspicuous the approach of enemies. Turkeys do not rise from snow easily or alight in it gracefully; as a result, they are inclined not to take wing when there is snow on the ground. Many a time I have followed these superb birds over the snow in the frozen forest; always it was possible to come within about a hundred and thirty yards of them, but no nearer. Like all other wild creatures that have had experience with hunters, they have learned to gauge rather nicely the range of a shotgun. As that vital distance is approached by the stalker, the birds will take wing.

In the wintry mountains there is no grander sight than that afforded by a flock of these majestic birds swarthily topping a white ridge to go volplaning down a long, forested slope, their wings making roaring music. I have timed turkeys in such coasting maneuvers, and their speed was not less than a hundred miles an hour. To check their perilous rush, they bank precisely as do airplanes, then turn, then glide softly downward. As soon as they are on the ground, they begin sweetly to call together. If I can see one such sight during a day in the lonely hills of winter, I am repaid for any discomfort that my trip has occasioned.

But it is not the mere sight of wild life alone that thrills me; there is something deeper: the certain consciousness that behind the snow, and the dark mountains, and all the life that we observe, there is a mighty Plan, and there is He who planned it. The observer of Nature must inevitably become a lover of God. No man who is reflective, no man who has the capacity to sense the beauty of the natural world, no man who is conscious of the nearness of the Creator will ever trouble himself much about the technicalities of creeds. An exhilarating devotion to Nature frees one from the fear of missing a man-made pathway. Surrounded by the loveliness and the majesty of the exquisite world, the human heart can say with childlike simplicity: "My Master made all this. God is Here. He is not Yonder."

A creed may be a good guide for a certain type of mind, yet, after all, it is an opinion imposed upon us by men who appropriated to themselves more authority in matters spiritual than is ever accorded mortals. No human being ever has the right to dictate spiritually to any other human being. The heart seems to have the divine capacity for direct communication with the Creator. On the fragrant bosom of Nature a man hears the warm and reassuring heartbeat of the Eternal, and he knows that he is a true son of the Almighty. The soul is a wild brother also, and far back in the snowy mountains of doubt it safely winters through, because it is so fashioned that it cannot escape God's love. Even such a thing as the flight of a turkey above the winter woods calls to mind the Infinite Compassion.

While the wild turkey winters through in good style, the ruffed grouse seems to use more genuine judgment in meeting the various problems occasioned by the cold. In one respect only is he inferior: he persists in roosting too low. I have never been able to understand why a bird so intelligent should roost at just the height most convenient for a wildcat or a fox to reach him. Of course, if he sleeps higher, there are other enemies to be encountered—notably the great horned owl; and, in the twilight and in the dusk of dawn, that arch-terror of the grouse, the duck hawk or peregrine falcon. During the Northern winter it is probable that this bird of prey destroys more grouse than all the hunters—perhaps more than all this noble game bird's other enemies combined. It is no wonder that forest rangers and game wardens have declared relentless war on this savage and beautiful bird of prey. Because it captures the flying grouse with imperious ease, and because it has been known scornfully to seize the Wilson snipe at the very pitch of his dizzy, enigmatic flight, this hawk probably can overtake anything that flies. And it is the very personification of keenness and silence. He is truly a fearsome enemy of the gentle and princely grouse. But against more cosmic enemies like the weather this wildwood aristocrat has that high intelligence that affords almost perfect protection.

Is the night likely to be cold and stormy? He dives beneath the snow for shelter. Is all the food on the ground buried deep in snowy drifts? He lives on the tender buds of the trees. Against all the rigors of winter he has the two capital talismans—the knowledge of how to get food and how to keep warm. It is not, I think, generally known that, while the grouse of the North are booted, having thick tufts of feathers all the way down their legs, those of the South have bare legs. To put it more accurately, as one travels down the Blue Ridge or the Alleghenies, the farther south one goes, the cleaner legs he will find on the grouse. Nor is this a variation in fashion; it is merely living, intelligent Nature accommodating itself to changes in climate. Nature has no fashions; they reflect the folly of men.

In any time of stress, wild things, like people, are likely to congregate. This fact is true of the Virginia deer—though when too hotly pursued, they separate. I recall seeing a beautiful herd of twenty-six that had gathered during a prodigious freshet. And in the winter, when weather conditions are something of a general menace, they herd. In the forests of the North and of Canada so-called "yarding" is common; that is, scores of deer, using the same trails through the snow, will come together in open yards that they have trampled down. In middle latitudes, in hard weather, they stay low on the mountains, on the southern slopes of benches and ravines.

I remember rousing a stag from the most attractive couch imaginable: he was warmly curled up in a sunny patch of mountain laurel on the warm slope of an otherwise bare ridge. On another occasion I followed a fine buck in a driving storm, his big, fresh tracks being barely discernible in the fast-obliterating snow. When at last I came upon him, he was standing under the fabulous shade of a mighty hemlock, calmly chewing the cud. He was in what Emerson would call "the tumultuous privacy of storm." I am sure that he traveled as he did in order to reach that particular shelter; I had followed him three miles, and his course had been purposefully straight. It is my belief that there are no wild creatures of any age or experience which do not keep constantly in mind places of shelter in times of heavy storms, as they do in times of other dangers. Certainly their clairvoyant knowledge of the woods which they range, and of the skies that they sentiently traverse, would lead one to suppose that they are familiar with every "covert from the wind." The safety of wild things depends largely upon just such knowledge and its precise use; in fact, with them such wisdom is incessantly a matter of life and death.

The whitetail deer is an omnivorous feeder, and in even the coldest and most stormy weather he can usually secure sufficient food of one kind or another. He will often paw the snow aside to get at moss and wild meadow hay and acorns; he will go down on his knees to get browsings on the ice of sheltering logs; he will stand on his hind legs and, balancing himself daintily, reach seven feet up in a sapling to crop the tender buds and twigs. (The rascal is entirely too fond of apple buds!) In the time of deep snow he practically lives on bark, leaves in their brown, tight-fisted, velvet sheathes and delicate twigs. A farmer in that wild tract known as Path Valley told me that one winter deer came regularly to his corncrib at night and nibbled at the ends of ears sticking out through the chinks. Time was when he used to eat chestnuts voraciously, but the fearful chestnut blight has put an end to one important source of the wild deer's winter food supply. However, he has sense enough to adapt himself admirably to changed conditions; we get along without chestnuts, and so does he. Calm adjustment to even the most disorderly and radical change is one of the master secrets of a serene existence.

That Nature herself comes partly to the assistance of her children who must winter it through is apparent when we consider the fur coats they wear. The deer of the Southern pinelands and swamps have in winter an ordinary lightweight coat, while the deer of the North have the kind that generous husbands give their wives when autumn comes. The coat of the Northern whitetail is so admirable that in zero weather he can lie down in the snow and feel no discomfort.

What is true of the deer is, of course, true also of all fur bearers; and the farther north they are found, the handsomer will be their winter furs. Prices paid for Southern furs are invariably lower than those allowed for pelts from blizzard-swept latitudes. Winter may be hard, but it is tremendously life-giving. The deer and the quail of the North are a little larger and burlier than their Southern cousins, who are not obliged to undergo the rigors of a long winter. Cold hurts, but it compensates—within reasonable limits: there are no supermen or superanimals at the Poles.

Despite a general belief to the contrary, the Northern forest is by no means a cheerless place in midwinter. Much of its charm comes from the activity of the wild things that are wintering through. Here will be a lively gray squirrel scampering across the gleaming snow to dig with miraculous precision for the acorn that he buried on last Thanksgiving Day. How he finds it under the immense stretch of that uniform white blanket is a matter which I shall not attempt to explain. But it is apparent that he has an almost uncanny memory and an equally perfect sense of direction. Nor do I know who selected him and taught him the principle of saving. He is a cunning and amiable little miser.

Here are the tracks of rabbits, of grouse, and of a solitary gobbler. Perched on a dead chestnut are three crows, not in the least perturbed by the glimmering wild landscape by which they are frostily ringed. I hear a cheerful, urchin sort of scuffling on bark, and a small flock of nuthatches appears. They are industrious and happy. Down in the rhododendron burn, where the ice-baffled stream gurgles and spurts crystally, a black-capped chickadee calls ringingly. He is among the permanent residents, and the winter woods are home to him.

Near a dewy tasseled patch of pines just where the mountain woods end there is a fine spring, deep-gushing from the heart of the great hill. The water from this must be warm, for even in the dead of winter there is green grass here. Robins know about this, and here a few of them always winter. Hundreds of thousands of the relatives of these birds have gone South for the cold months. Why have these stayed? Apparently they prefer winter and home to travel in countries unfamiliar and beautiful. The strangest of all migrants that I ever knew to winter in the North was a mocking bird—a somewhat rare summer visitor above the line. He wintered safely in a boxwood garden in the heart of Pennsylvania. Curiously enough, when spring came, he vanished—probably to find a mate.

Some wild brothers have the advantage of all others (and of man as well) in wintering through: they sleep. Bears, reptiles, frogs, and many insects just curl up and doze the entire winter through. It is an ideal and a marvelous provision of Nature. There is a somewhat vague line running, let us say, from Charleston, South Carolina, to San Diego, California, south of which these creatures do not hibernate. Along the line they may go to sleep in dead earnest, but they may wake up before the winter is half over. Though the alligator is supposed to hibernate in South Carolina, he is abroad in Florida all winter; and in the former state I have heard him, in mid-January, blaring his monstrous, pleistocene bellow across the lonely marsh-hung wastes of the Santee delta. The snakes along the line of hibernation seem to sleep through the cold spells and waken in the warm ones. These hibernators of the line do not manifest that enthusiasm for sleep which, it is alleged, is characteristic of dwellers in the South.

The coming of winter has been, from time immemorial, a period of dramatic change. Whole continents adjust themselves, in so far as their living inhabitants are concerned, to the epic sweep of the world away from the sun, and to the chilling tilt of its axis. But despite winter and its attendant storms, life remains life; and its passion for survival is such that all its strength and resourcefulness will, in times of stress, be used for its preservation. Nor is it at all certain that the non-migrants fare worse than their travel-loving friends. No country is a paradise for anybody or anything. Dangers are everywhere, and an escape from mere cold may mean the encountering of worse perils.

Small birds in myriads migrate. But so do hawks. I suppose that a wild stay-at-home puts, in effect, to himself with some satisfaction Hamlet's question as to whether it is always a wise plan to try to escape dangers of which one is aware, if, in so doing, one is liable "to fly to others that we know not of."

The winter rains, the snows, the faint but kindly sunshine, the wrathful winds—these are but displays of those same forces which produce, under slightly altered conditions, that melting loveliness that we know as springtime. And these wild brothers of ours, having a strange and ancient wisdom, accept winter with a serenity of spirit that puts man to shame. Whether it is in soft, weepy April or in bleak December, they have the same hearty joy in life. Those that cannot stand the winter go South; those that can bear it stay at home. If they do not fully appreciate the patent miracle of such an arrangement, we should; for it beautifully manifests that the Lord of the Universe makes life, at its worst, bearable—as He makes it, at its best, delectable.

THE END